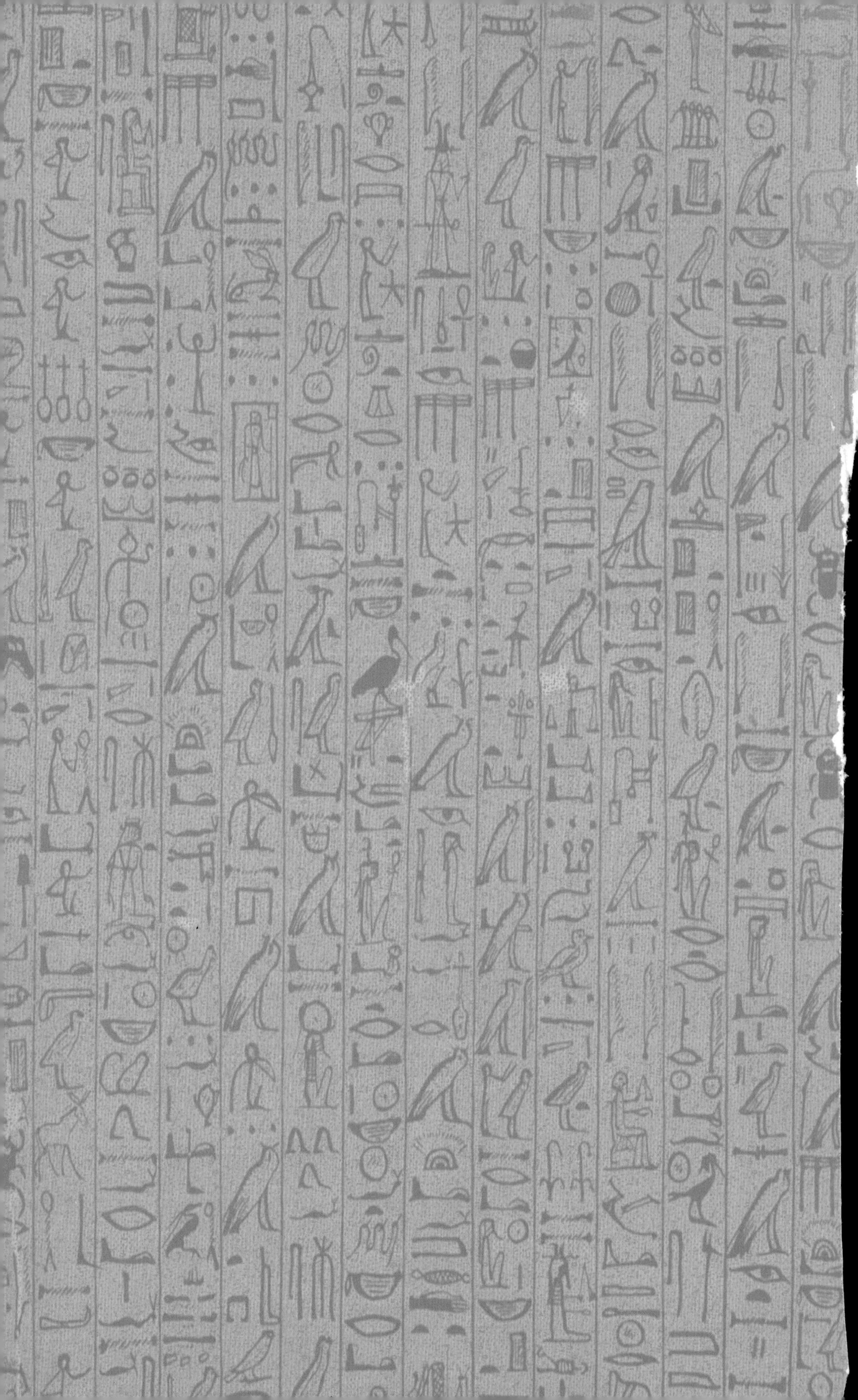

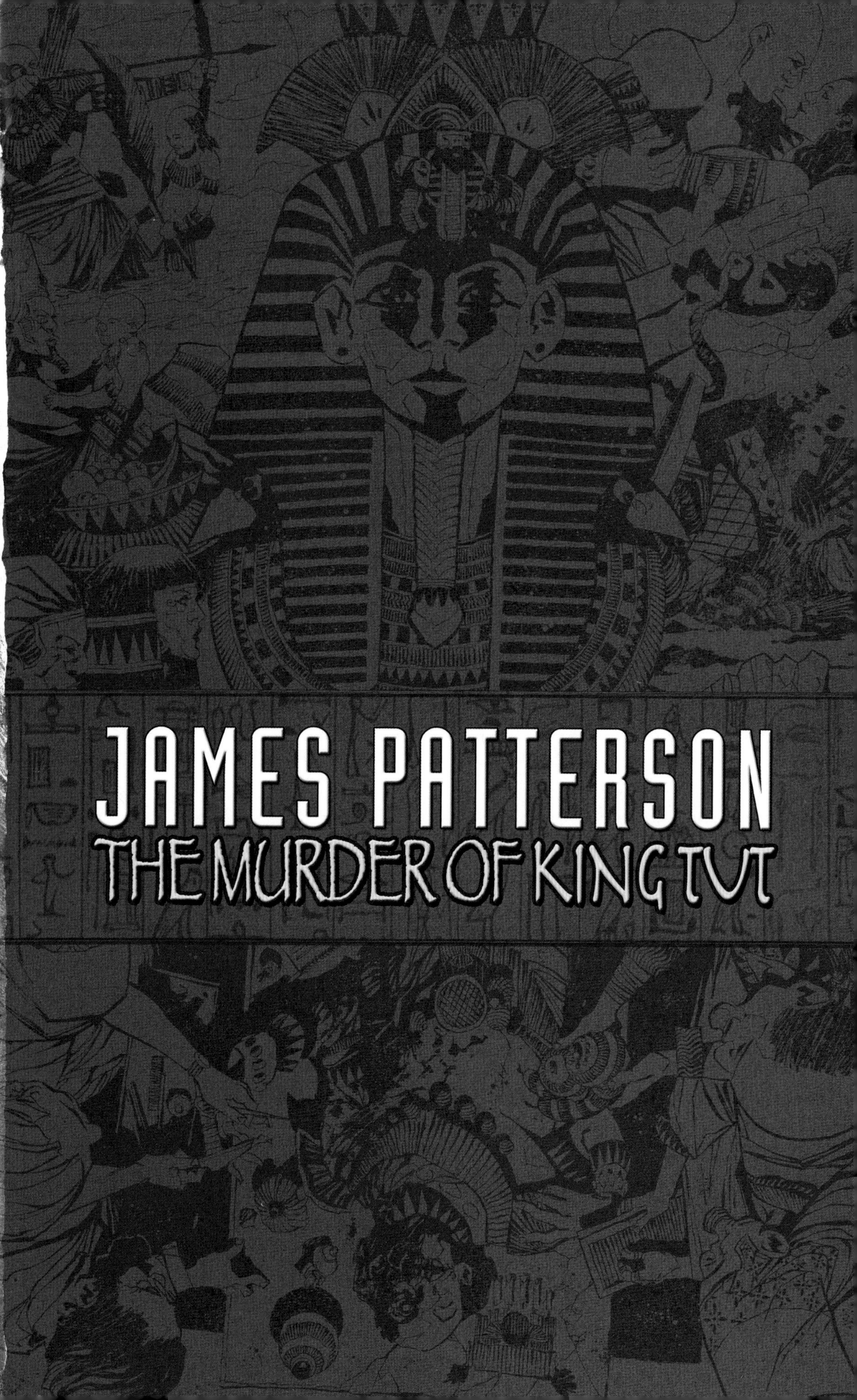
JAMES PATTERSON
THE MURDER OF KING TUT

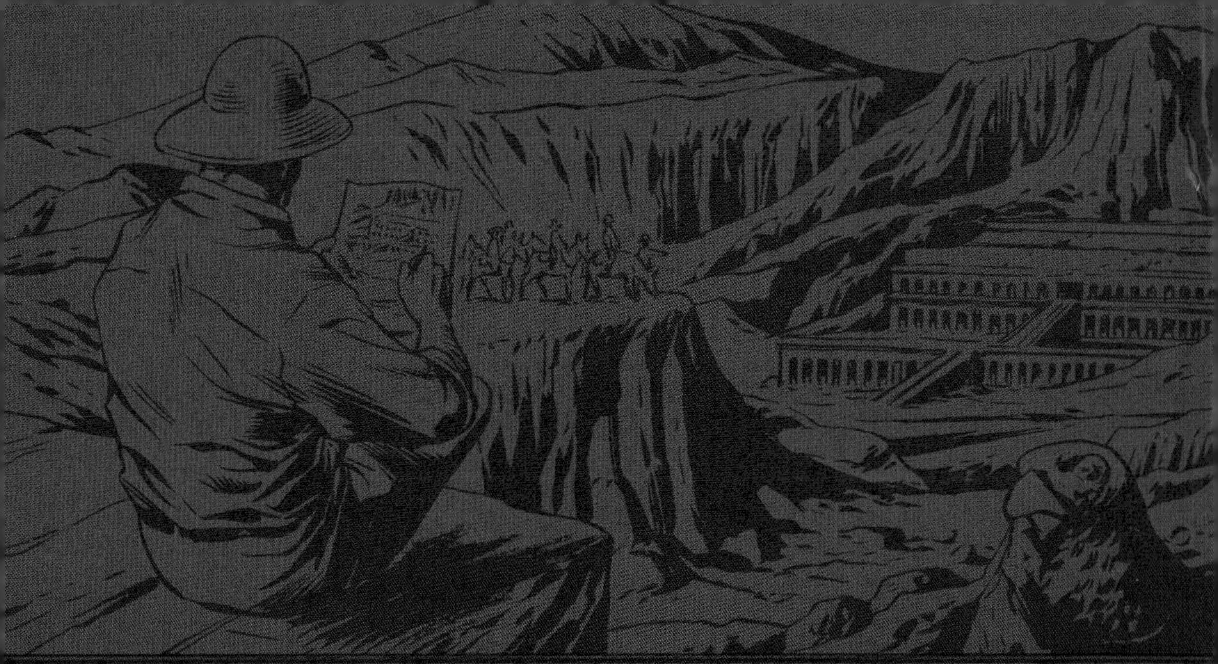

~ The Murder of King Tut ~

Egypt, 1336 BC: The iconoclastic pharaoh Akhenaten dies, leaving the throne to his five-year-old bastard son, Tutankhamen. The boy will transform Egypt before dying as a teenager, buried in an anonymous tomb and erased from the history of Egypt by his enemies. His death will remain a mystery for more than three thousand years...

Egypt, 1891 AD: A teenage artist named Howard Carter arrives in Egypt as an assistant to the Egyptologist Percy Newberry. Thus begins a thirty-year quest that culminates in the most famous discovery in the history of the Valley of Kings... the tomb of the near-mythical Tutankhamen.

The present day: Carter's discovery shines forth in a shocking new light as contemporary forensics and detective work reveal the truth about the boy pharaoh's death... and bring Howard Carter's long quest to its definitive end.

BASED ON "THE MURDER OF KING TUT" BY JAMES PATTERSON & MARTIN DUGARD

ADAPTED BY
ALEXANDER IRVINE

ARTIST
RON RANDALL
HOWARD CARTER'S EXPLOITS

ARTIST
CHRISTOPHER MITTEN
ANCIENT EGYPT SAGA

LETTERS NEIL UYETAKE • COLORS DOM REGAN • EDITOR BOB SCHRECK
COLLECTION EDITS JUSTIN EISINGER • COLLECTION DESIGN SHAWN LEE
COLLECTION COVER DAVE DORMAN

www.IDWPUBLISHING.com

ISBN: 978-1-60010-780-1 13 12 11 10 1 2 3 4

IDW

IDW Publishing is: Operations: Ted Adams, CEO & Publisher • Greg Goldstein, Chief Operating Officer • Matthew Ruzicka, CPA, Chief Financial Officer • Alan Payne, VP of Sales • Lorelei Bunjes, Director of Digital Services • Jeff Webber, Director of ePublishing • AnnaMaria White, Dir., Marketing and Public Relations • Dirk Wood, Dir., Retail Marketing • Marci Hubbard, Executive Assistant • Alonzo Simon, Shipping Manager • Angela Loggins, Staff Accountant • Cherrie Go, Assistant Web Designer • Editorial: Chris Ryall, Chief Creative Officer, Editor-In-Chief • Scott Dunbier, Senior Editor, Special Projects • Andy Schmidt, Senior Editor • Bob Schreck, Senior Editor • Justin Eisinger, Senior Editor, Books • Kris Oprisko, Editor/Foreign Lic. • Denton J. Tipton, Editor • Tom Waltz, Editor • Mariah Huehner, Editor • Carlos Guzman, Assistant Editor • Bobby Curnow, Assistant Editor • Design: Robbie Robbins, EVP/Sr. Graphic Artist • Neil Uyetake, Senior Art Director • Chris Mowry, Senior Graphic Artist • Amauri Osorio, Graphic Artist • Gilberto Lazcano, Production Assistant • Shawn Lee, Graphic Artist

Originally published as JAMES PATTERSON'S THE MURDER OF KING TUT Issues #1–5.

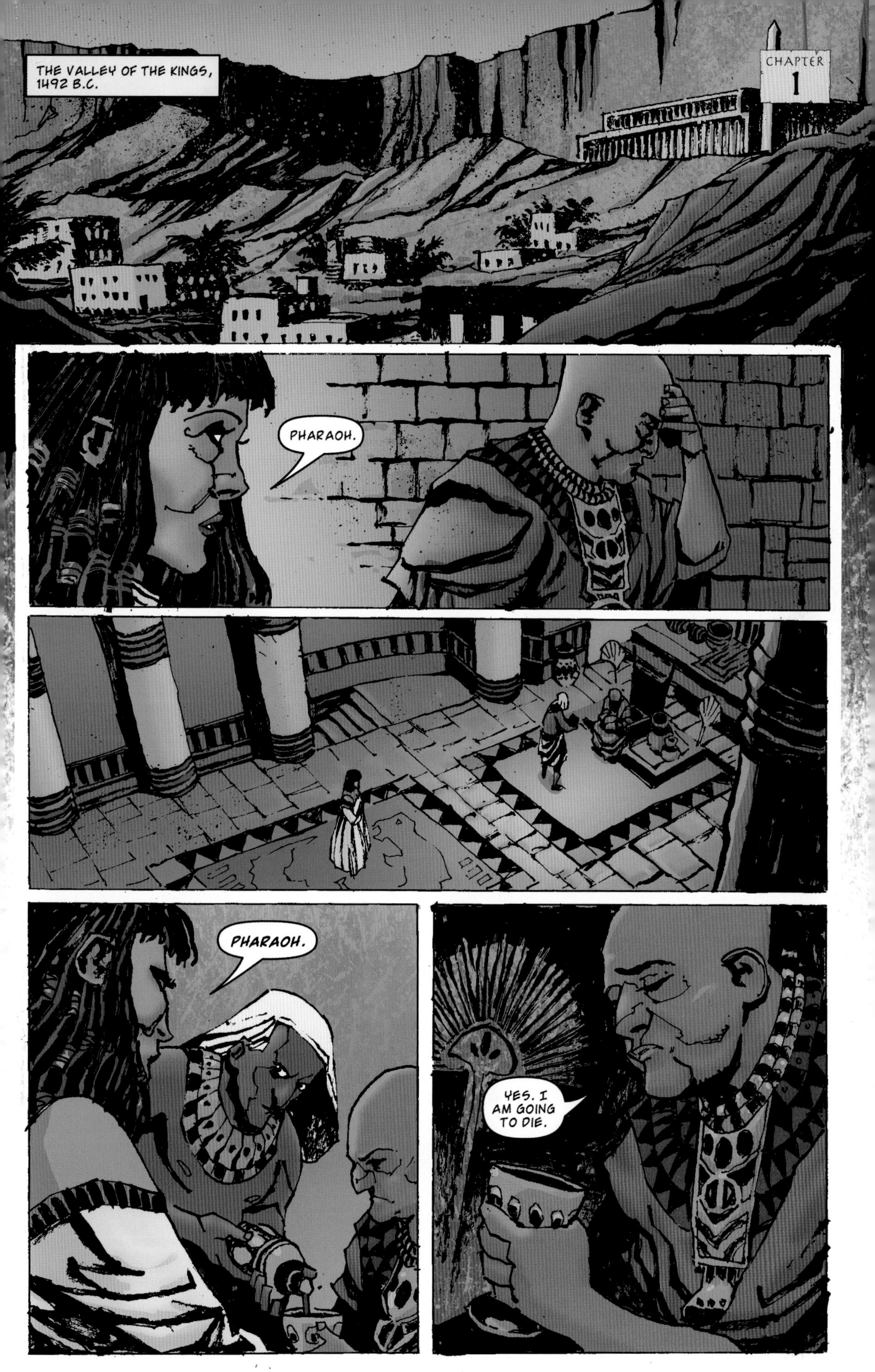
THE VALLEY OF THE KINGS, 1492 B.C.
CHAPTER 1
PHARAOH.
PHARAOH.
YES. I AM GOING TO DIE.

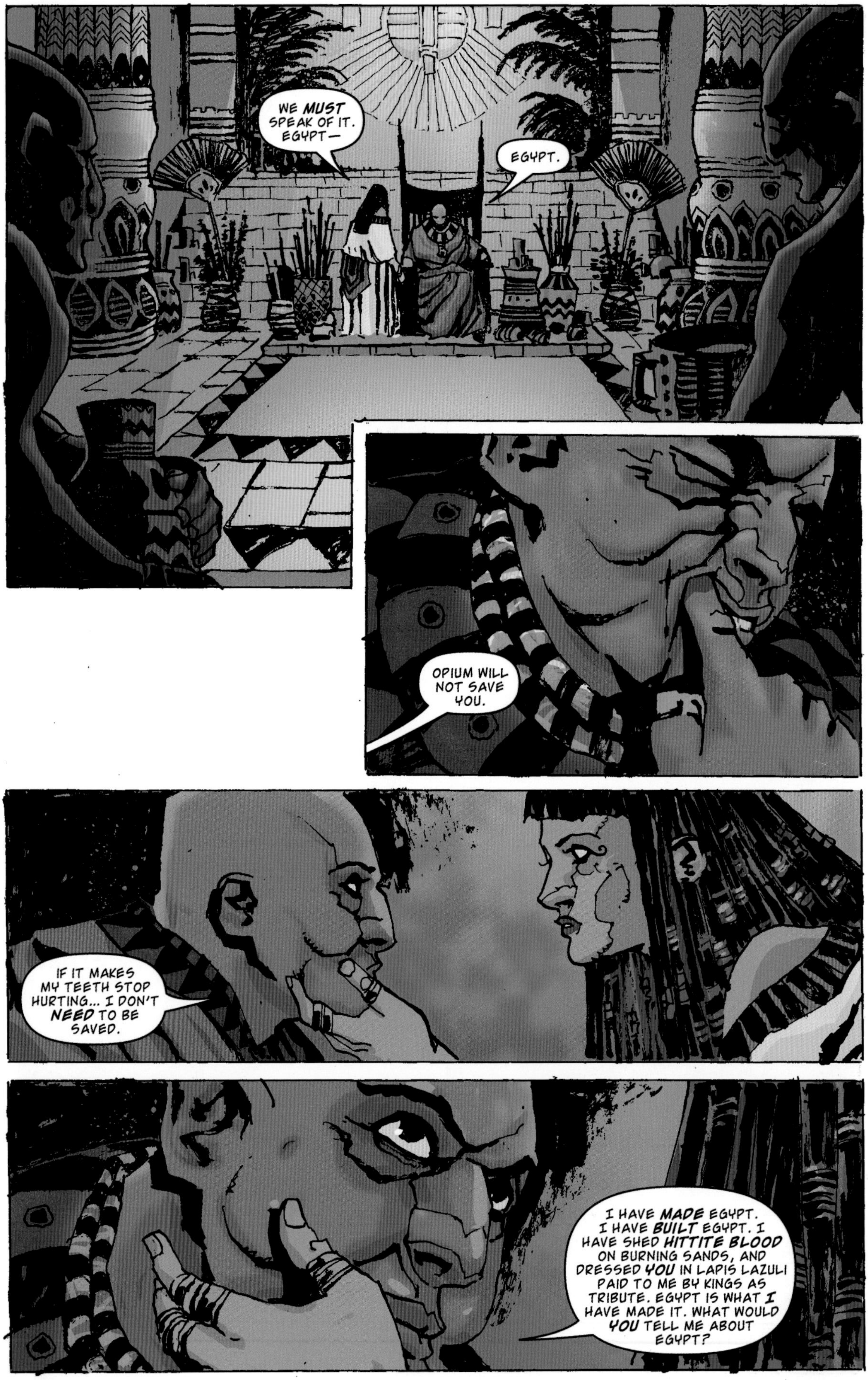
WE MUST SPEAK OF IT. EGYPT—
EGYPT.
OPIUM WILL NOT SAVE YOU.
IF IT MAKES MY TEETH STOP HURTING... I DON'T NEED TO BE SAVED.
I HAVE MADE EGYPT. I HAVE BUILT EGYPT. I HAVE SHED HITTITE BLOOD ON BURNING SANDS, AND DRESSED YOU IN LAPIS LAZULI PAID TO ME BY KINGS AS TRIBUTE. EGYPT IS WHAT I HAVE MADE IT. WHAT WOULD YOU TELL ME ABOUT EGYPT?

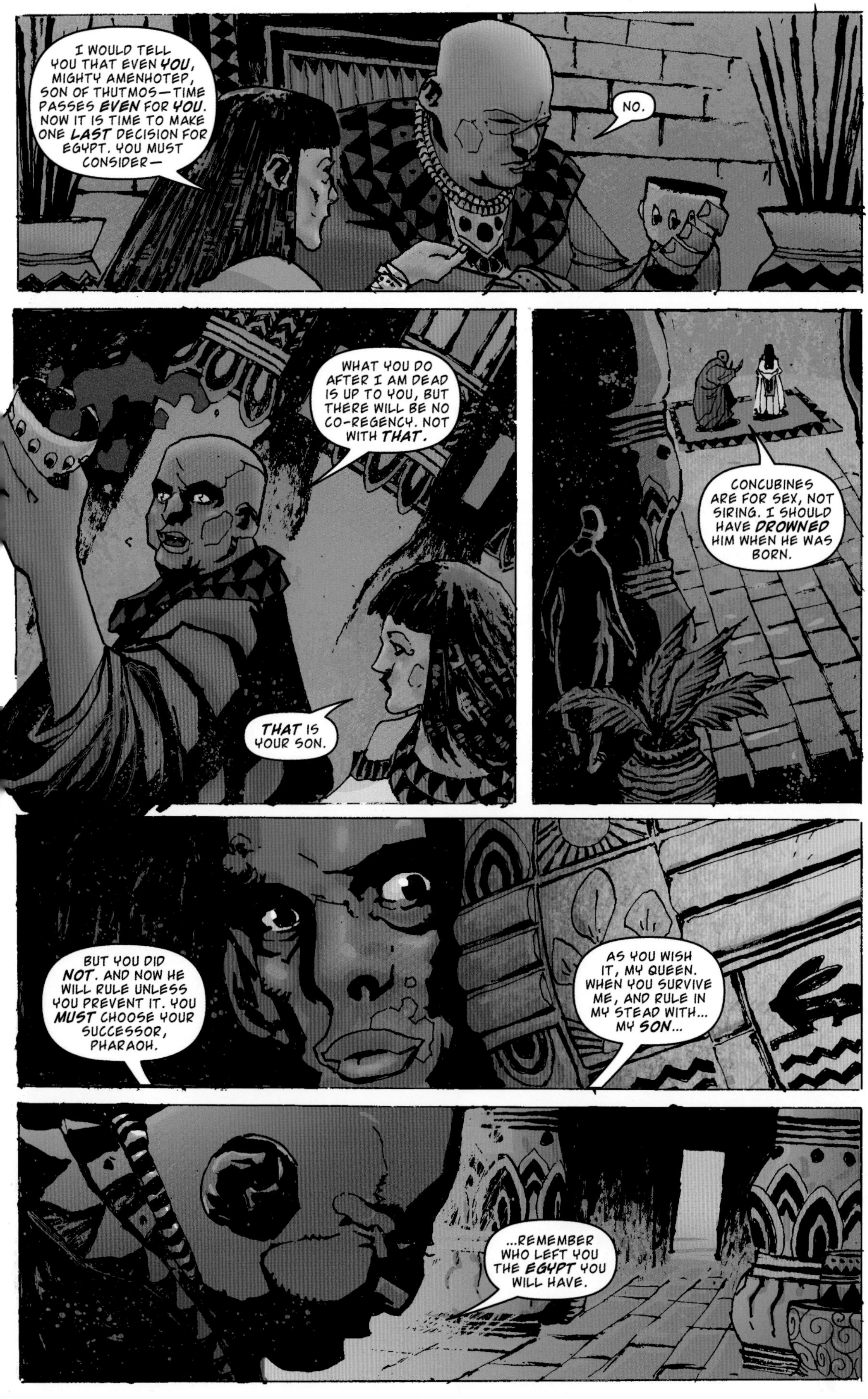
I WOULD TELL YOU THAT EVEN YOU, MIGHTY AMENHOTEP, SON OF THUTMOS—TIME PASSES EVEN FOR YOU. NOW IT IS TIME TO MAKE ONE LAST DECISION FOR EGYPT. YOU MUST CONSIDER—
NO.
WHAT YOU DO AFTER I AM DEAD IS UP TO YOU, BUT THERE WILL BE NO CO-REGENCY. NOT WITH THAT.
THAT IS YOUR SON.
CONCUBINES ARE FOR SEX, NOT SIRING. I SHOULD HAVE DROWNED HIM WHEN HE WAS BORN.
BUT YOU DID NOT. AND NOW HE WILL RULE UNLESS YOU PREVENT IT. YOU MUST CHOOSE YOUR SUCCESSOR, PHARAOH.
AS YOU WISH IT, MY QUEEN. WHEN YOU SURVIVE ME, AND RULE IN MY STEAD WITH... MY SON...
...REMEMBER WHO LEFT YOU THE EGYPT YOU WILL HAVE.

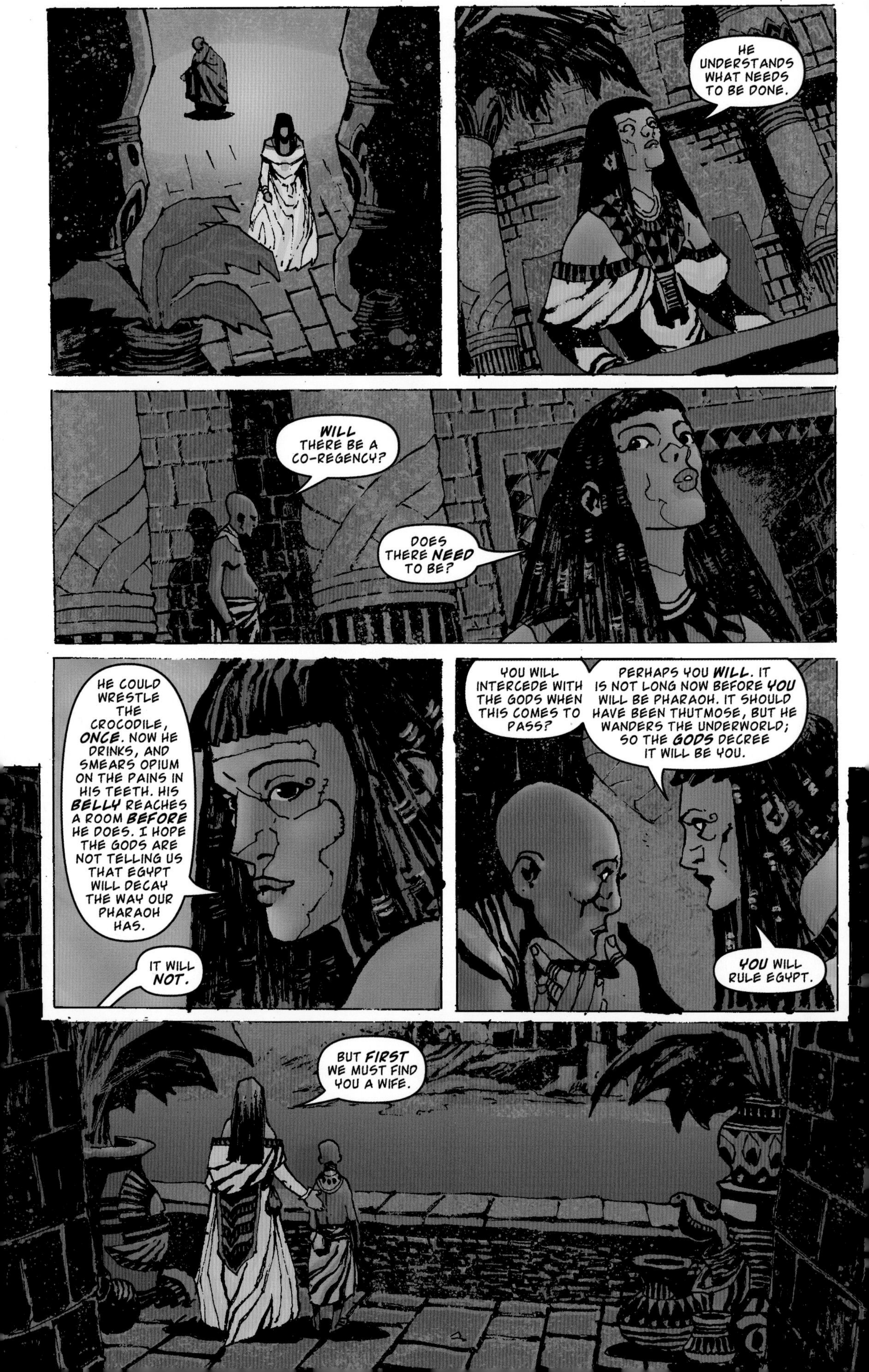
HE UNDERSTANDS WHAT NEEDS TO BE DONE.
WILL THERE BE A CO-REGENCY?
DOES THERE NEED TO BE?
HE COULD WRESTLE THE CROCODILE, ONCE. NOW HE DRINKS, AND SMEARS OPIUM ON THE PAINS IN HIS TEETH. HIS BELLY REACHES A ROOM BEFORE HE DOES. I HOPE THE GODS ARE NOT TELLING US THAT EGYPT WILL DECAY THE WAY OUR PHARAOH HAS.
IT WILL NOT.
YOU WILL INTERCEDE WITH THE GODS WHEN THIS COMES TO PASS?
PERHAPS YOU WILL. IT IS NOT LONG NOW BEFORE YOU WILL BE PHARAOH. IT SHOULD HAVE BEEN THUTMOSE, BUT HE WANDERS THE UNDERWORLD; SO THE GODS DECREE IT WILL BE YOU.
YOU WILL RULE EGYPT.
BUT FIRST WE MUST FIND YOU A WIFE.

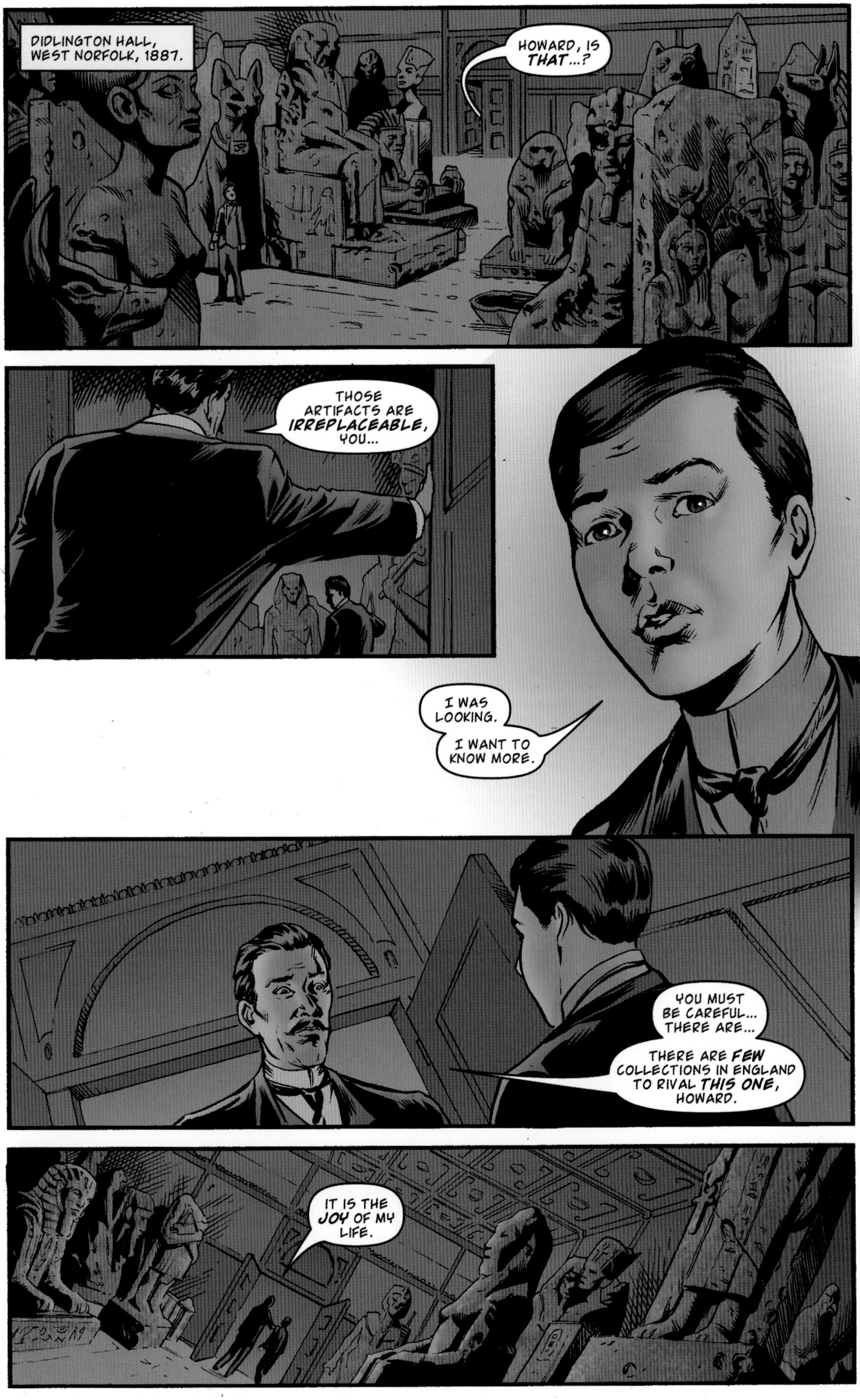
DIDLINGTON HALL, WEST NORFOLK, 1887.
HOWARD, IS THAT...?
THOSE ARTIFACTS ARE IRREPLACEABLE, YOU...
I WAS LOOKING.
I WANT TO KNOW MORE.
YOU MUST BE CAREFUL... THERE ARE...
THERE ARE FEW COLLECTIONS IN ENGLAND TO RIVAL THIS ONE, HOWARD.
IT IS THE JOY OF MY LIFE.

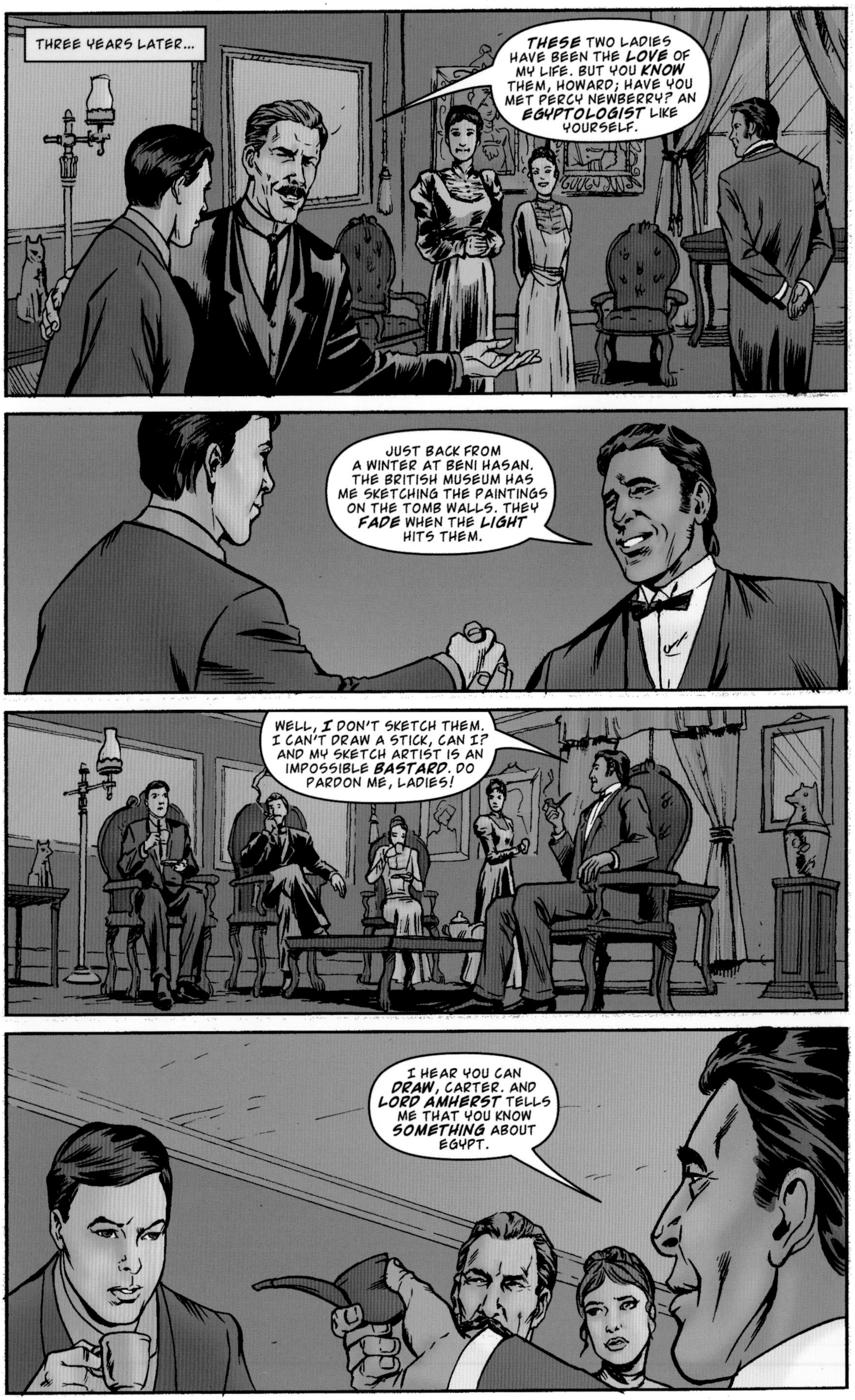
THREE YEARS LATER...
THESE TWO LADIES HAVE BEEN THE LOVE OF MY LIFE. BUT YOU KNOW THEM, HOWARD; HAVE YOU MET PERCY NEWBERRY? AN EGYPTOLOGIST LIKE YOURSELF.
JUST BACK FROM A WINTER AT BENI HASAN. THE BRITISH MUSEUM HAS ME SKETCHING THE PAINTINGS ON THE TOMB WALLS. THEY FADE WHEN THE LIGHT HITS THEM.
WELL, I DON'T SKETCH THEM. I CAN'T DRAW A STICK, CAN I? AND MY SKETCH ARTIST IS AN IMPOSSIBLE BASTARD. DO PARDON ME, LADIES!
I HEAR YOU CAN DRAW, CARTER. AND LORD AMHERST TELLS ME THAT YOU KNOW SOMETHING ABOUT EGYPT.

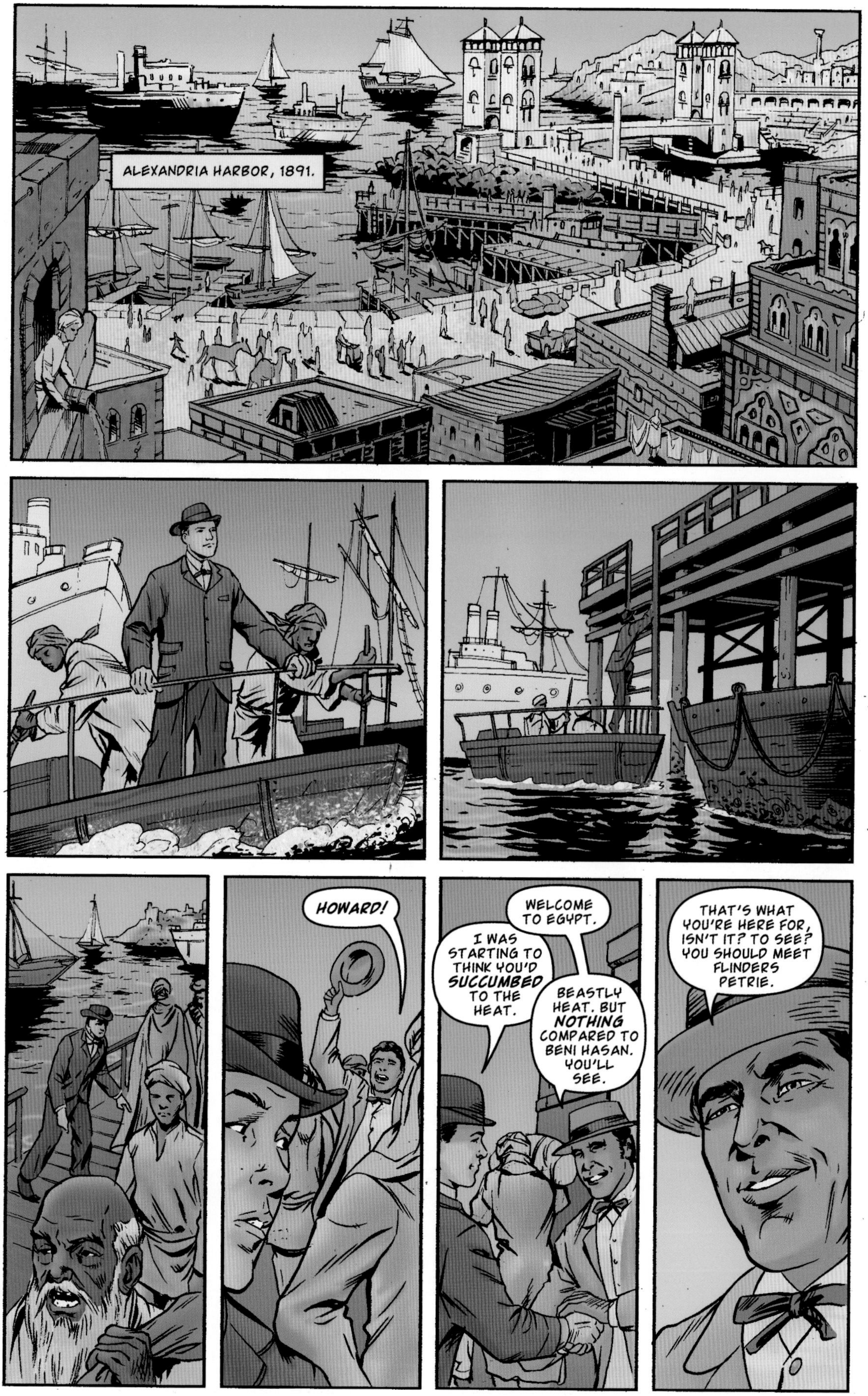

ALEXANDRIA HARBOR, 1891.
HOWARD!
I WAS STARTING TO THINK YOU'D SUCCUMBED TO THE HEAT.
WELCOME TO EGYPT.
BEASTLY HEAT. BUT NOTHING COMPARED TO BENI HASAN. YOU'LL SEE.
THAT'S WHAT YOU'RE HERE FOR, ISN'T IT? TO SEE? YOU SHOULD MEET FLINDERS PETRIE.

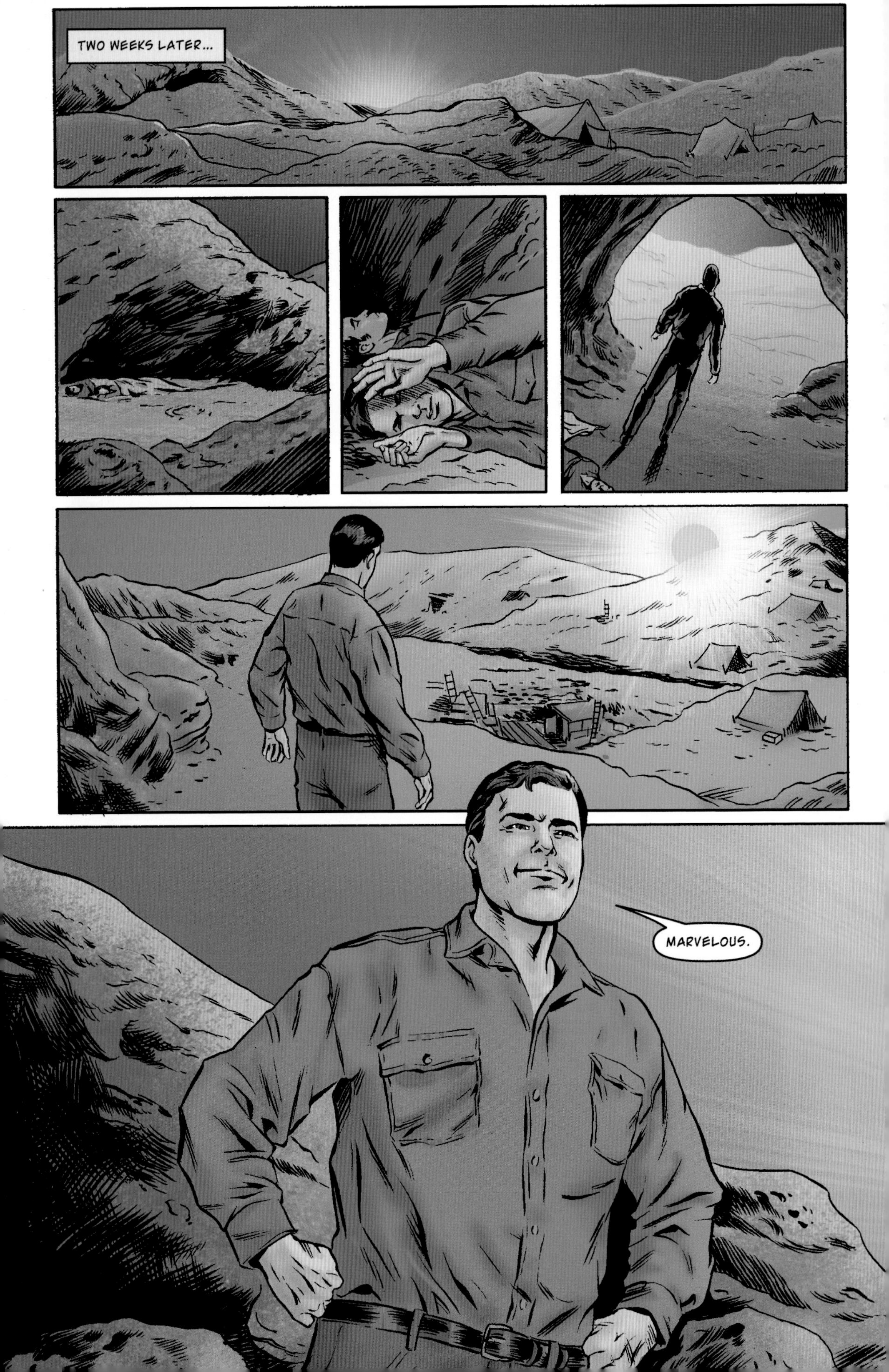
TWO WEEKS LATER...
MARVELOUS.

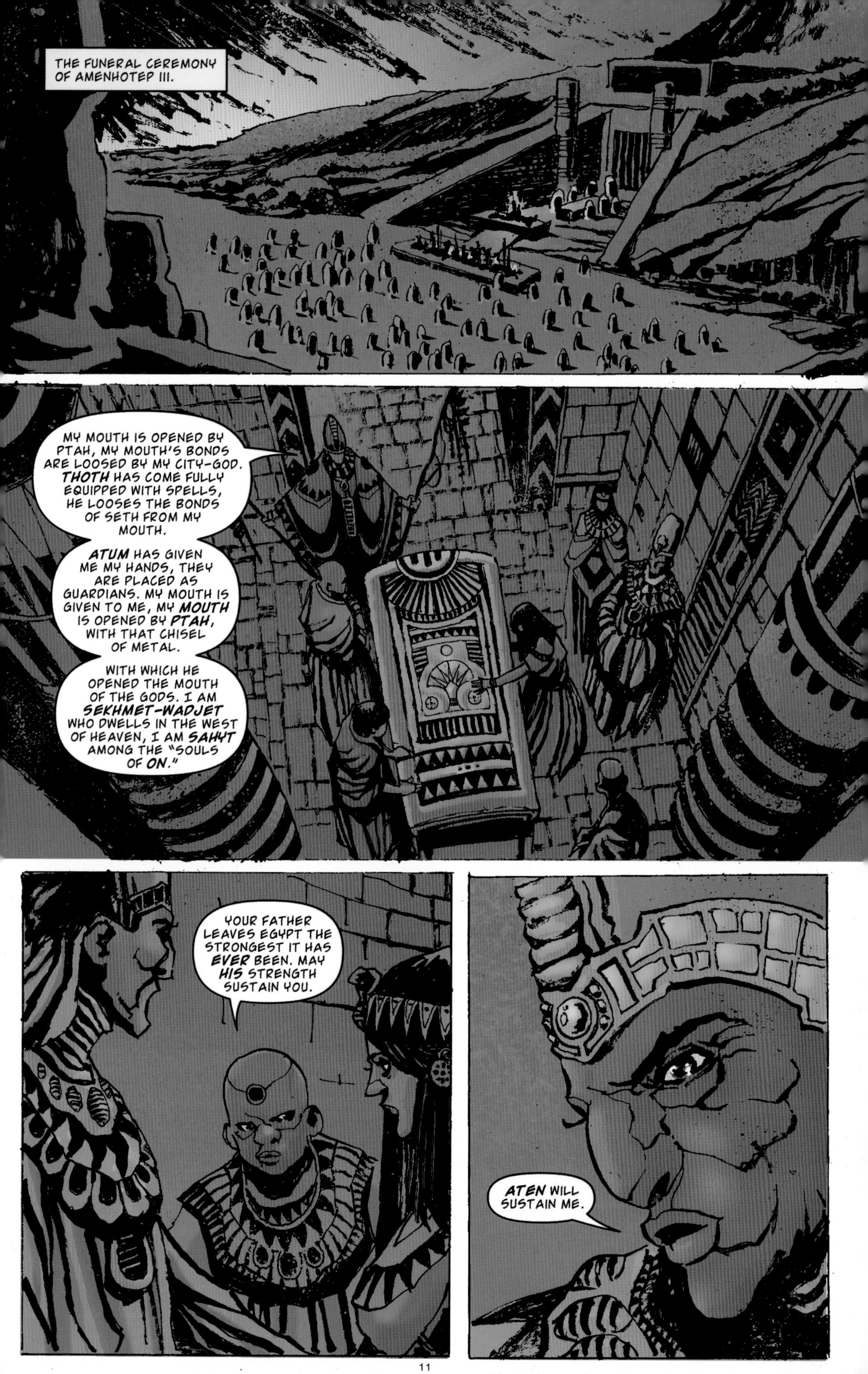
THE FUNERAL CEREMONY OF AMENHOTEP III.
MY MOUTH IS OPENED BY PTAH, MY MOUTH'S BONDS ARE LOOSED BY MY CITY-GOD. THOTH HAS COME FULLY EQUIPPED WITH SPELLS, HE LOOSES THE BONDS OF SETH FROM MY MOUTH.
ATUM HAS GIVEN ME MY HANDS, THEY ARE PLACED AS GUARDIANS. MY MOUTH IS GIVEN TO ME, MY MOUTH IS OPENED BY PTAH, WITH THAT CHISEL OF METAL.
WITH WHICH HE OPENED THE MOUTH OF THE GODS. I AM SEKHMET-WADJET WHO DWELLS IN THE WEST OF HEAVEN, I AM SAHYT AMONG THE "SOULS OF ON."
YOUR FATHER LEAVES EGYPT THE STRONGEST IT HAS EVER BEEN. MAY HIS STRENGTH SUSTAIN YOU.
ATEN WILL SUSTAIN ME.

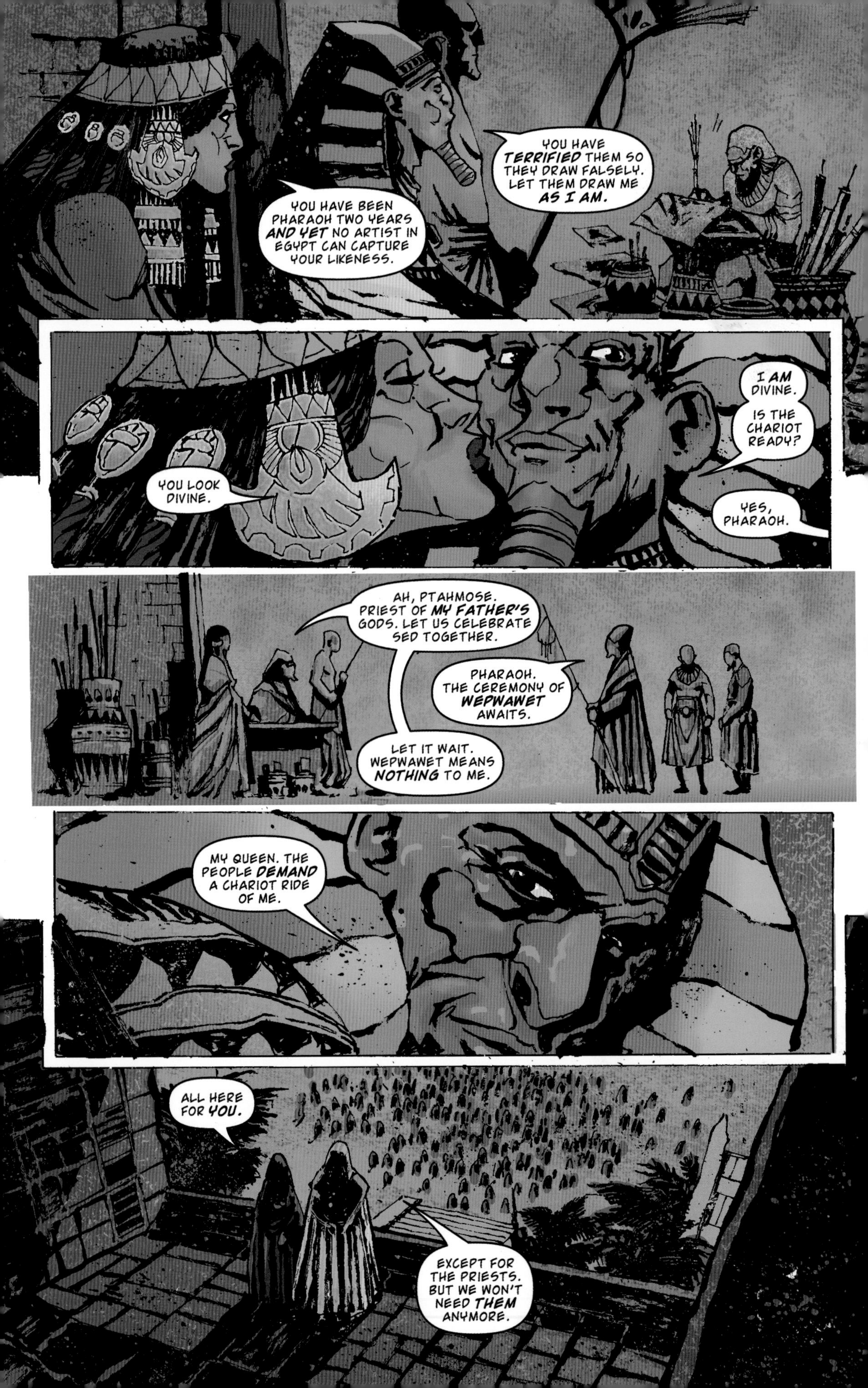
YOU HAVE BEEN PHARAOH TWO YEARS AND YET NO ARTIST IN EGYPT CAN CAPTURE YOUR LIKENESS.
YOU HAVE TERRIFIED THEM SO THEY DRAW FALSELY. LET THEM DRAW ME AS I AM.
YOU LOOK DIVINE.
I AM DIVINE.
IS THE CHARIOT READY?
YES, PHARAOH.
AH, PTAHMOSE. PRIEST OF MY FATHER'S GODS. LET US CELEBRATE SED TOGETHER.
PHARAOH. THE CEREMONY OF WEPWAWET AWAITS.
LET IT WAIT. WEPWAWET MEANS NOTHING TO ME.
MY QUEEN. THE PEOPLE DEMAND A CHARIOT RIDE OF ME.
ALL HERE FOR YOU.
EXCEPT FOR THE PRIESTS. BUT WE WON'T NEED THEM ANYMORE.

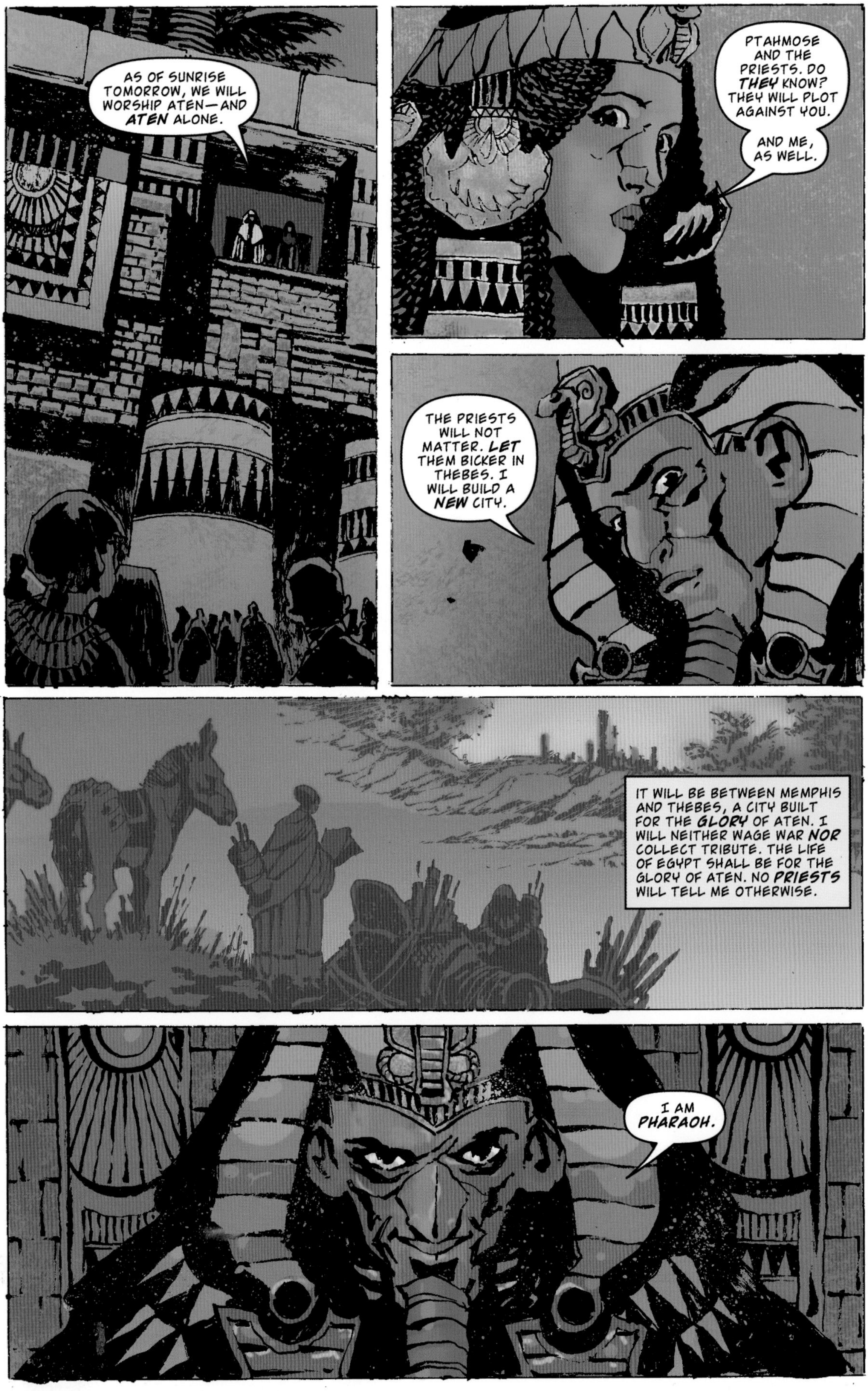
AS OF SUNRISE TOMORROW, WE WILL WORSHIP ATEN—AND ATEN ALONE.
PTAHMOSE AND THE PRIESTS. DO THEY KNOW? THEY WILL PLOT AGAINST YOU.
AND ME, AS WELL.
THE PRIESTS WILL NOT MATTER. LET THEM BICKER IN THEBES. I WILL BUILD A NEW CITY.
IT WILL BE BETWEEN MEMPHIS AND THEBES, A CITY BUILT FOR THE GLORY OF ATEN. I WILL NEITHER WAGE WAR NOR COLLECT TRIBUTE. THE LIFE OF EGYPT SHALL BE FOR THE GLORY OF ATEN. NO PRIESTS WILL TELL ME OTHERWISE.
I AM PHARAOH.

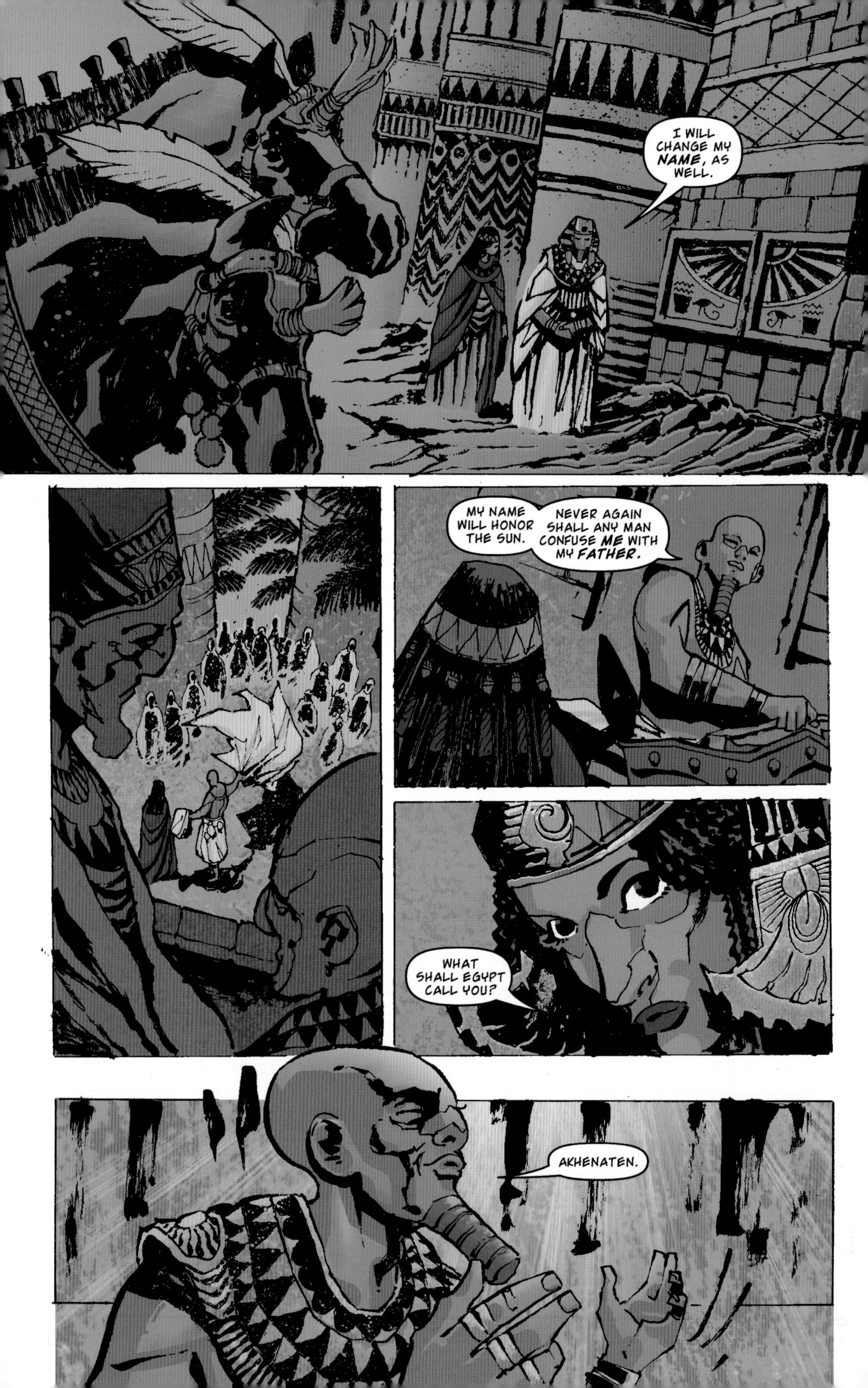
I WILL CHANGE MY NAME, AS WELL.
MY NAME WILL HONOR THE SUN.
NEVER AGAIN SHALL ANY MAN CONFUSE ME WITH MY FATHER.
WHAT SHALL EGYPT CALL YOU?
AKHENATEN.

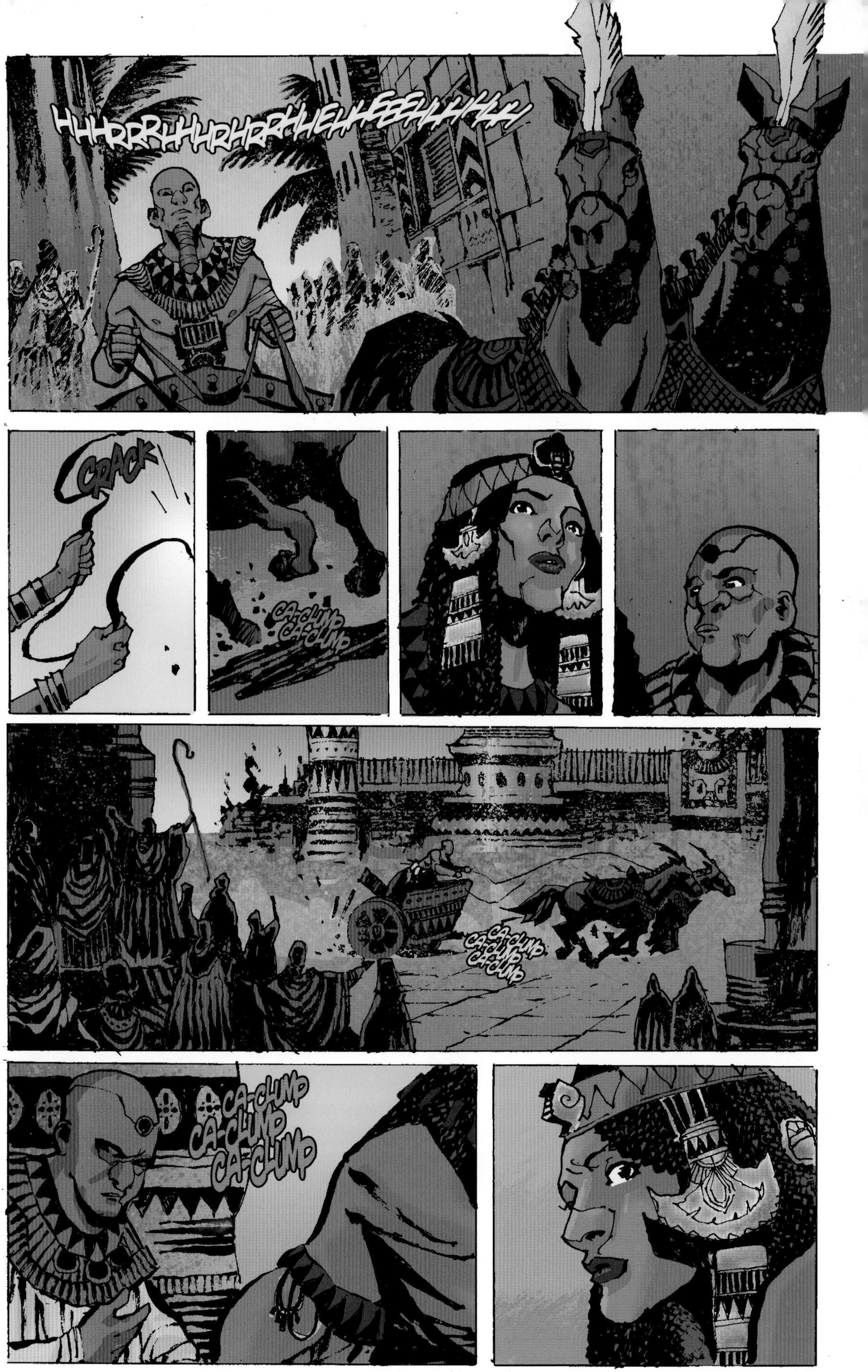
HHHRRRHHHRHRRHHEHHEEEHHHHH
CRACK
CA-CLUMP CA-CLUMP
CA-CLUMP CA-CLUMP CA-CLUMP
CA-CLUMP CA-CLUMP CA-CLUMP

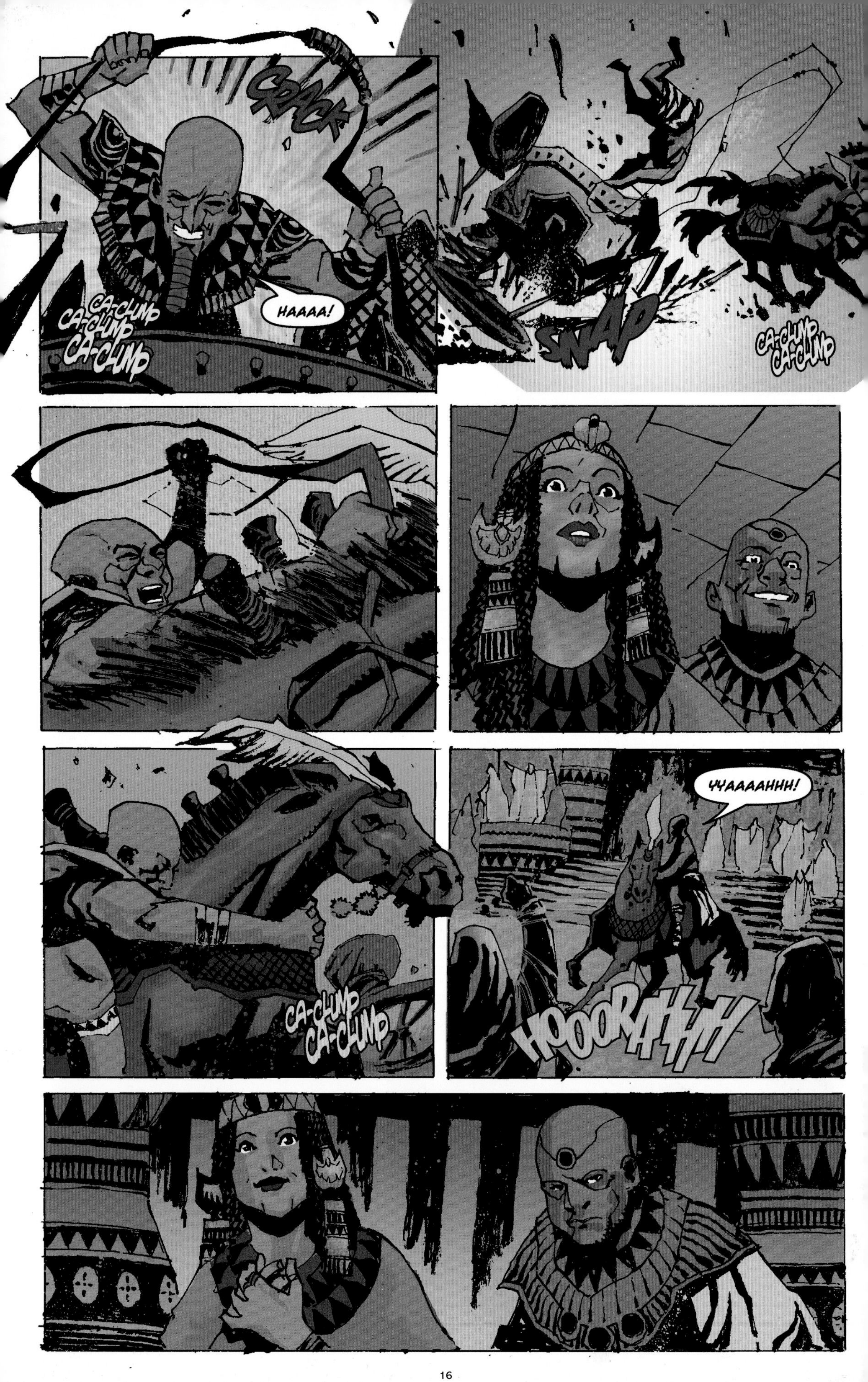
CRACK
CA-CLUMP CA-CLUMP CA-CLUMP
HAAAA!
SNAP
CA-CLUMP CA-CLUMP
CA-CLUMP CA-CLUMP
YYAAAAHHH!
HOOORAHHH

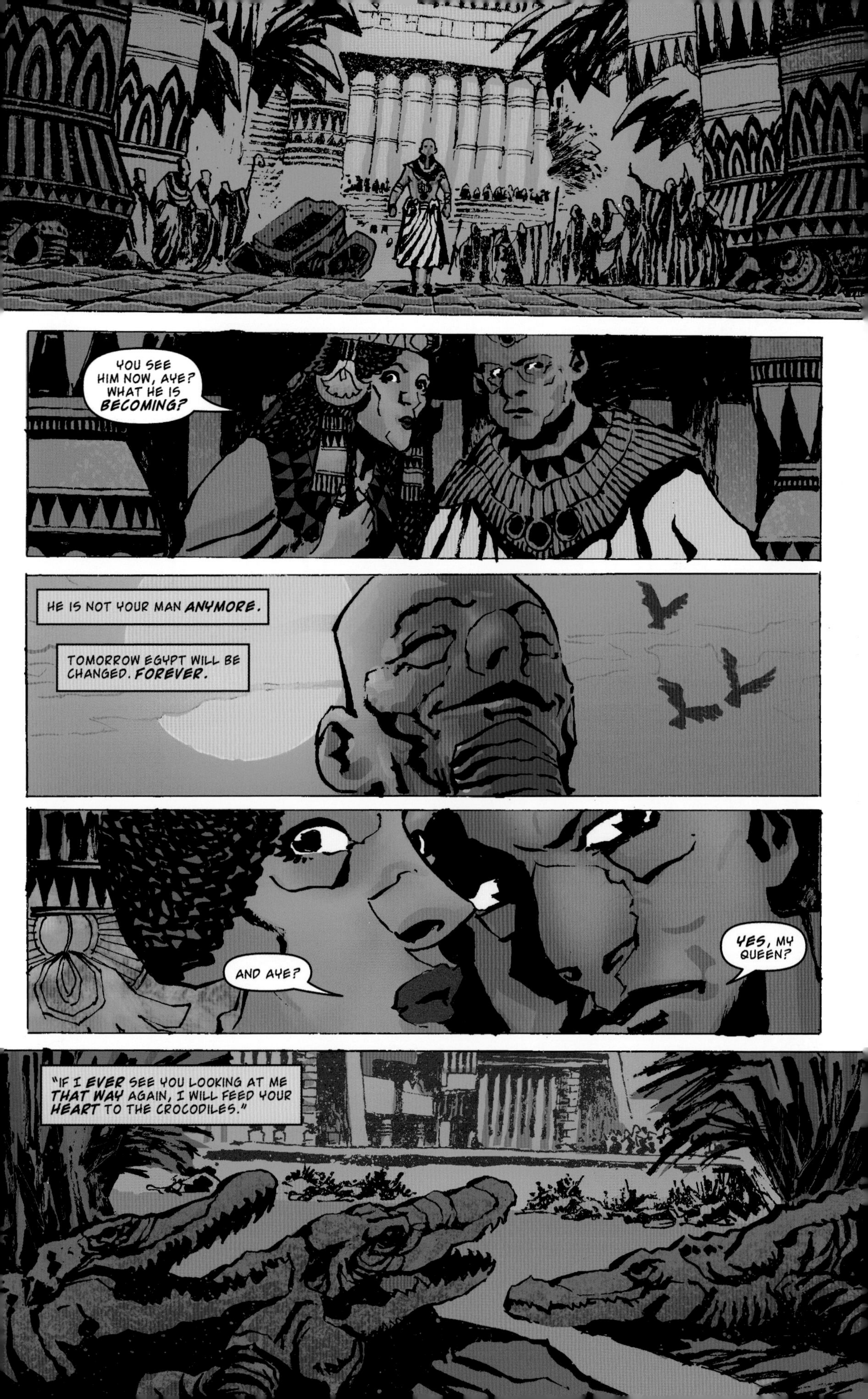
YOU SEE HIM NOW, AYE? WHAT HE IS *BECOMING?*
HE IS NOT YOUR MAN *ANYMORE.*
TOMORROW EGYPT WILL BE CHANGED. *FOREVER.*
AND AYE?
YES, MY QUEEN?
"IF I *EVER* SEE YOU LOOKING AT ME *THAT WAY* AGAIN, I WILL FEED YOUR *HEART* TO THE CROCODILES."

TWO YEARS. NO CITY HAS *EVER* BEEN BUILT FASTER.

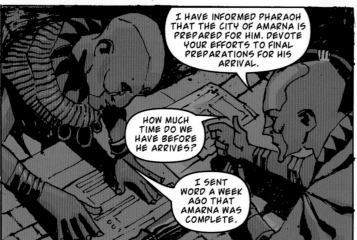

I HAVE INFORMED PHARAOH THAT THE CITY OF AMARNA IS PREPARED FOR HIM. DEVOTE YOUR EFFORTS TO FINAL PREPARATIONS FOR HIS ARRIVAL.

HOW MUCH TIME DO WE HAVE BEFORE HE ARRIVES?

I SENT WORD A WEEK AGO THAT AMARNA WAS COMPLETE.

BUT IT IS *NOT* READY. IT IS NOTHING *CLOSE* TO READY. NOT FOR PHARAOH.

IT *MUST* BE. HE WILL ARRIVE IN TWO WEEKS. PERHAPS THREE. HE HAS A *GREAT MANY* SUN-WORSHIPPING MINIONS TO MOBILIZE.

ALL STRENGTH COMES FROM ATEN.

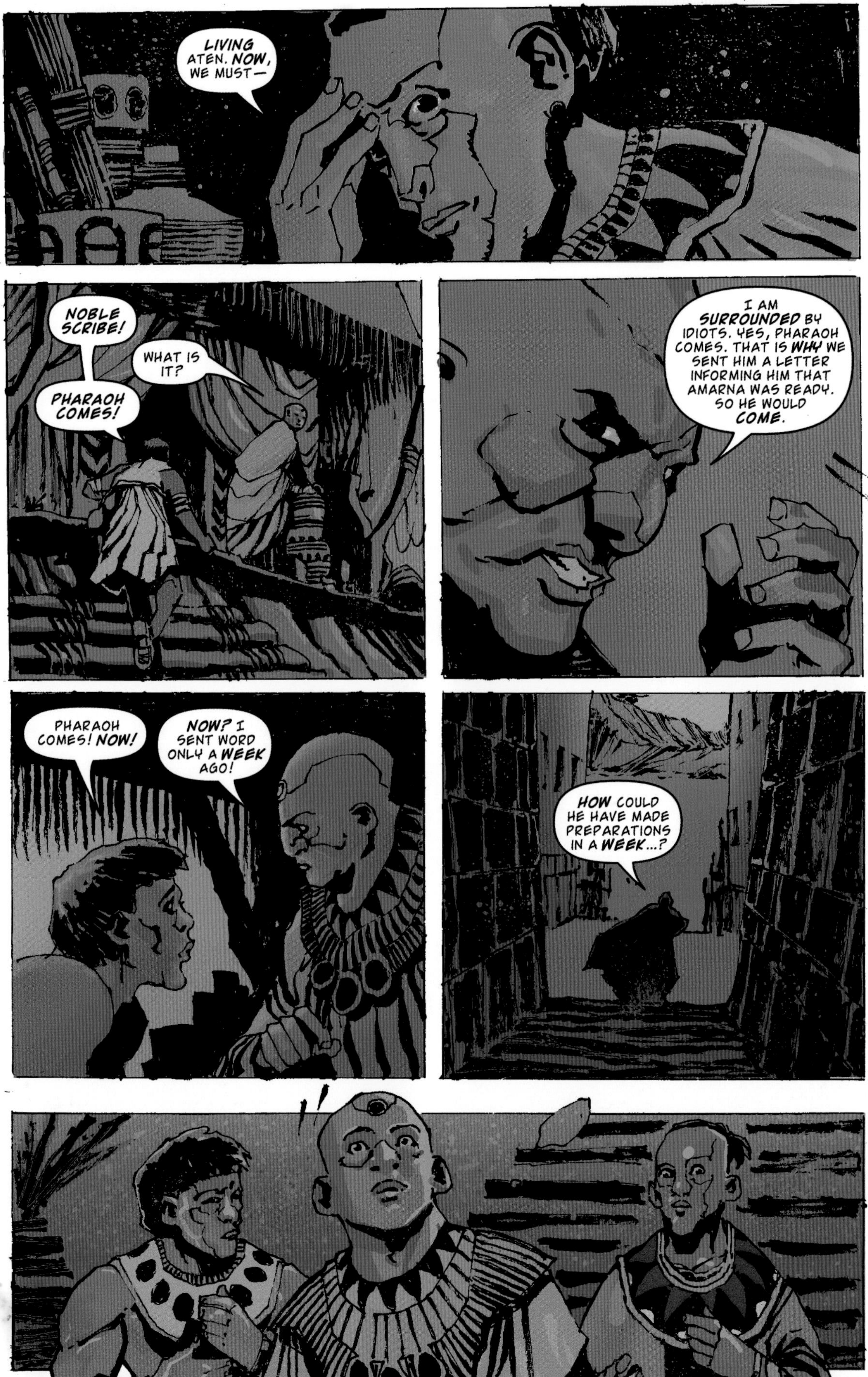
LIVING ATEN. NOW, WE MUST—
NOBLE SCRIBE!
PHARAOH COMES!
WHAT IS IT?
I AM SURROUNDED BY IDIOTS. YES, PHARAOH COMES. THAT IS WHY WE SENT HIM A LETTER INFORMING HIM THAT AMARNA WAS READY. SO HE WOULD COME.
PHARAOH COMES! NOW!
NOW? I SENT WORD ONLY A WEEK AGO!
HOW COULD HE HAVE MADE PREPARATIONS IN A WEEK...?

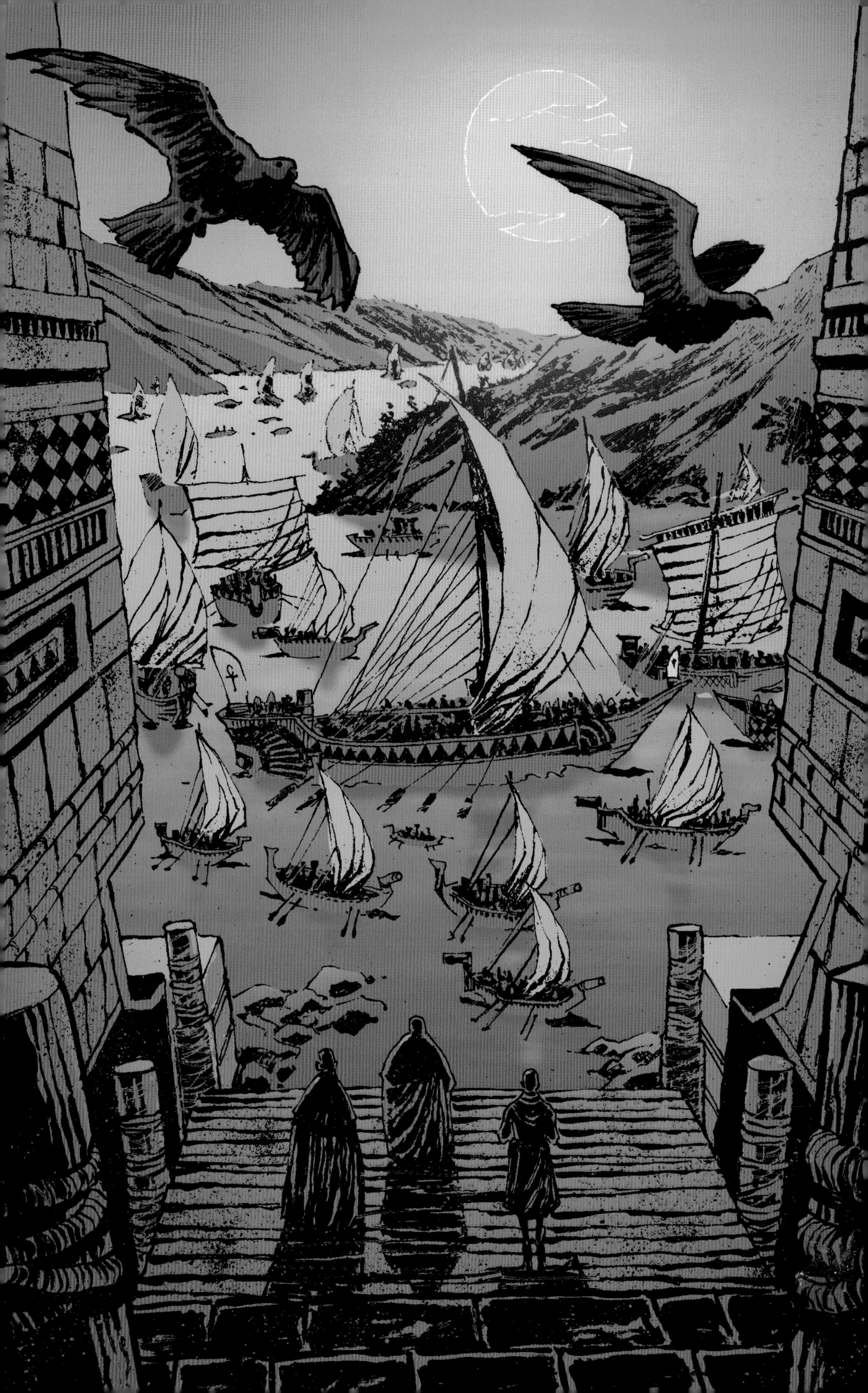

OUR CITY.

I BUILT IT FOR *YOU.*

YOU *BUILT IT* TO GET *AYE* OUT OF THEBES.

THAT WAS FOR YOU, TOO.

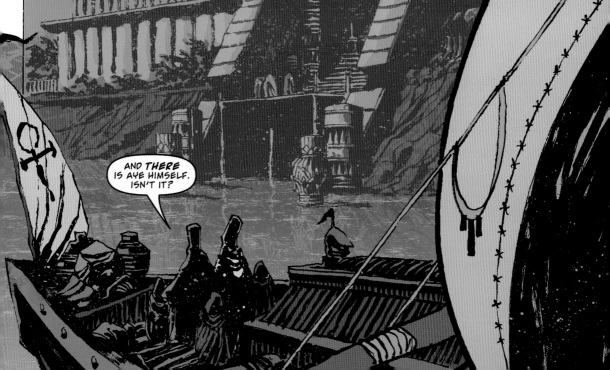

AND *THERE* IS AYE HIMSELF. ISN'T IT?

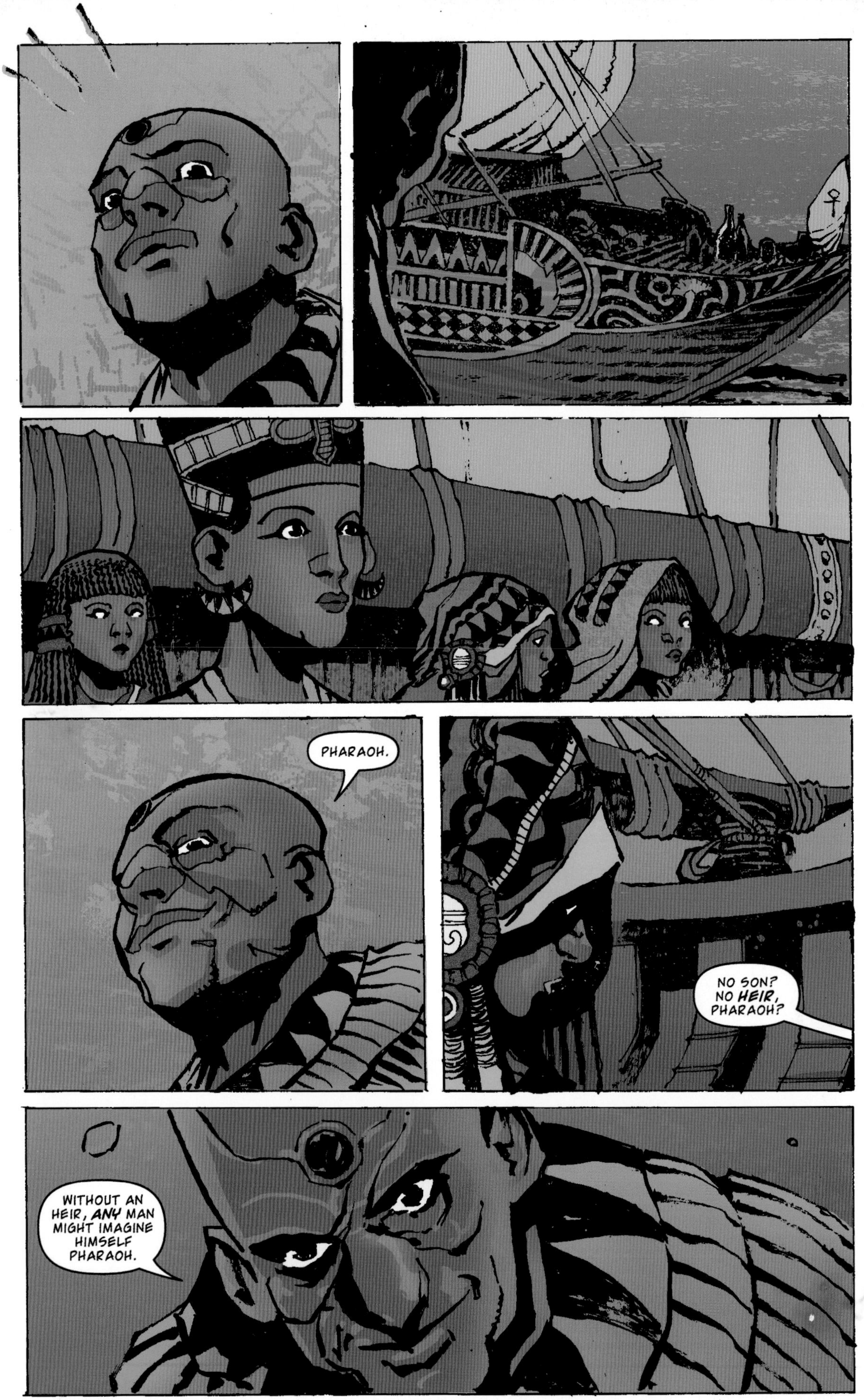
PHARAOH.
NO SON? NO HEIR, PHARAOH?
WITHOUT AN HEIR, ANY MAN MIGHT IMAGINE HIMSELF PHARAOH.

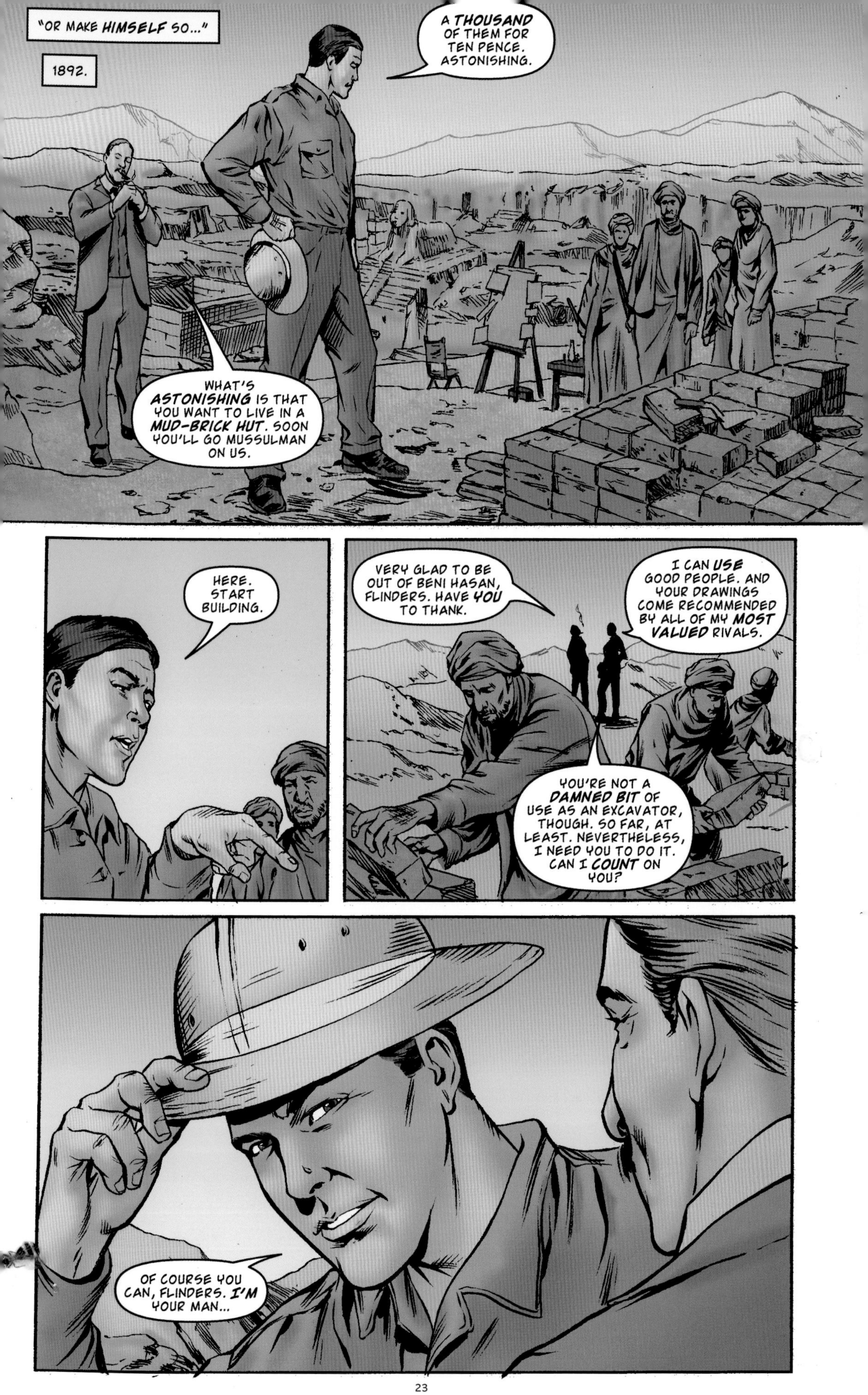
"OR MAKE HIMSELF SO..."
1892.
A THOUSAND OF THEM FOR TEN PENCE. ASTONISHING.
WHAT'S ASTONISHING IS THAT YOU WANT TO LIVE IN A MUD-BRICK HUT. SOON YOU'LL GO MUSSULMAN ON US.
HERE. START BUILDING.
VERY GLAD TO BE OUT OF BENI HASAN, FLINDERS. HAVE YOU TO THANK.
I CAN USE GOOD PEOPLE. AND YOUR DRAWINGS COME RECOMMENDED BY ALL OF MY MOST VALUED RIVALS.
YOU'RE NOT A DAMNED BIT OF USE AS AN EXCAVATOR, THOUGH. SO FAR, AT LEAST. NEVERTHELESS, I NEED YOU TO DO IT. CAN I COUNT ON YOU?
OF COURSE YOU CAN, FLINDERS. I'M YOUR MAN...

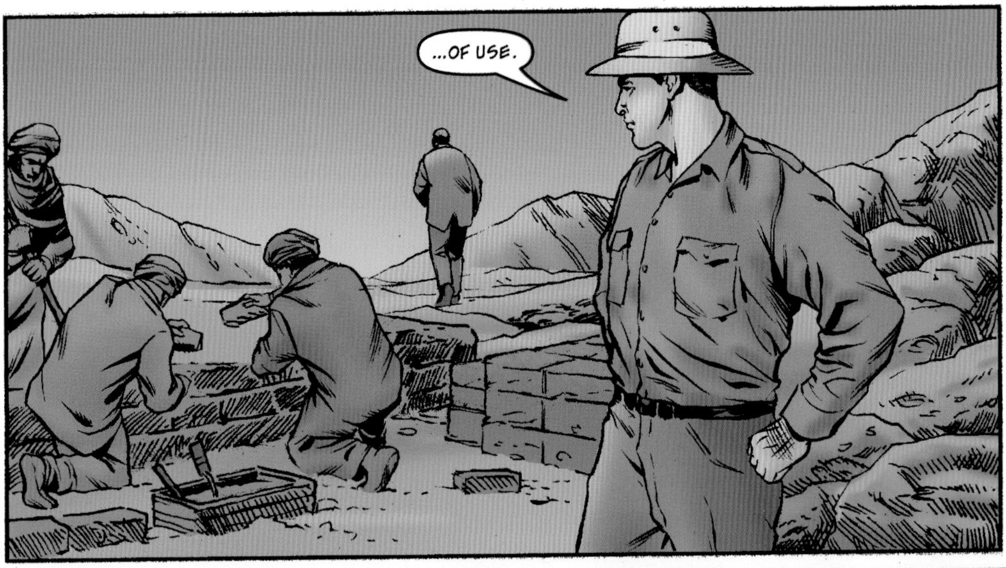
...OF USE.

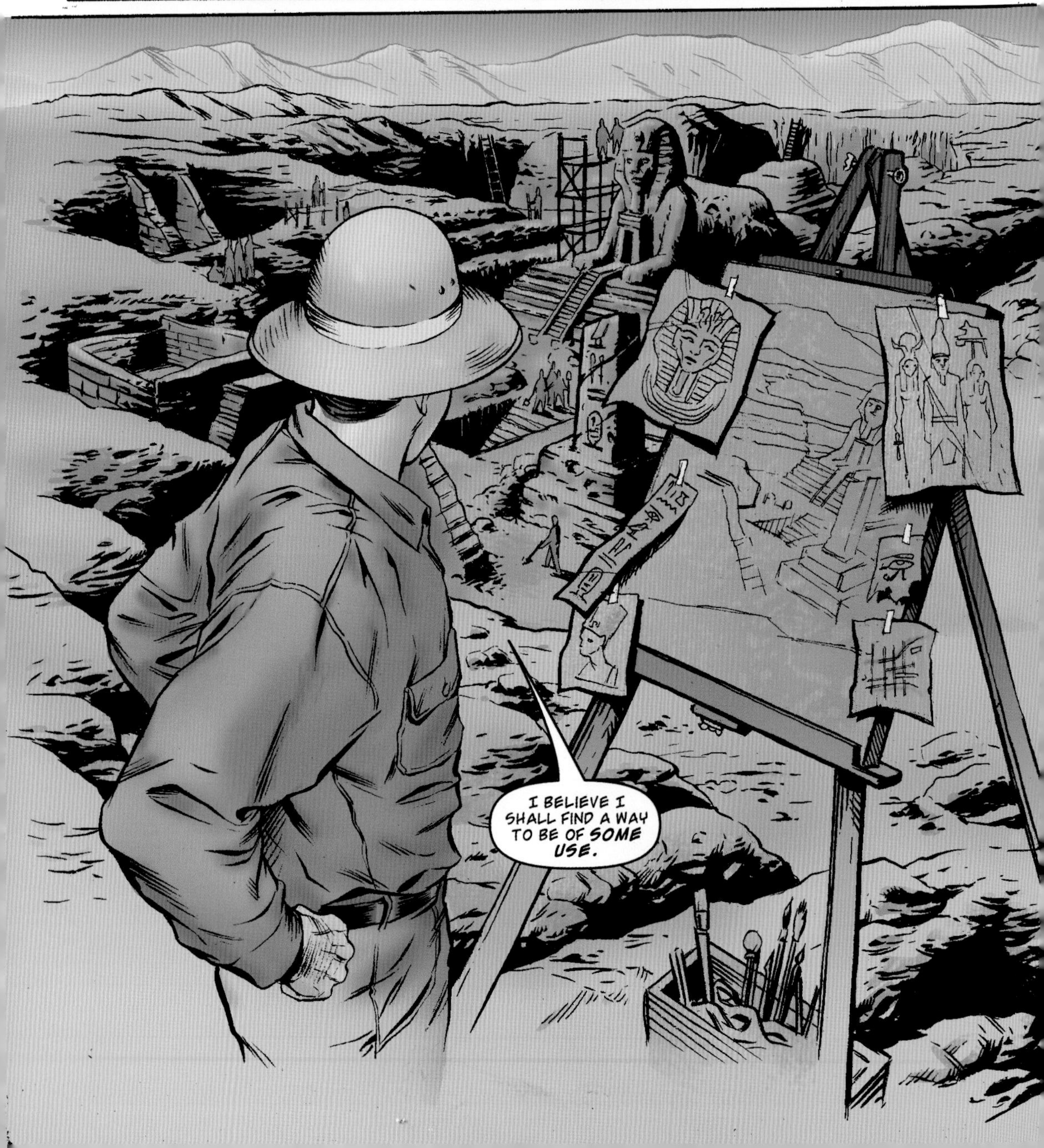
I BELIEVE I SHALL FIND A WAY TO BE OF **SOME USE**.

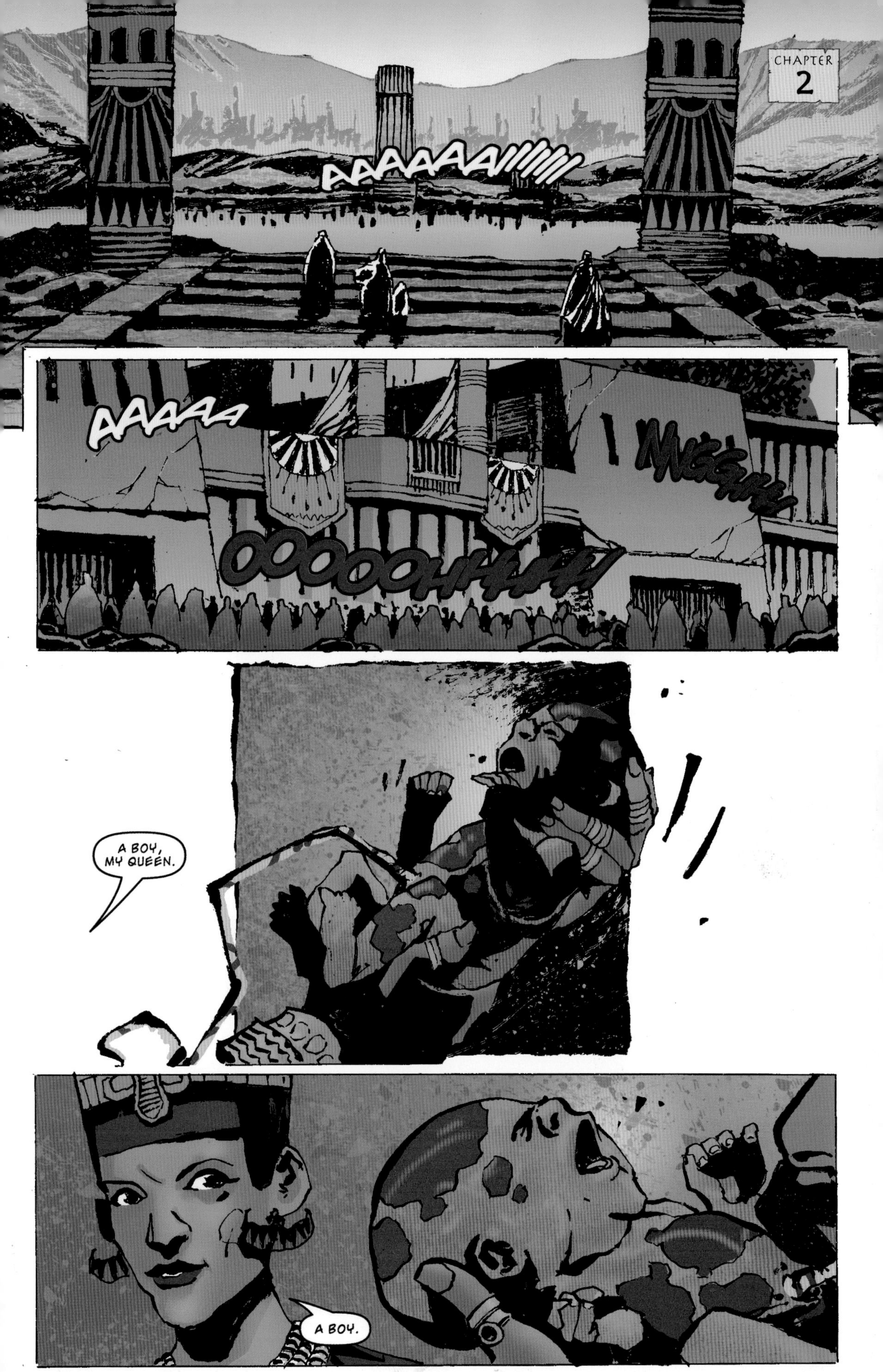
CHAPTER
2
AAAAAAIIIIIIII
AAAAA
NNGGHHH
OOOOOOHHHHH
A BOY, MY QUEEN.
A BOY.

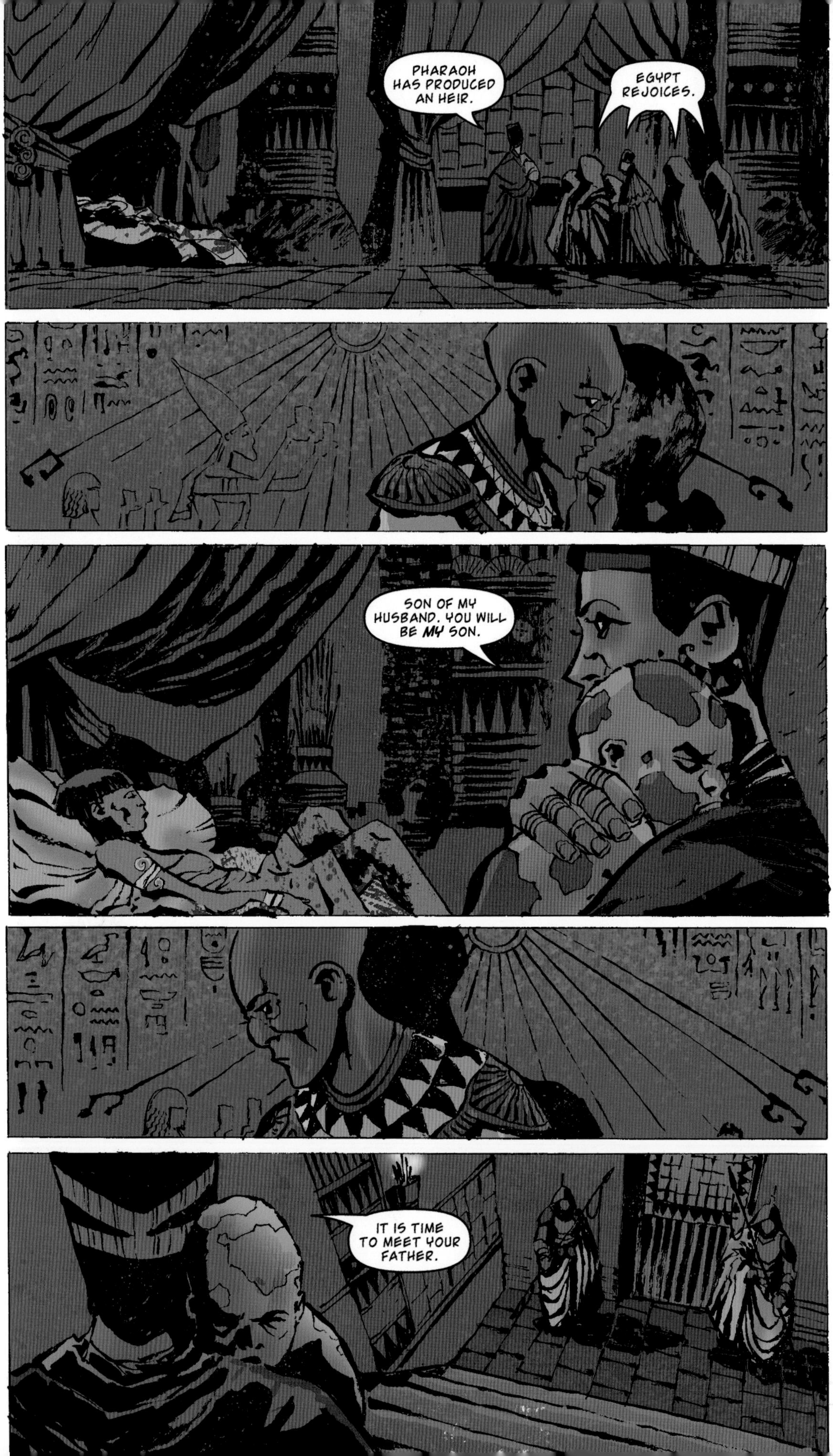
PHARAOH HAS PRODUCED AN HEIR.
EGYPT REJOICES.
SON OF MY HUSBAND. YOU WILL BE *MY* SON.
IT IS TIME TO MEET YOUR FATHER.

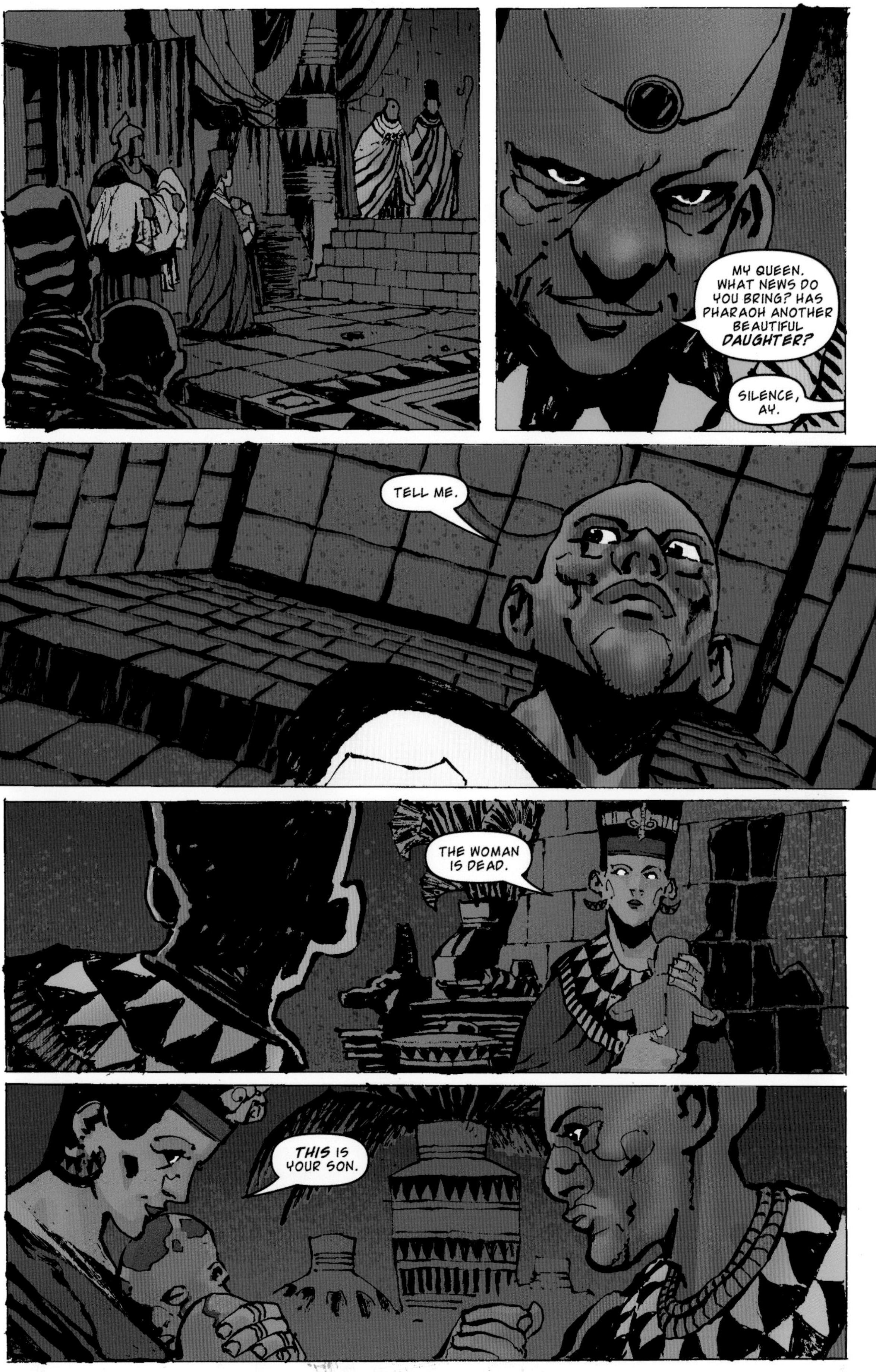
MY QUEEN. WHAT NEWS DO YOU BRING? HAS PHARAOH ANOTHER BEAUTIFUL DAUGHTER?
SILENCE, AY.
TELL ME.
THE WOMAN IS DEAD.
THIS IS YOUR SON.

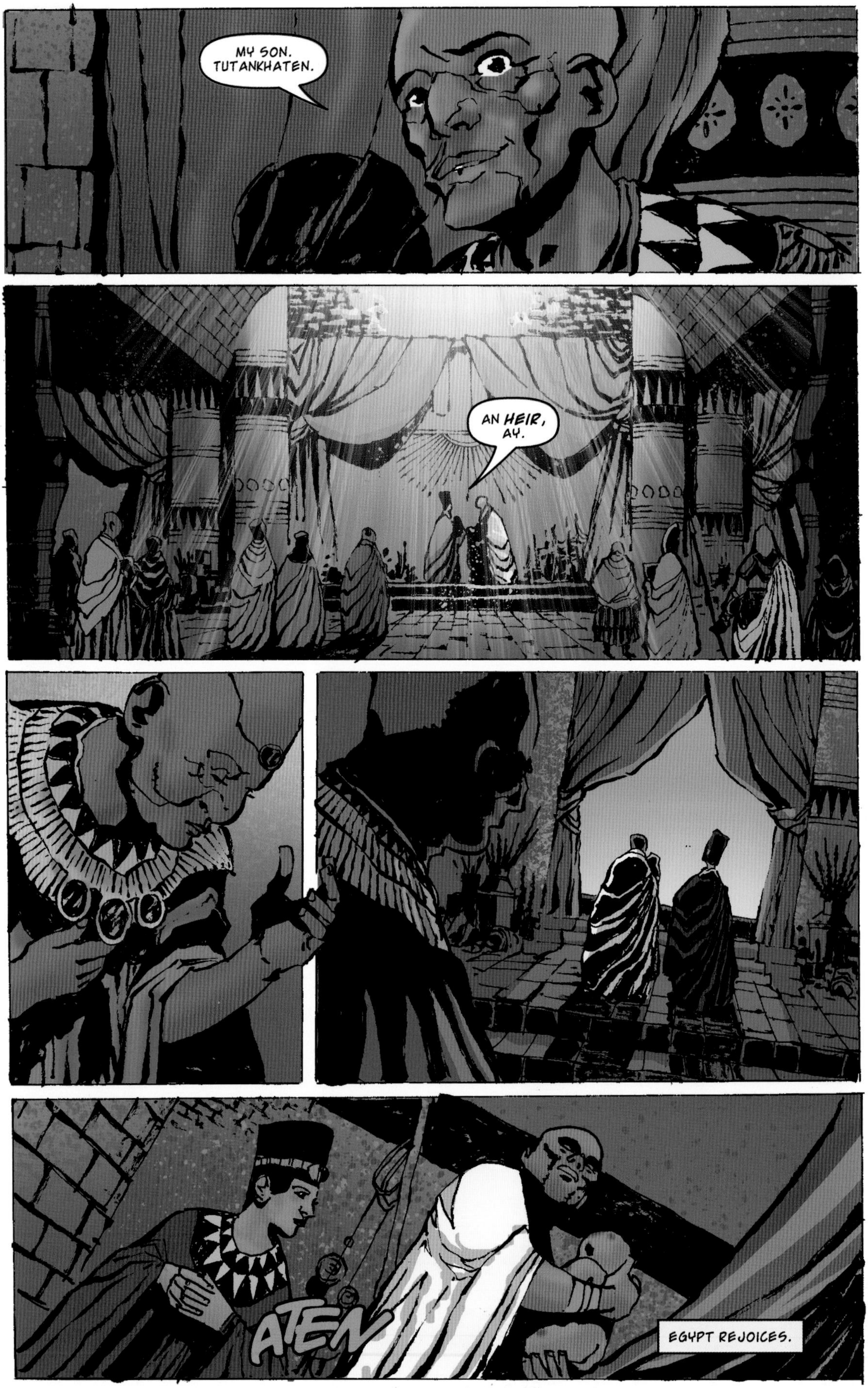
MY SON. TUTANKHATEN.
AN HEIR, AY.
ATEN
EGYPT REJOICES.

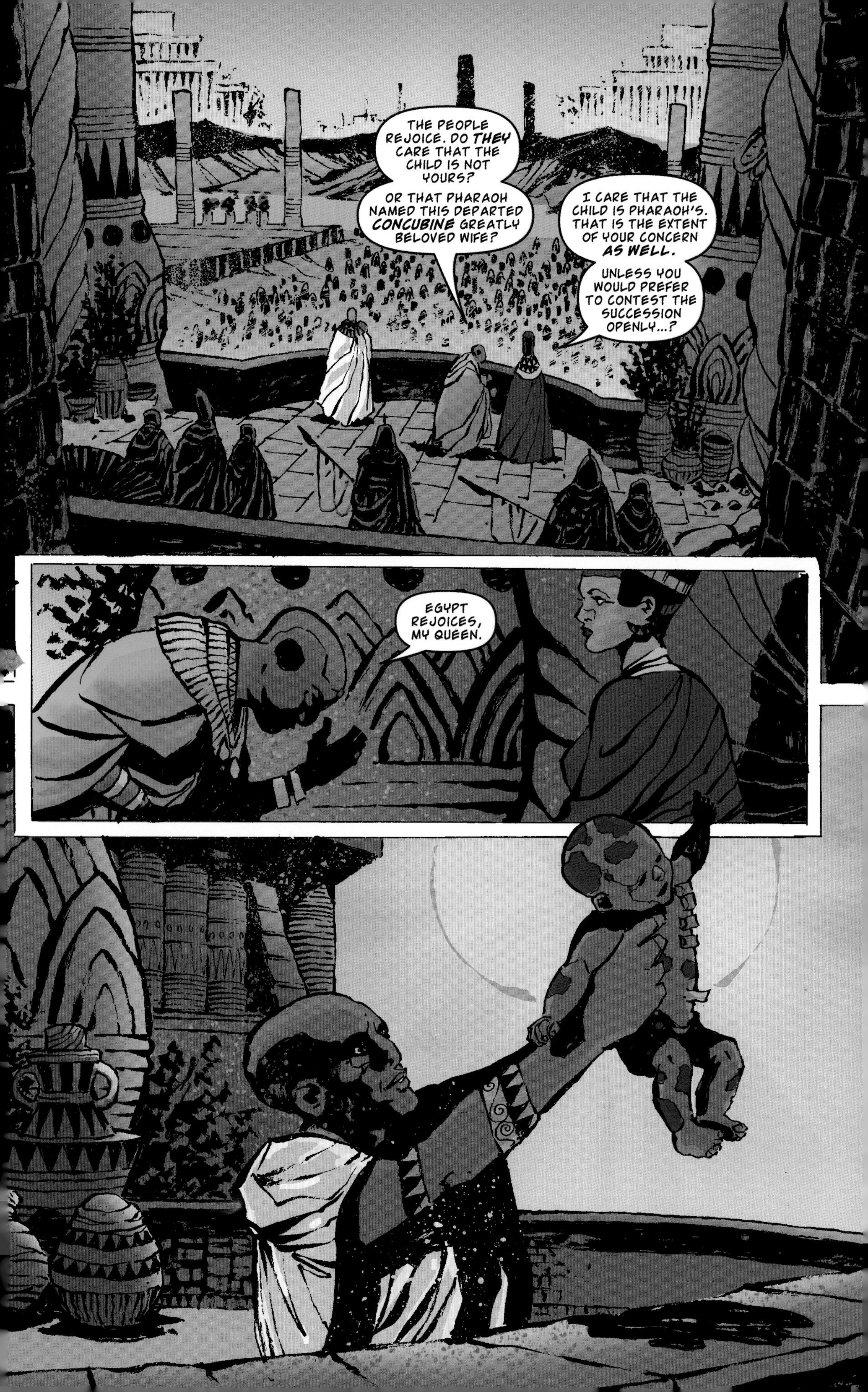
THE PEOPLE REJOICE. DO THEY CARE THAT THE CHILD IS NOT YOURS?
OR THAT PHARAOH NAMED THIS DEPARTED CONCUBINE GREATLY BELOVED WIFE?
I CARE THAT THE CHILD IS PHARAOH'S. THAT IS THE EXTENT OF YOUR CONCERN AS WELL.
UNLESS YOU WOULD PREFER TO CONTEST THE SUCCESSION OPENLY...?
EGYPT REJOICES, MY QUEEN.

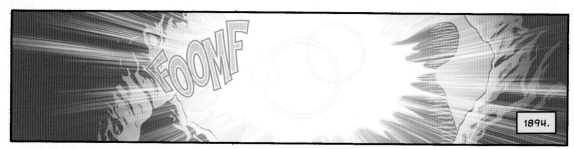

FOOMF

1894.

DID YOU GET IT?

HARD TO KNOW UNTIL IT'S DEVELOPED, WOULDN'T YOU SAY?

WELL, LET'S FIND OUT, SHALL WE? NOTHING ELSE IS GOING TO HAPPEN TODAY, WHAT WITH RAMADAN.

TOUR GUIDE. THAT'S THE JOB TO HAVE.

ONLY IF YOU'D RATHER TALK THAN WORK.

I THINK I WOULD. PLUS THE WOMEN...

30

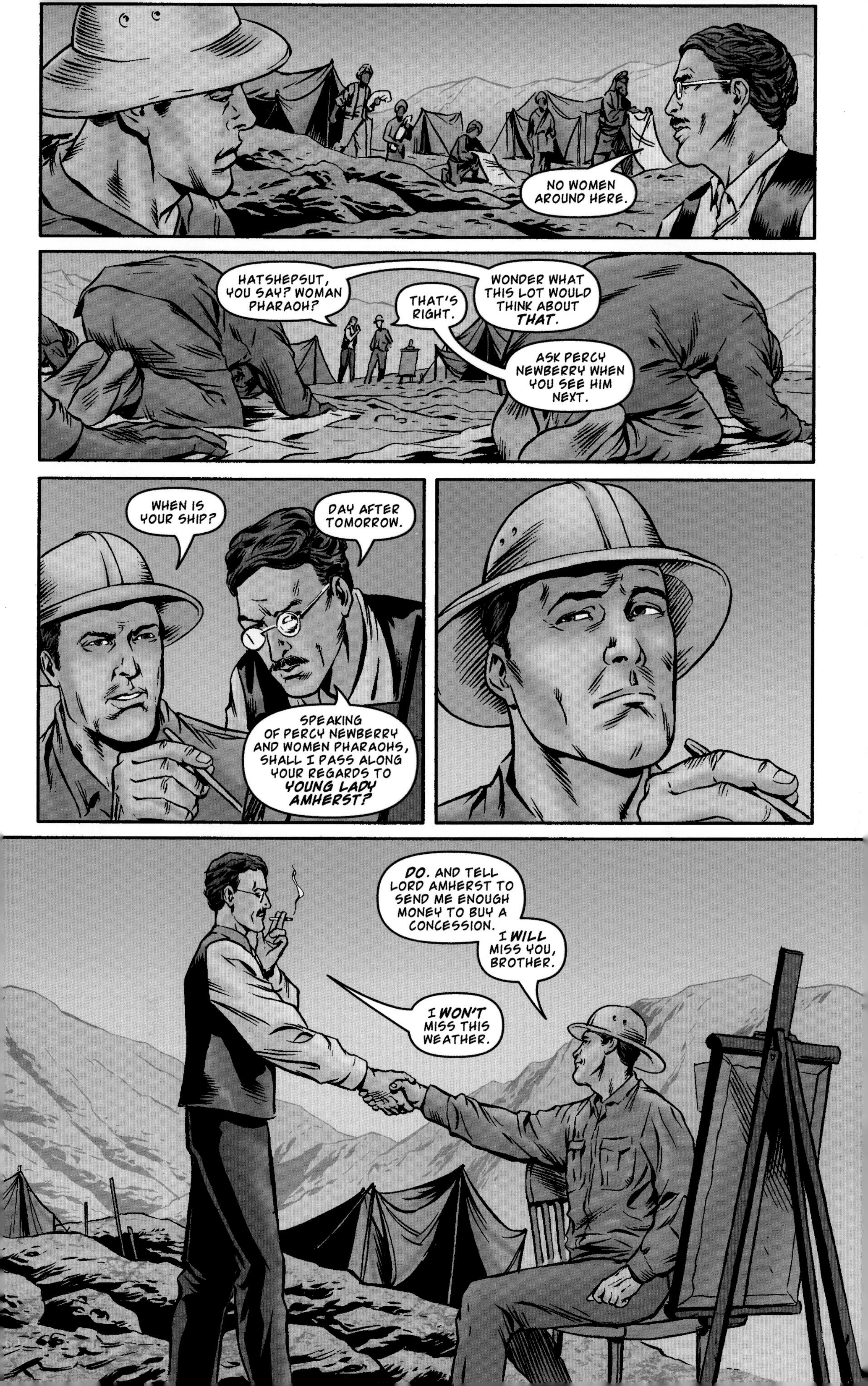
NO WOMEN AROUND HERE.
HATSHEPSUT, YOU SAY? WOMAN PHARAOH?
THAT'S RIGHT.
WONDER WHAT THIS LOT WOULD THINK ABOUT *THAT*.
ASK PERCY NEWBERRY WHEN YOU SEE HIM NEXT.
WHEN IS YOUR SHIP?
DAY AFTER TOMORROW.
SPEAKING OF PERCY NEWBERRY AND WOMEN PHARAOHS, SHALL I PASS ALONG YOUR REGARDS TO *YOUNG LADY AMHERST?*
DO. AND TELL LORD AMHERST TO SEND ME ENOUGH MONEY TO BUY A CONCESSION.
I *WILL* MISS YOU, BROTHER.
I *WON'T* MISS THIS WEATHER.

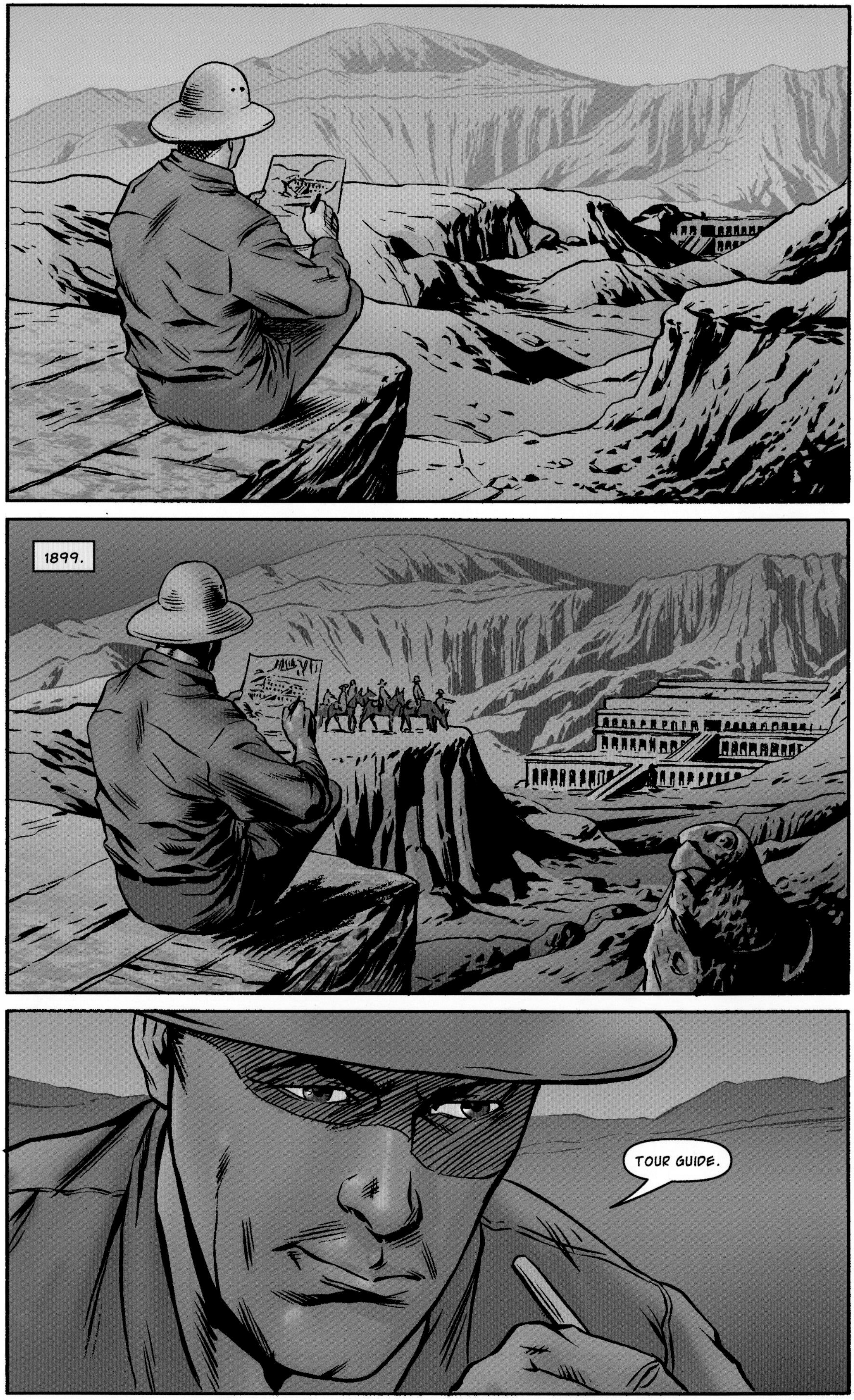
1899.
TOUR GUIDE.

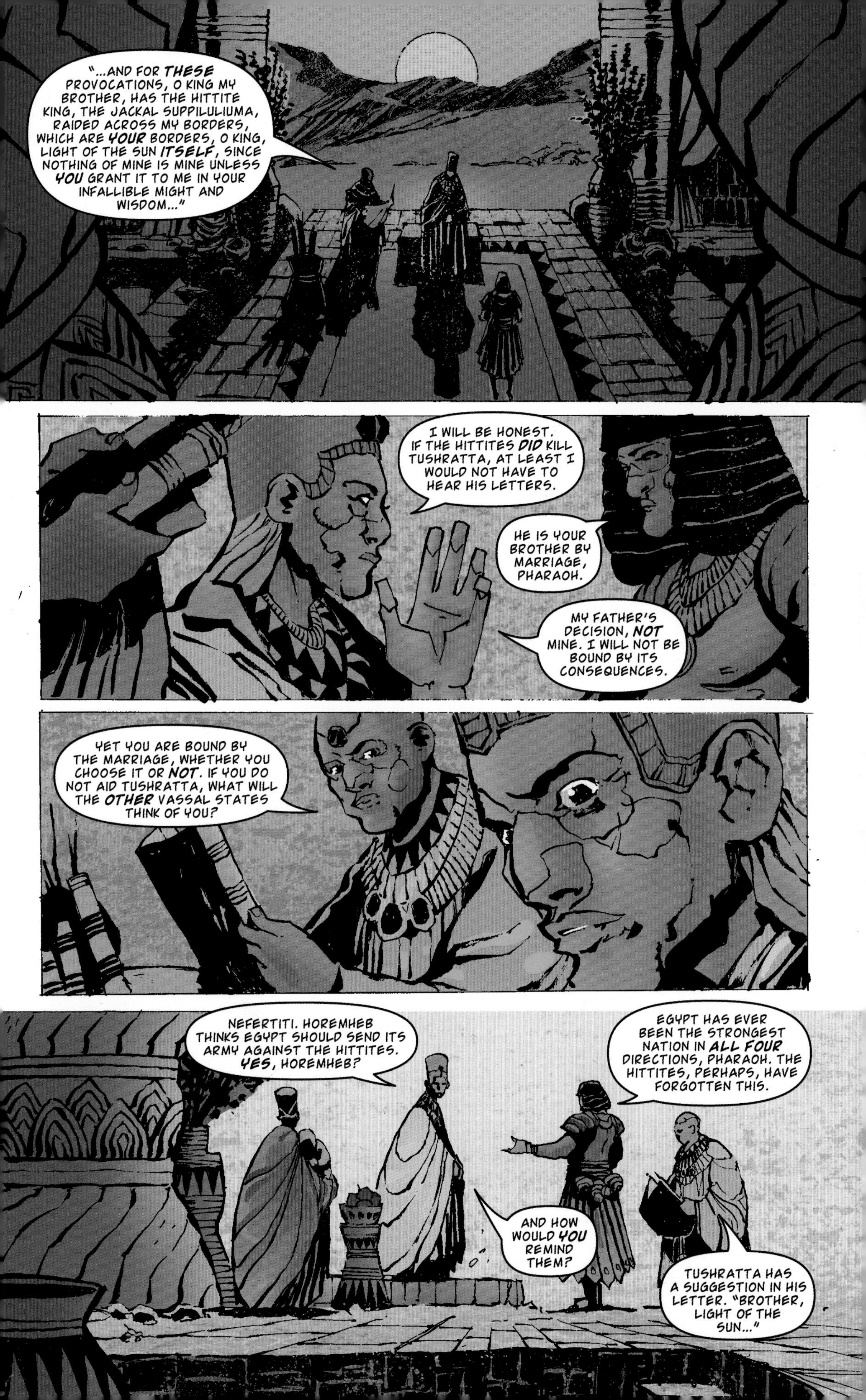
"...AND FOR THESE PROVOCATIONS, O KING MY BROTHER, HAS THE HITTITE KING, THE JACKAL SUPPILULIUMA, RAIDED ACROSS MY BORDERS, WHICH ARE YOUR BORDERS, O KING, LIGHT OF THE SUN ITSELF, SINCE NOTHING OF MINE IS MINE UNLESS YOU GRANT IT TO ME IN YOUR INFALLIBLE MIGHT AND WISDOM..."
I WILL BE HONEST. IF THE HITTITES DID KILL TUSHRATTA, AT LEAST I WOULD NOT HAVE TO HEAR HIS LETTERS.
HE IS YOUR BROTHER BY MARRIAGE, PHARAOH.
MY FATHER'S DECISION, NOT MINE. I WILL NOT BE BOUND BY ITS CONSEQUENCES.
YET YOU ARE BOUND BY THE MARRIAGE, WHETHER YOU CHOOSE IT OR NOT. IF YOU DO NOT AID TUSHRATTA, WHAT WILL THE OTHER VASSAL STATES THINK OF YOU?
NEFERTITI. HOREMHEB THINKS EGYPT SHOULD SEND ITS ARMY AGAINST THE HITTITES. YES, HOREMHEB?
EGYPT HAS EVER BEEN THE STRONGEST NATION IN ALL FOUR DIRECTIONS, PHARAOH. THE HITTITES, PERHAPS, HAVE FORGOTTEN THIS.
AND HOW WOULD YOU REMIND THEM?
TUSHRATTA HAS A SUGGESTION IN HIS LETTER. "BROTHER, LIGHT OF THE SUN..."

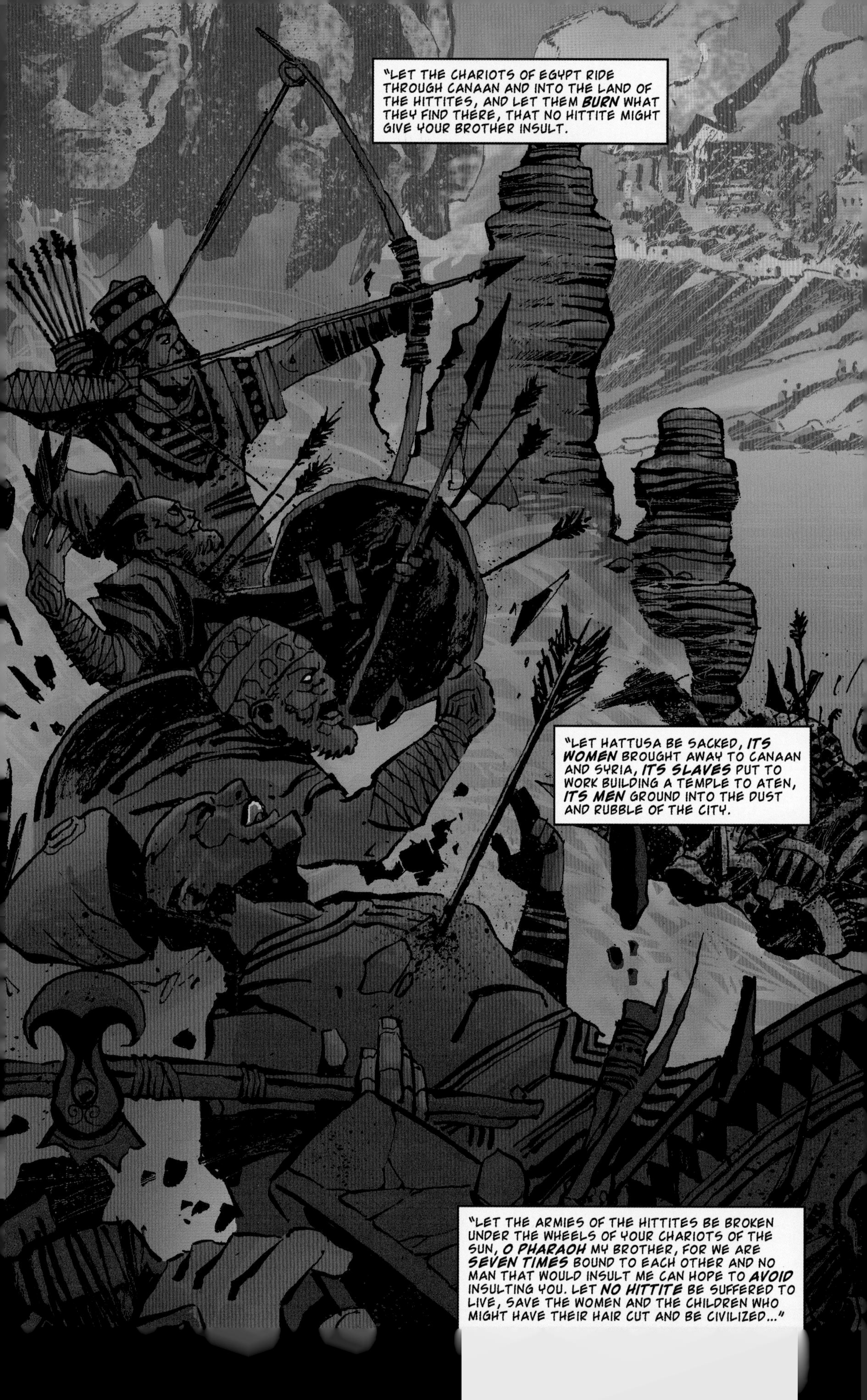
"LET THE CHARIOTS OF EGYPT RIDE THROUGH CANAAN AND INTO THE LAND OF THE HITTITES, AND LET THEM **BURN** WHAT THEY FIND THERE, THAT NO HITTITE MIGHT GIVE YOUR BROTHER INSULT.
"LET HATTUSA BE SACKED, **ITS WOMEN** BROUGHT AWAY TO CANAAN AND SYRIA, **ITS SLAVES** PUT TO WORK BUILDING A TEMPLE TO ATEN, **ITS MEN** GROUND INTO THE DUST AND RUBBLE OF THE CITY.
"LET THE ARMIES OF THE HITTITES BE BROKEN UNDER THE WHEELS OF YOUR CHARIOTS OF THE SUN, **O PHARAOH** MY BROTHER, FOR WE ARE **SEVEN TIMES** BOUND TO EACH OTHER AND NO MAN THAT WOULD INSULT ME CAN HOPE TO **AVOID** INSULTING YOU. LET **NO HITTITE** BE SUFFERED TO LIVE, SAVE THE WOMEN AND THE CHILDREN WHO MIGHT HAVE THEIR HAIR CUT AND BE CIVILIZED..."

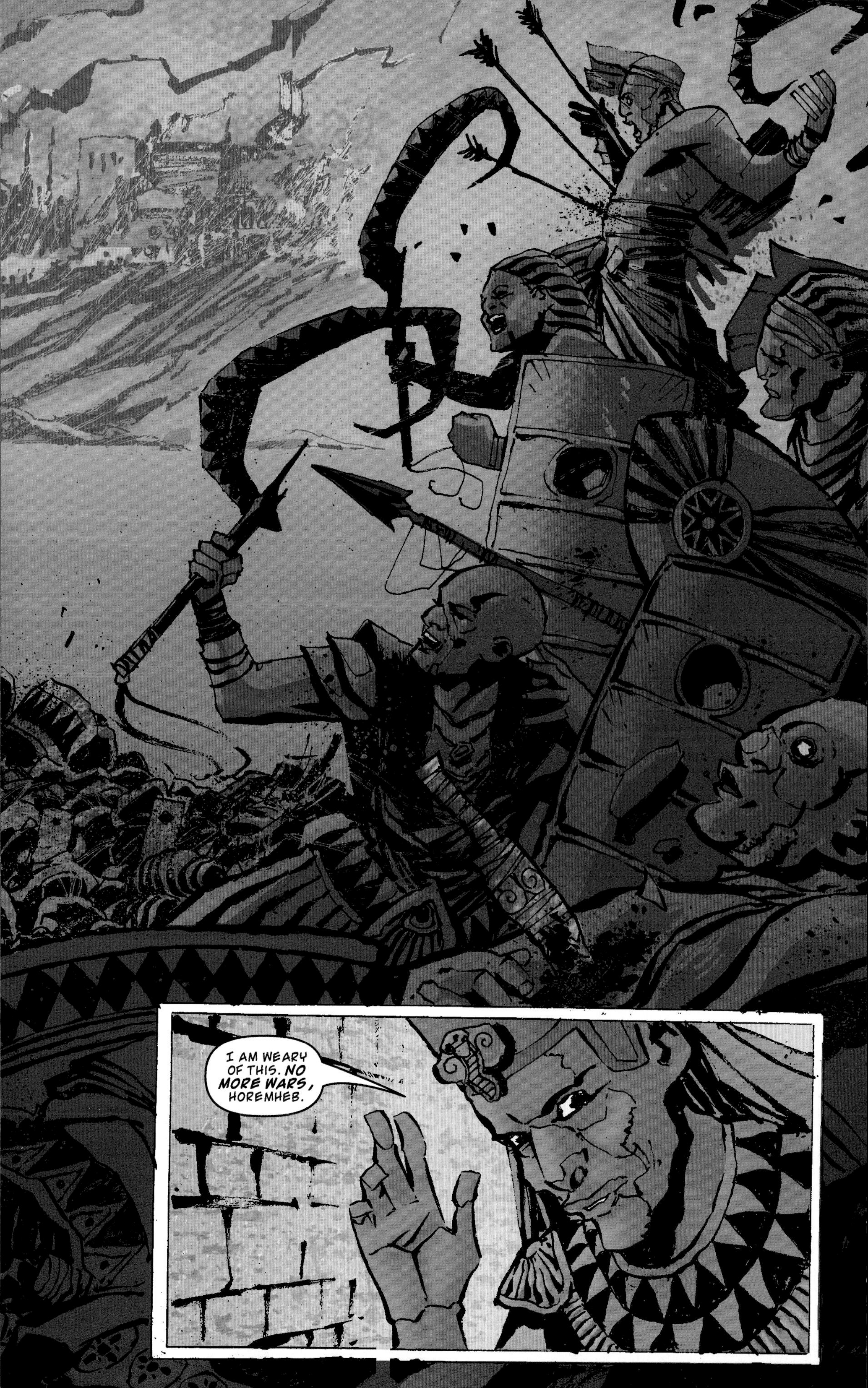
I AM WEARY OF THIS. NO MORE WARS, HOREMHEB.

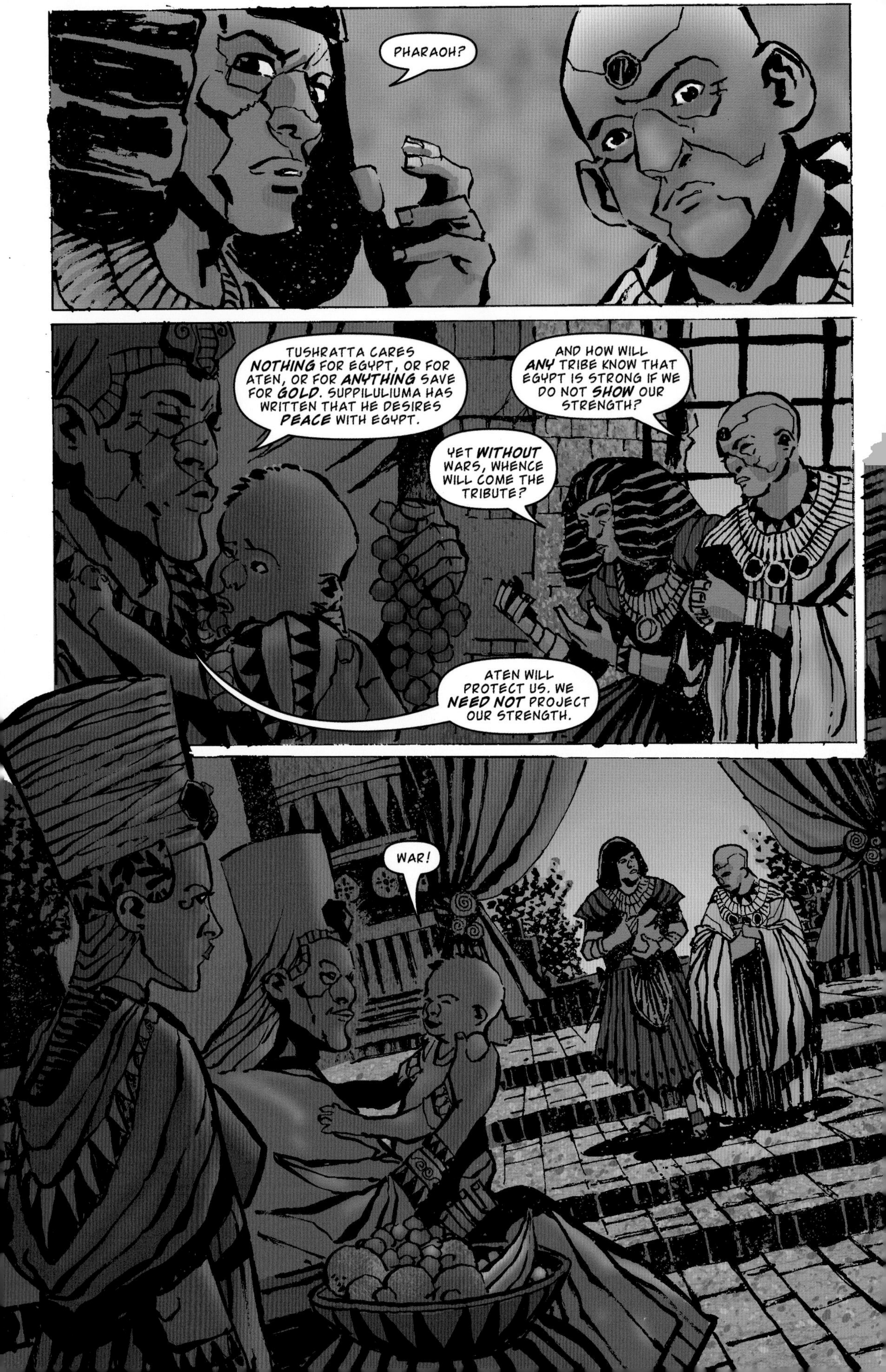
PHARAOH?
TUSHRATTA CARES NOTHING FOR EGYPT, OR FOR ATEN, OR FOR ANYTHING SAVE FOR GOLD. SUPPILULIUMA HAS WRITTEN THAT HE DESIRES PEACE WITH EGYPT.
AND HOW WILL ANY TRIBE KNOW THAT EGYPT IS STRONG IF WE DO NOT SHOW OUR STRENGTH?
YET WITHOUT WARS, WHENCE WILL COME THE TRIBUTE?
ATEN WILL PROTECT US. WE NEED NOT PROJECT OUR STRENGTH.
WAR!

GENTLEMEN ARE INVITED TO TAKE OFF THEIR COATS. LADIES, I'M AFRAID YOU'LL HAVE TO SETTLE FOR REMOVING YOUR HATS.

DEAREST LADY AMHERST, I HAVE RECENTLY PROCURED A **MUCH-DESIRED** POSITION OF STABILITY AND INFLUENCE WITHIN THE EGYPTOLOGIST HIERARCHY. I AM NOW **CHIEF INSPECTOR** FOR THE ANTIQUITIES SERVICE IN UPPER EGYPT.

THE VALLEY OF THE KINGS, AS IT IS KNOWN, IS MINE TO INSPECT. WHATEVER WONDERS MAY COME FROM ITS PACKED AND RECALCITRANT SOIL, I AM TO CURATE THEM.

VALLEY OF THE KINGS, 1900.

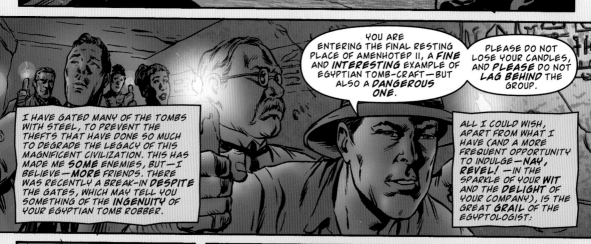

YOU ARE ENTERING THE FINAL RESTING PLACE OF AMENHOTEP II, A **FINE** AND **INTERESTING** EXAMPLE OF EGYPTIAN TOMB-CRAFT—BUT ALSO A **DANGEROUS ONE**.

PLEASE DO NOT LOSE YOUR CANDLES, AND **PLEASE** DO NOT **LAG BEHIND** THE GROUP.

I HAVE GATED MANY OF THE TOMBS WITH STEEL, TO PREVENT THE THEFTS THAT HAVE DONE SO MUCH TO DEGRADE THE LEGACY OF THIS MAGNIFICENT CIVILIZATION. THIS HAS MADE ME **SOME** ENEMIES, BUT—I BELIEVE—**MORE** FRIENDS. THERE WAS RECENTLY A BREAK-IN **DESPITE** THE GATES, WHICH MAY TELL YOU SOMETHING OF THE **INGENUITY** OF YOUR EGYPTIAN TOMB ROBBER.

ALL I COULD WISH, APART FROM WHAT I HAVE (AND A MORE FREQUENT OPPORTUNITY TO INDULGE—NAY, **REVEL!**—IN THE SPARKLE OF YOUR **WIT** AND THE **DELIGHT** OF YOUR COMPANY), IS THE GREAT **GRAIL** OF THE EGYPTOLOGIST:

PAY CAREFUL ATTENTION TO **EACH** AND **EVERY** STEP, PLEASE.

A CONCESSION OF MY OWN.

WHAT THE DEVIL'S **WITH** THESE PITS? SOME "**REST IN PEACE**."

MOSTLY, I BELIEVE, THEY ARE THERE TO DRAIN OFF EXCESS RAIN.

BUT IF THEY DRAIN OFF AN OCCASIONAL **TOMB ROBBER**, NO EGYPTIAN WOULD BE BROKEN-HEARTED.

IT IS **POSSIBLE** THAT I HAVE, AT LAST, MET THE MAN WHO MIGHT POSSESS BOTH THE FINANCIAL WHEREWITHAL AND THE PIONEER RECKLESSNESS TO MAKE THAT HAPPEN. HIS NAME IS THEODORE DAVIS, AND **OF COURSE** HE IS AN AMERICAN.

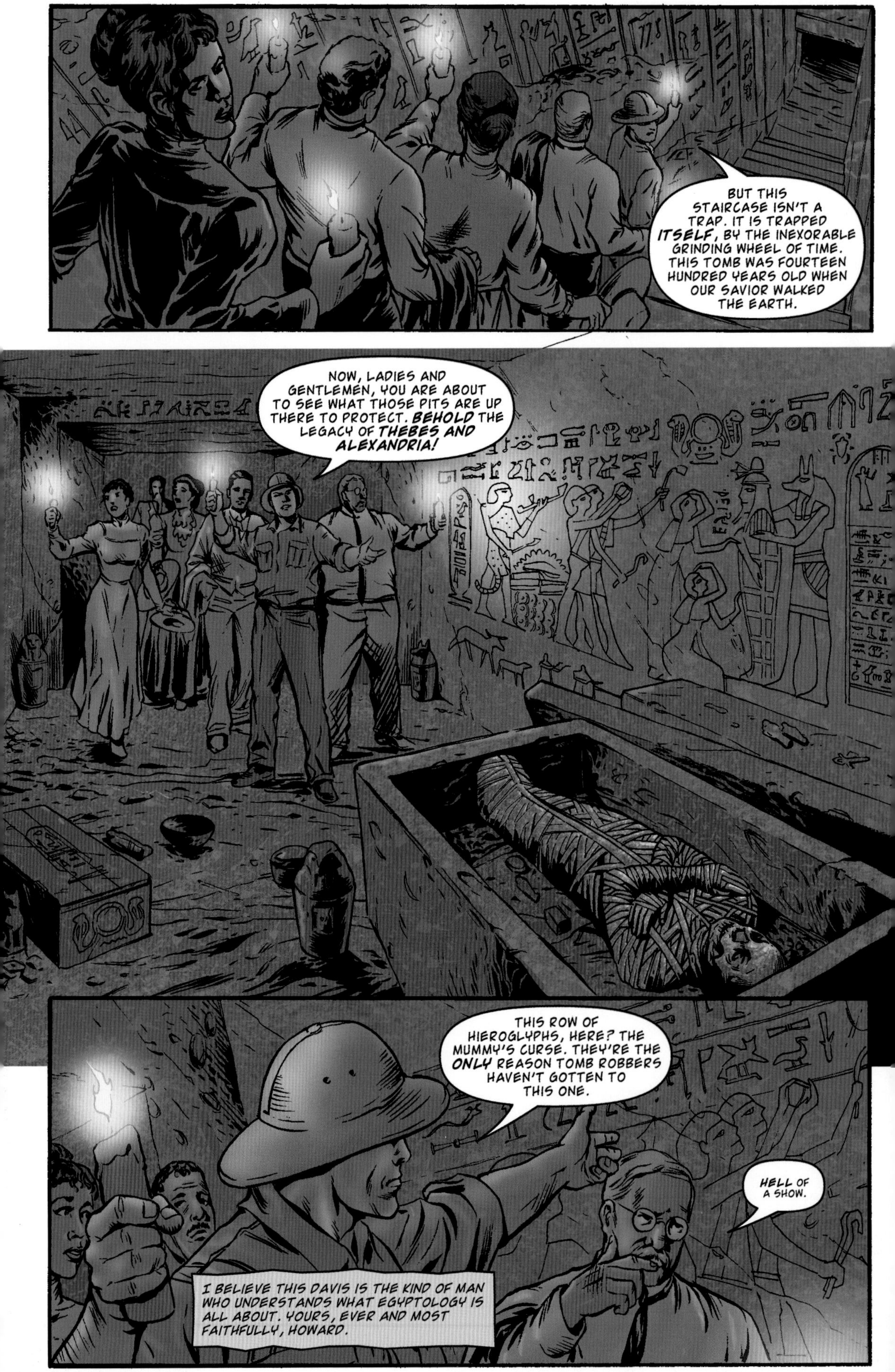

BUT THIS STAIRCASE ISN'T A TRAP. IT IS TRAPPED ITSELF, BY THE INEXORABLE GRINDING WHEEL OF TIME. THIS TOMB WAS FOURTEEN HUNDRED YEARS OLD WHEN OUR SAVIOR WALKED THE EARTH.
NOW, LADIES AND GENTLEMEN, YOU ARE ABOUT TO SEE WHAT THOSE PITS ARE UP THERE TO PROTECT. BEHOLD THE LEGACY OF THEBES AND ALEXANDRIA!
THIS ROW OF HIEROGLYPHS, HERE? THE MUMMY'S CURSE. THEY'RE THE ONLY REASON TOMB ROBBERS HAVEN'T GOTTEN TO THIS ONE.
HELL OF A SHOW.
I BELIEVE THIS DAVIS IS THE KIND OF MAN WHO UNDERSTANDS WHAT EGYPTOLOGY IS ALL ABOUT. YOURS, EVER AND MOST FAITHFULLY, HOWARD.

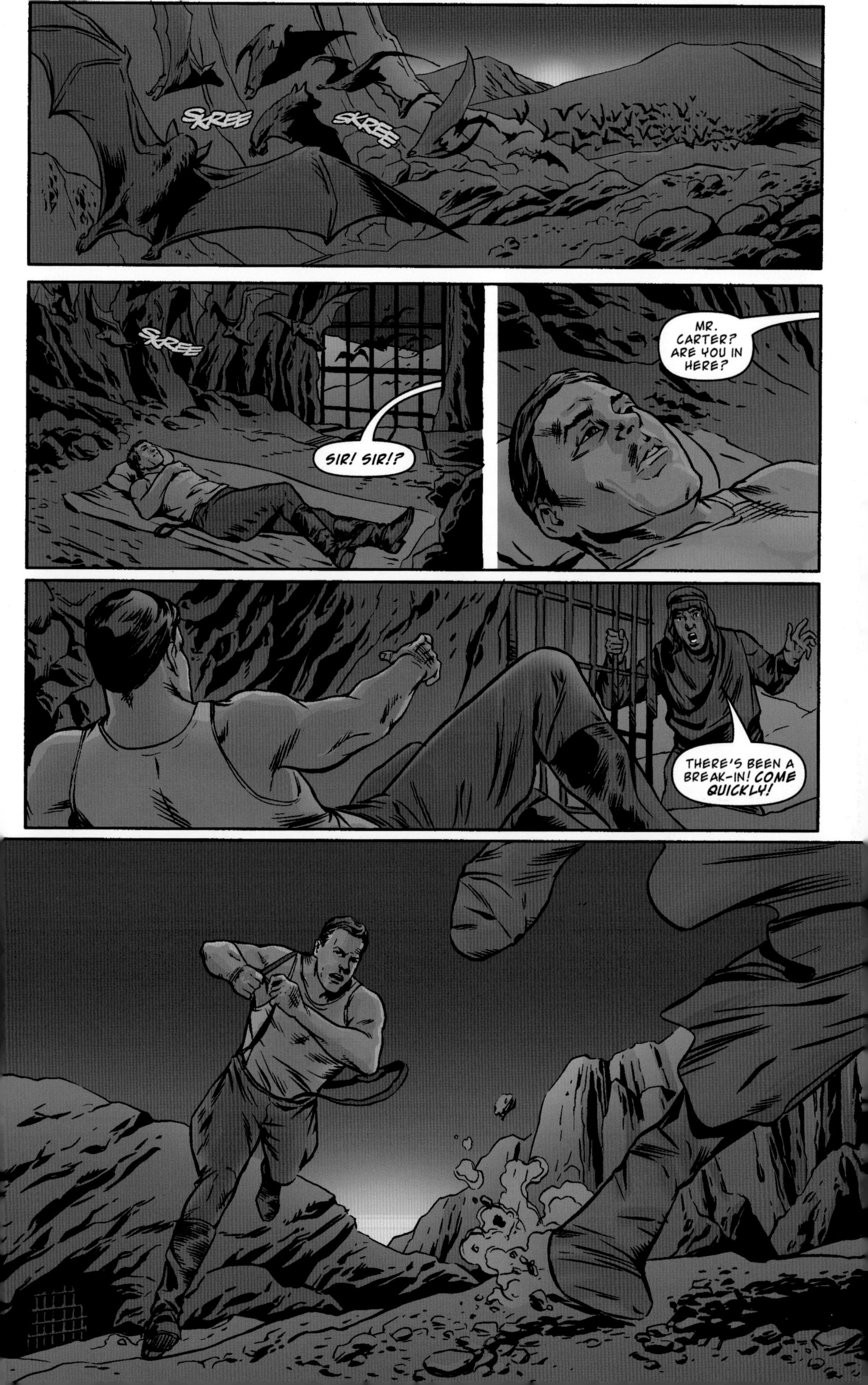
SKREE
SKREE
SKREE
SIR! SIR!?
MR. CARTER? ARE YOU IN HERE?
THERE'S BEEN A BREAK-IN! COME QUICKLY!

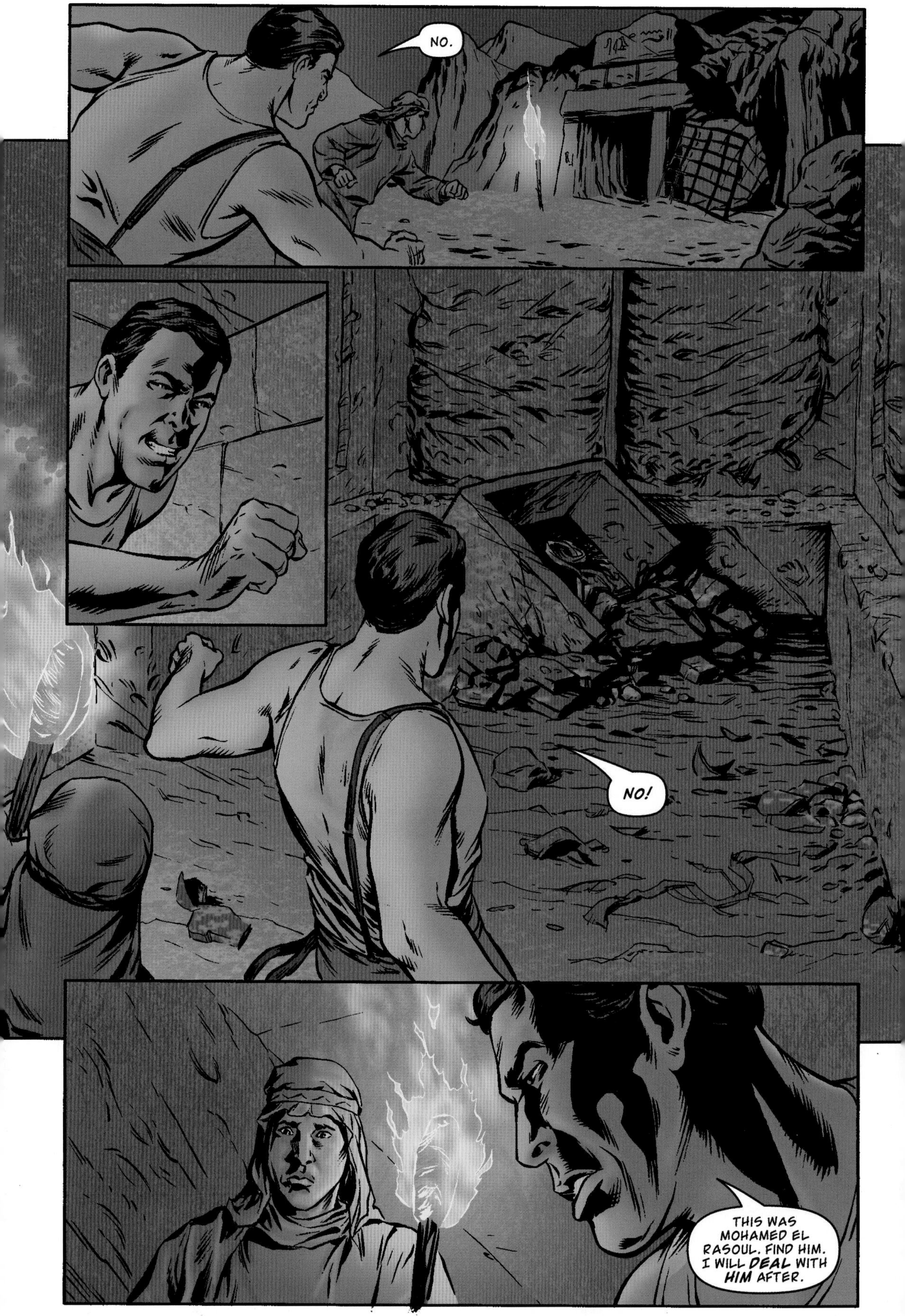
NO.
NO!
THIS WAS MOHAMED EL RASOUL. FIND HIM. I WILL DEAL WITH HIM AFTER.

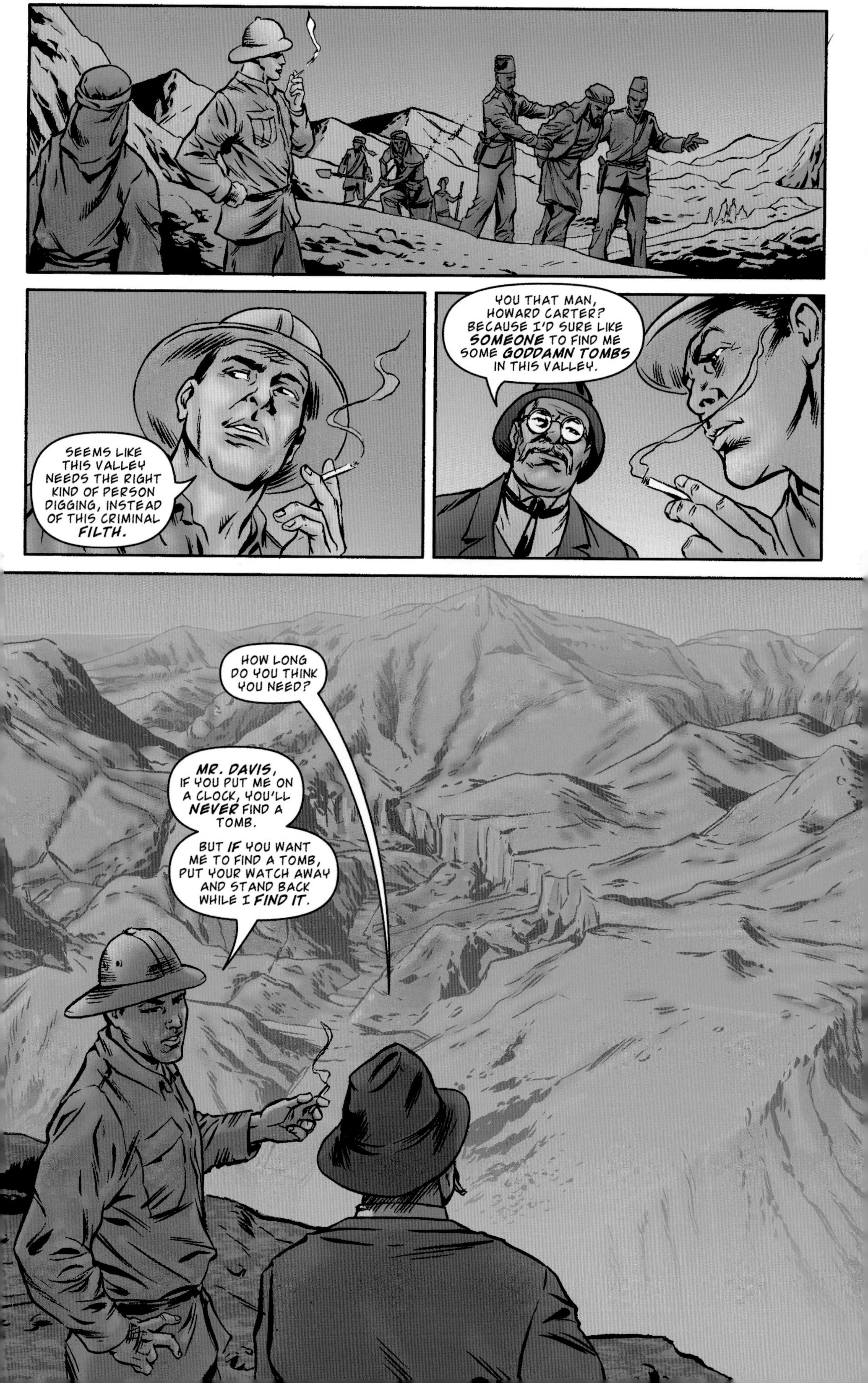
SEEMS LIKE THIS VALLEY NEEDS THE RIGHT KIND OF PERSON DIGGING, INSTEAD OF THIS CRIMINAL **FILTH**.
YOU THAT MAN, HOWARD CARTER? BECAUSE I'D SURE LIKE **SOMEONE** TO FIND ME SOME **GODDAMN TOMBS** IN THIS VALLEY.
HOW LONG DO YOU THINK YOU NEED?
MR. DAVIS, IF YOU PUT ME ON A CLOCK, YOU'LL **NEVER** FIND A TOMB.
BUT **IF** YOU WANT ME TO FIND A TOMB, PUT YOUR WATCH AWAY AND STAND BACK WHILE I **FIND IT**.

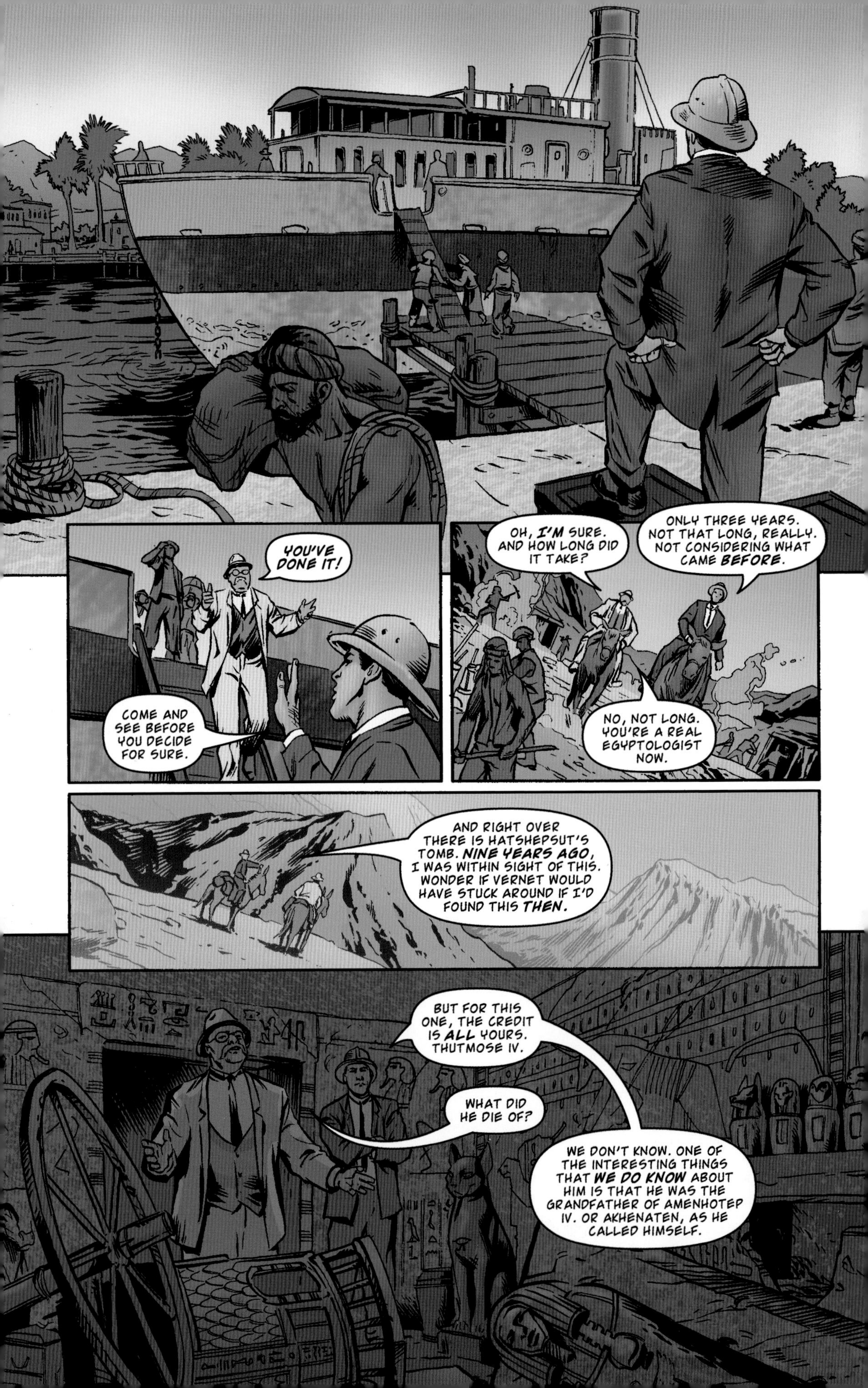
YOU'VE DONE IT!
COME AND SEE BEFORE YOU DECIDE FOR SURE.
OH, I'M SURE. AND HOW LONG DID IT TAKE?
ONLY THREE YEARS. NOT THAT LONG, REALLY. NOT CONSIDERING WHAT CAME BEFORE.
NO, NOT LONG. YOU'RE A REAL EGYPTOLOGIST NOW.
AND RIGHT OVER THERE IS HATSHEPSUT'S TOMB. NINE YEARS AGO, I WAS WITHIN SIGHT OF THIS. WONDER IF VERNET WOULD HAVE STUCK AROUND IF I'D FOUND THIS THEN.
BUT FOR THIS ONE, THE CREDIT IS ALL YOURS. THUTMOSE IV.
WHAT DID HE DIE OF?
WE DON'T KNOW. ONE OF THE INTERESTING THINGS THAT WE DO KNOW ABOUT HIM IS THAT HE WAS THE GRANDFATHER OF AMENHOTEP IV. OR AKHENATEN, AS HE CALLED HIMSELF.

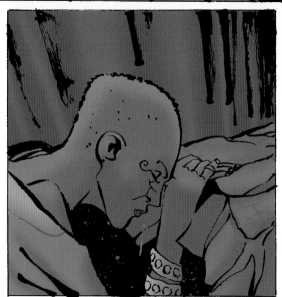

GUARD!

YES, MY—

BRING ME AY. IMMEDIATELY.

PHARAOH HAS JOINED HIS ANCESTORS.

WHAT DID HE DIE OF?

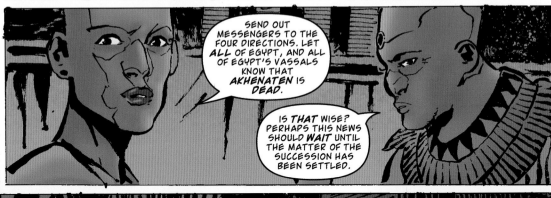

SEND OUT MESSENGERS TO THE FOUR DIRECTIONS. LET *ALL* OF EGYPT, AND ALL OF EGYPT'S VASSALS KNOW THAT *AKHENATEN* IS *DEAD*.

IS *THAT* WISE? PERHAPS THIS NEWS SHOULD *WAIT* UNTIL THE MATTER OF THE SUCCESSION HAS BEEN SETTLED.

THERE IS *NO QUESTION* OF SUCCESSION. I WILL PREPARE TUTANKHAMEN, AND WHEN HE IS READY, HE WILL ASSUME *HIS FATHER'S THRONE*. UNTIL THEN, I WILL RULE *WITH* HIM.

NOW, AY. NOTIFY THE PRIESTS. PREPARATIONS FOR HIS BURIAL *MUST* BEGIN.

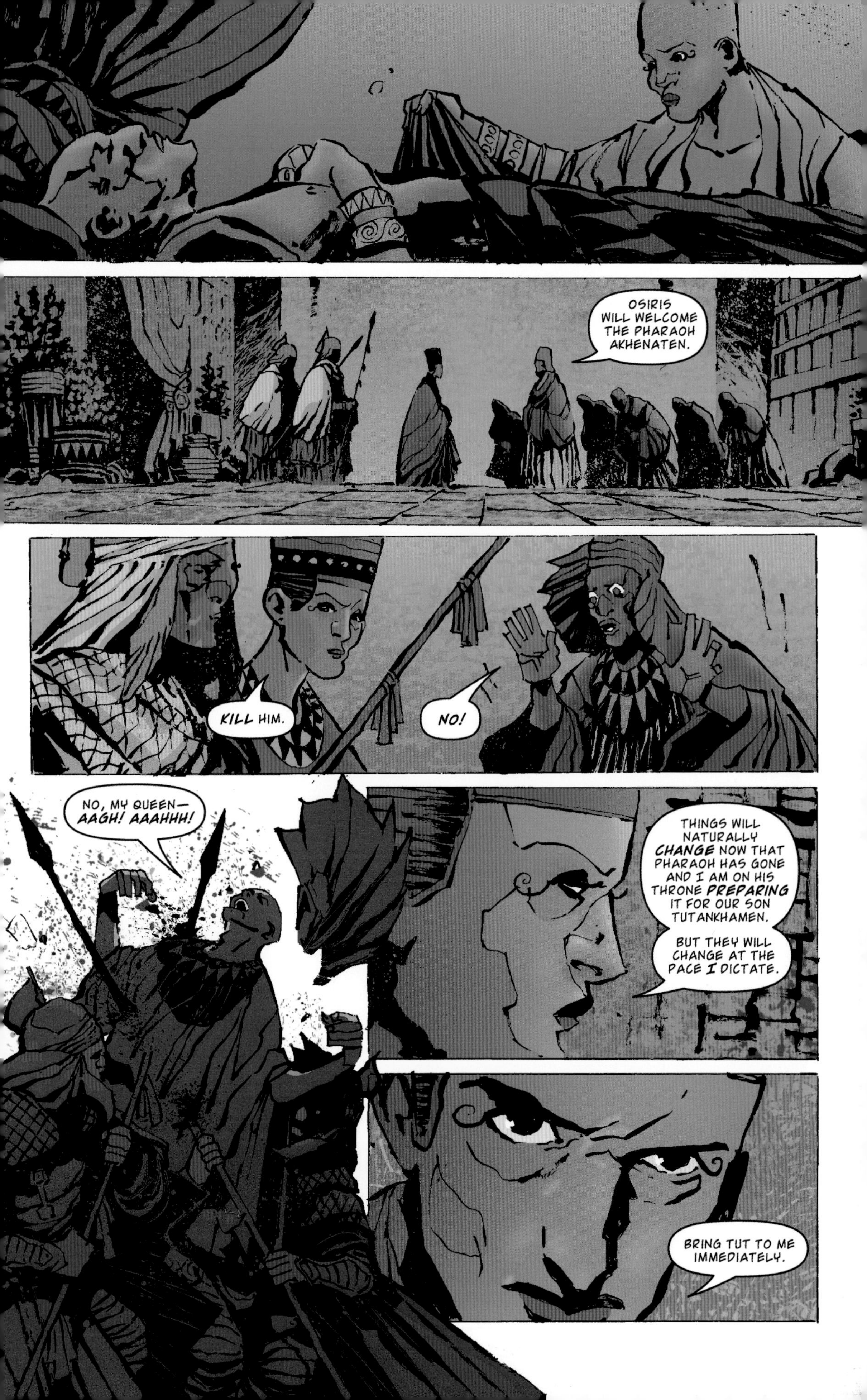
OSIRIS WILL WELCOME THE PHARAOH AKHENATEN.
KILL HIM.
NO!
NO, MY QUEEN— AAGH! AAAHHH!
THINGS WILL NATURALLY CHANGE NOW THAT PHARAOH HAS GONE AND I AM ON HIS THRONE PREPARING IT FOR OUR SON TUTANKHAMEN.
BUT THEY WILL CHANGE AT THE PACE I DICTATE.
BRING TUT TO ME IMMEDIATELY.

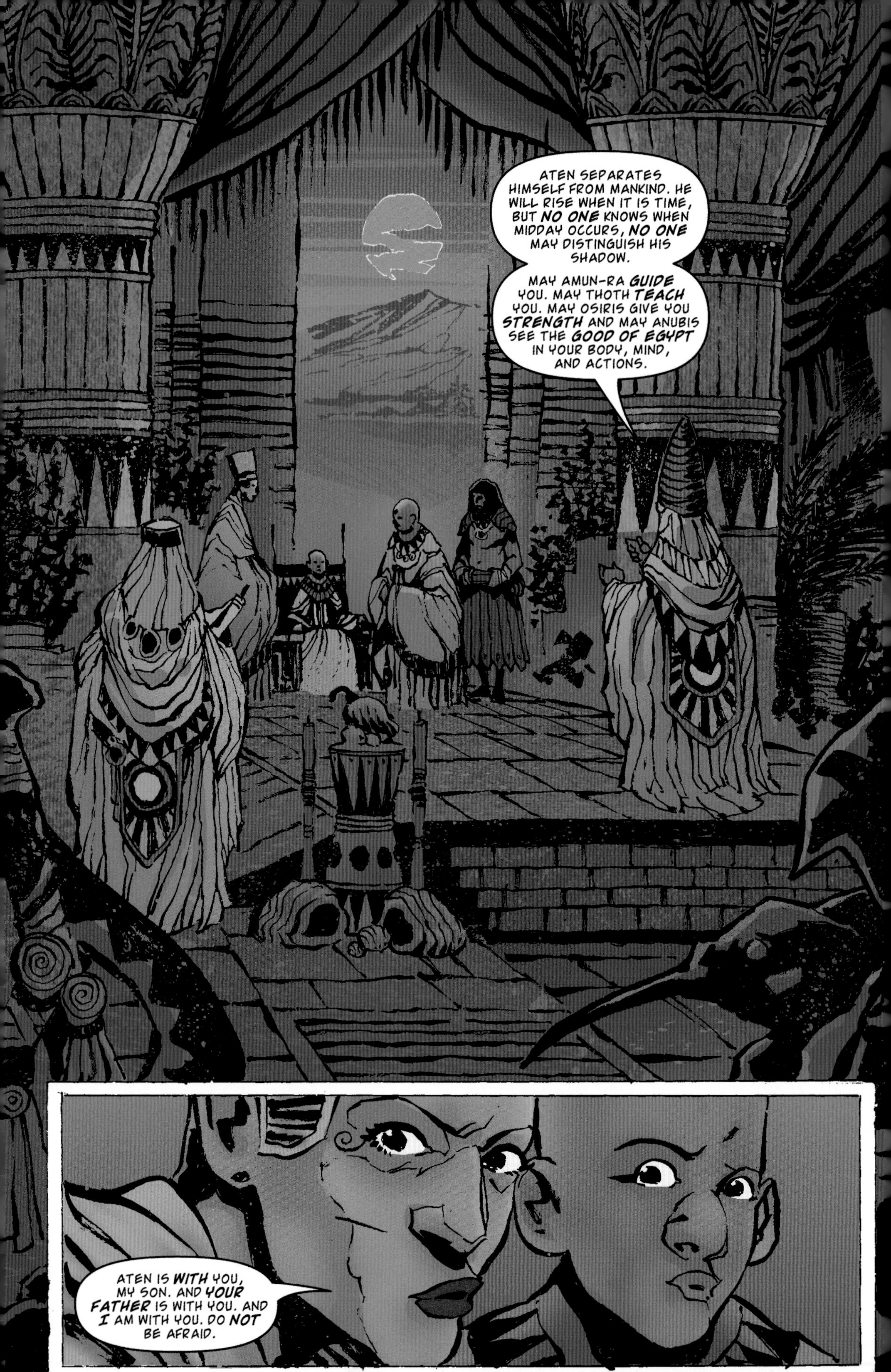
ATEN SEPARATES HIMSELF FROM MANKIND. HE WILL RISE WHEN IT IS TIME, BUT NO ONE KNOWS WHEN MIDDAY OCCURS, NO ONE MAY DISTINGUISH HIS SHADOW.
MAY AMUN-RA GUIDE YOU. MAY THOTH TEACH YOU. MAY OSIRIS GIVE YOU STRENGTH AND MAY ANUBIS SEE THE GOOD OF EGYPT IN YOUR BODY, MIND, AND ACTIONS.
ATEN IS WITH YOU, MY SON. AND YOUR FATHER IS WITH YOU. AND I AM WITH YOU. DO NOT BE AFRAID.

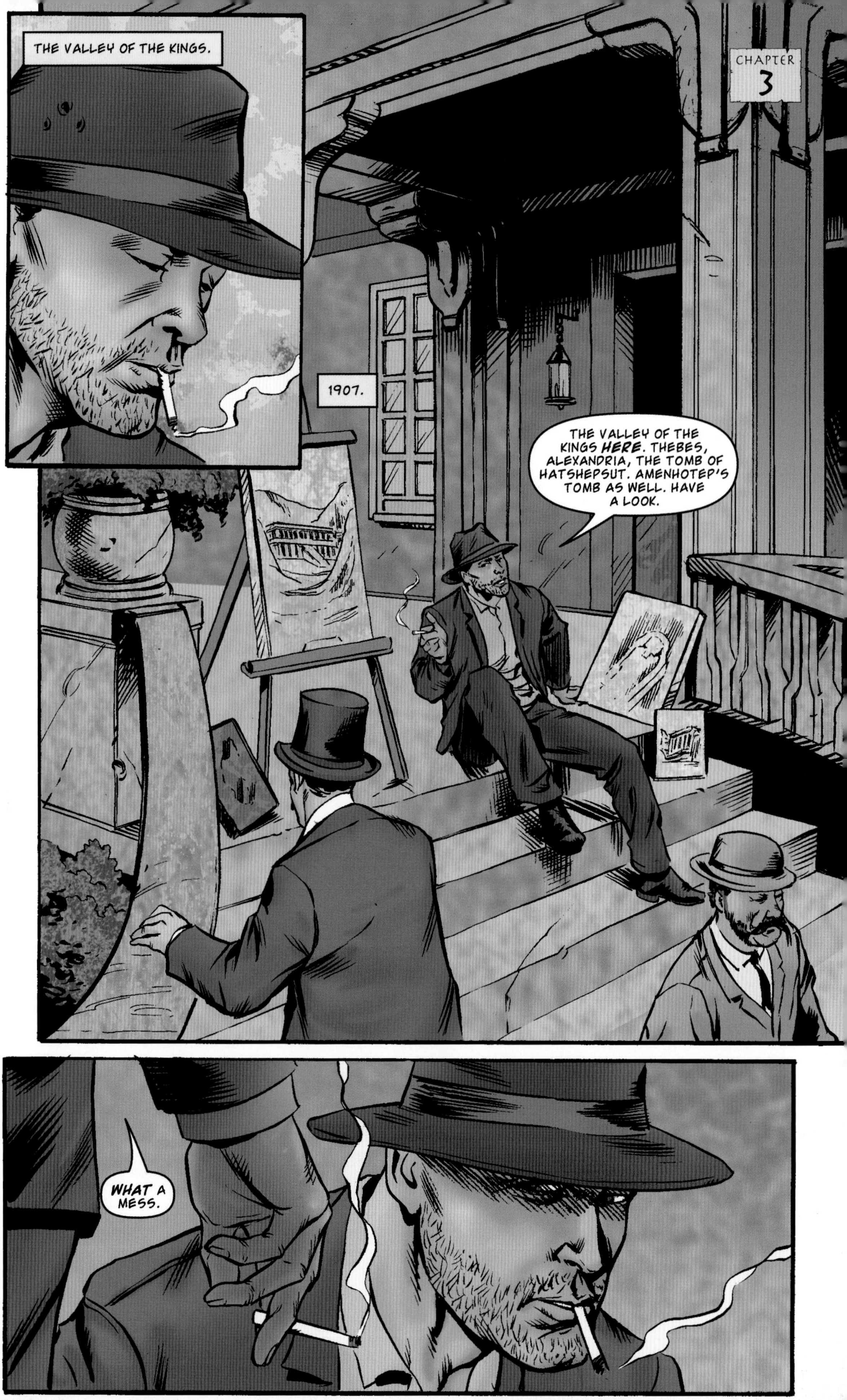
CHAPTER 3
THE VALLEY OF THE KINGS.
1907.
THE VALLEY OF THE KINGS HERE. THEBES, ALEXANDRIA, THE TOMB OF HATSHEPSUT. AMENHOTEP'S TOMB AS WELL. HAVE A LOOK.
WHAT A MESS.

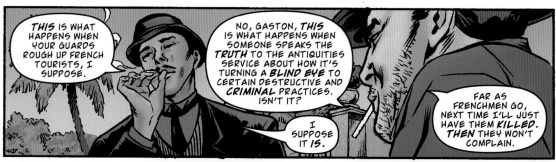

THIS IS WHAT HAPPENS WHEN YOUR GUARDS ROUGH UP FRENCH TOURISTS, I SUPPOSE.

NO, GASTON, THIS IS WHAT HAPPENS WHEN SOMEONE SPEAKS THE TRUTH TO THE ANTIQUITIES SERVICE ABOUT HOW IT'S TURNING A BLIND EYE TO CERTAIN DESTRUCTIVE AND CRIMINAL PRACTICES. ISN'T IT?

FAR AS FRENCHMEN GO, NEXT TIME I'LL JUST HAVE THEM KILLED. THEN THEY WON'T COMPLAIN.

I SUPPOSE IT IS.

I HEARD ABOUT THEODORE DAVIS AND HIS BLUE FAÏENCE CUP. WHO HASN'T? I'M SURPRISED, FRANKLY, THAT HE DIDN'T BREAK IT.

OUI. BONNE IDEE.

YOU WERE A TERRIBLE ADMINISTRATOR. INTERESTING TIMES OUT THERE. YOU'VE HEARD ABOUT THIS TUTANKHAMEN, NE C'EST PAS?

WELL, YOU'RE NOT GOING TO FIND HIM SITTING HERE, ARE YOU, MR. CARTER? LET ME ASK YOU SOMETHING.

HAS FOUR YEARS AWAY FROM THE TOMBS TAUGHT YOU ANY MANNERS AT ALL?

COME UPSTAIRS. THERE'S SOMEONE YOU SHOULD MEET. IF YOU OFFEND HIM, THIS IS THE LAST FAVOR I WILL EVER DO YOU.

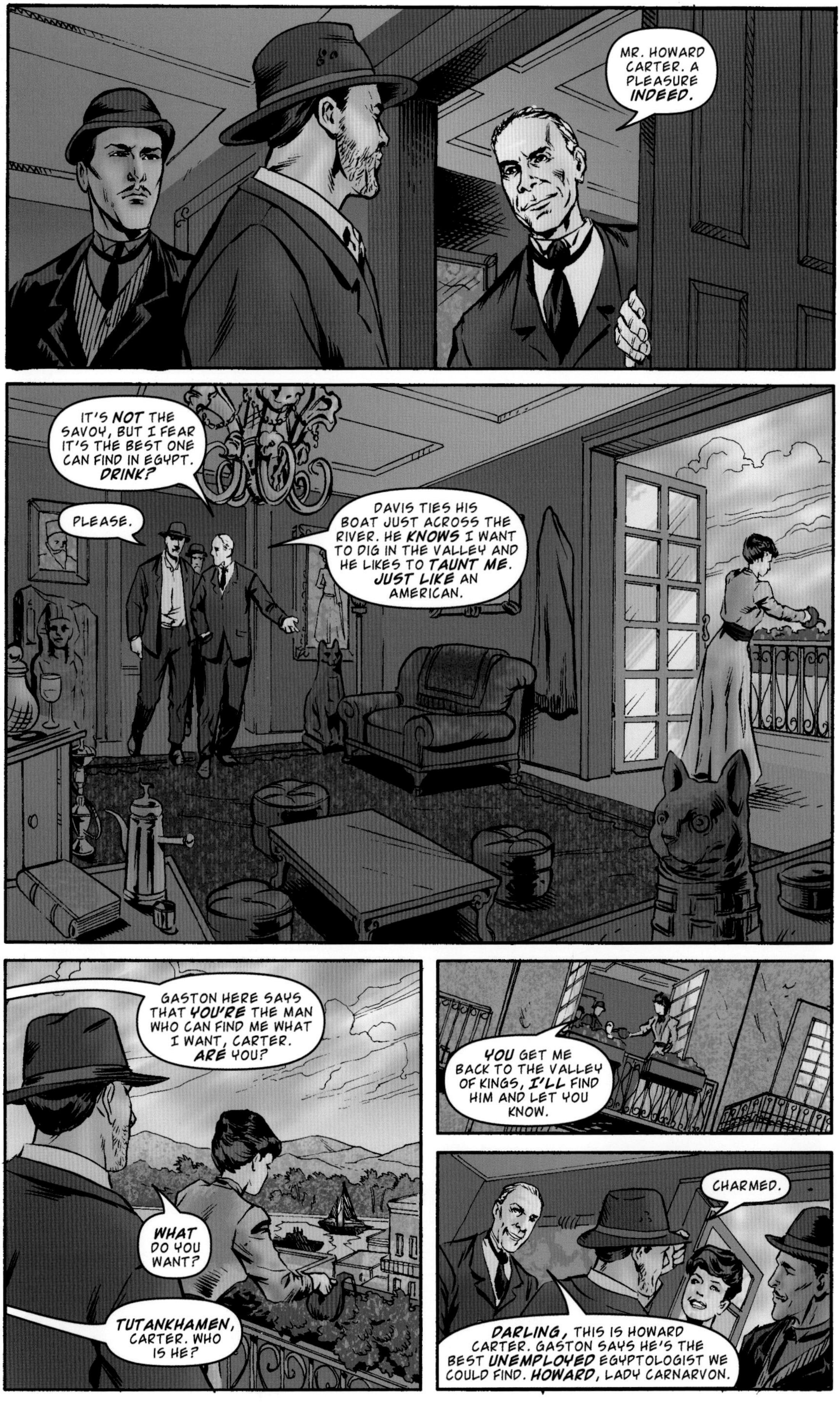

MR. HOWARD CARTER. A PLEASURE INDEED.
IT'S NOT THE SAVOY, BUT I FEAR IT'S THE BEST ONE CAN FIND IN EGYPT. DRINK?
PLEASE.
DAVIS TIES HIS BOAT JUST ACROSS THE RIVER. HE KNOWS I WANT TO DIG IN THE VALLEY AND HE LIKES TO TAUNT ME. JUST LIKE AN AMERICAN.
GASTON HERE SAYS THAT YOU'RE THE MAN WHO CAN FIND ME WHAT I WANT, CARTER. ARE YOU?
WHAT DO YOU WANT?
TUTANKHAMEN, CARTER. WHO IS HE?
YOU GET ME BACK TO THE VALLEY OF KINGS, I'LL FIND HIM AND LET YOU KNOW.
CHARMED.
DARLING, THIS IS HOWARD CARTER. GASTON SAYS HE'S THE BEST UNEMPLOYED EGYPTOLOGIST WE COULD FIND. HOWARD, LADY CARNARVON.

I'VE BEEN DIGGING FOR *THREE YEARS* NOW, AND YOU KNOW WHAT I'VE *FOUND?*

A MUMMIFIED *CAT.*

IT'S A *DARLING* LITTLE THING, BUT *NOT* WHAT GEORGE IS AFTER.

GASTON THINKS THAT *DESPITE* YOUR HOT TEMPER, *YOU'RE* THE MAN TO GET ME WHAT I WANT.

WHAT *WAS IT* YOU SAID, GASTON? CARTER, HOWARD. IT WAS IN *FRENCH,* HOWARD. I CAN UNDERSTAND IT WHEN I *HEAR* IT, BUT I *NEVER* REMEMBER A THING. ANOTHER VERSION OF L'ESPRIT DE L'ESCALIER, *NO?*

THE VALLEY IS *RIDDLED* WITH UNDISCOVERED TOMBS. IT *MUST* BE. THIS WILL BE A *GREAT* OPPORTUNITY FOR YOU TO GET *EVEN* WITH DAVIS.

YOU MEAN FOR *YOU* TO GET EVEN WITH DAVIS, *DON'T* YOU, CARTER?

PERHAPS. AND THEN I'LL STILL *OWE* YOU.

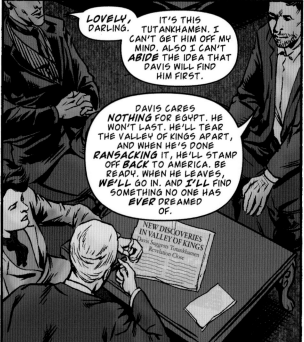

LOVELY, DARLING.

IT'S THIS TUTANKHAMEN. I CAN'T GET HIM OFF MY MIND. ALSO I CAN'T *ABIDE* THE IDEA THAT DAVIS WILL FIND HIM FIRST.

DAVIS CARES *NOTHING* FOR EGYPT. HE WON'T LAST. HE'LL TEAR THE VALLEY OF KINGS APART, AND WHEN HE'S DONE *RANSACKING* IT, HE'LL STAMP OFF *BACK* TO AMERICA. BE READY. WHEN HE LEAVES, *WE'LL* GO IN. AND *I'LL* FIND SOMETHING NO ONE HAS *EVER* DREAMED OF.

NEW DISCOVERIES IN VALLEY OF KINGS
Davis Suggests Tutankhamen Revelation Close

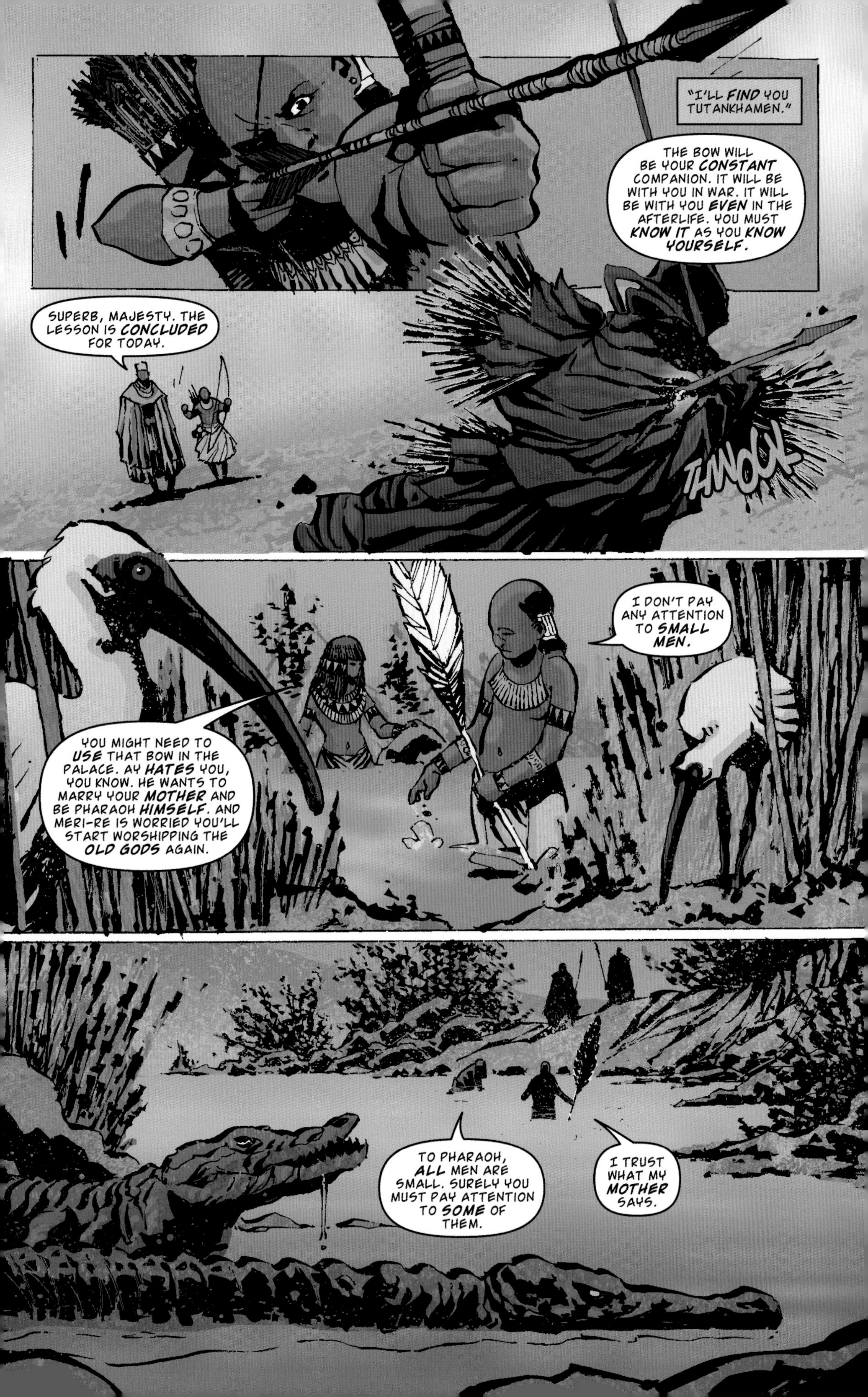
"I'LL FIND YOU TUTANKHAMEN."
THE BOW WILL BE YOUR CONSTANT COMPANION. IT WILL BE WITH YOU IN WAR. IT WILL BE WITH YOU EVEN IN THE AFTERLIFE. YOU MUST KNOW IT AS YOU KNOW YOURSELF.
SUPERB, MAJESTY. THE LESSON IS CONCLUDED FOR TODAY.
THWOCK
I DON'T PAY ANY ATTENTION TO SMALL MEN.
YOU MIGHT NEED TO USE THAT BOW IN THE PALACE. AY HATES YOU, YOU KNOW. HE WANTS TO MARRY YOUR MOTHER AND BE PHARAOH HIMSELF. AND MERI-RE IS WORRIED YOU'LL START WORSHIPPING THE OLD GODS AGAIN.
TO PHARAOH, ALL MEN ARE SMALL. SURELY YOU MUST PAY ATTENTION TO SOME OF THEM.
I TRUST WHAT MY MOTHER SAYS.

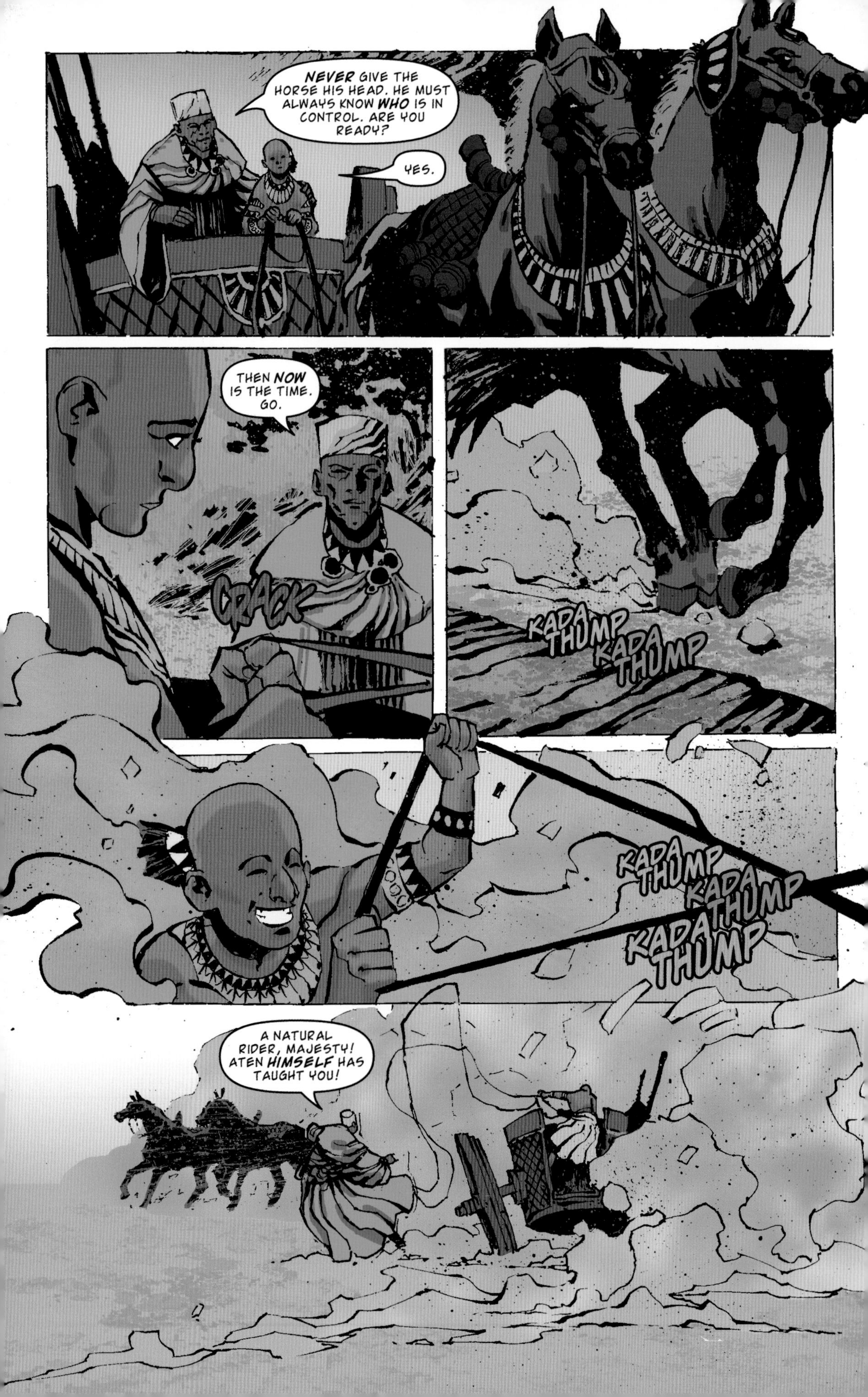
NEVER GIVE THE HORSE HIS HEAD. HE MUST ALWAYS KNOW WHO IS IN CONTROL. ARE YOU READY?
YES.
THEN NOW IS THE TIME. GO.
CRACK
KADA THUMP KADA THUMP
KADA THUMP KADA THUMP KADA THUMP
A NATURAL RIDER, MAJESTY! ATEN HIMSELF HAS TAUGHT YOU!

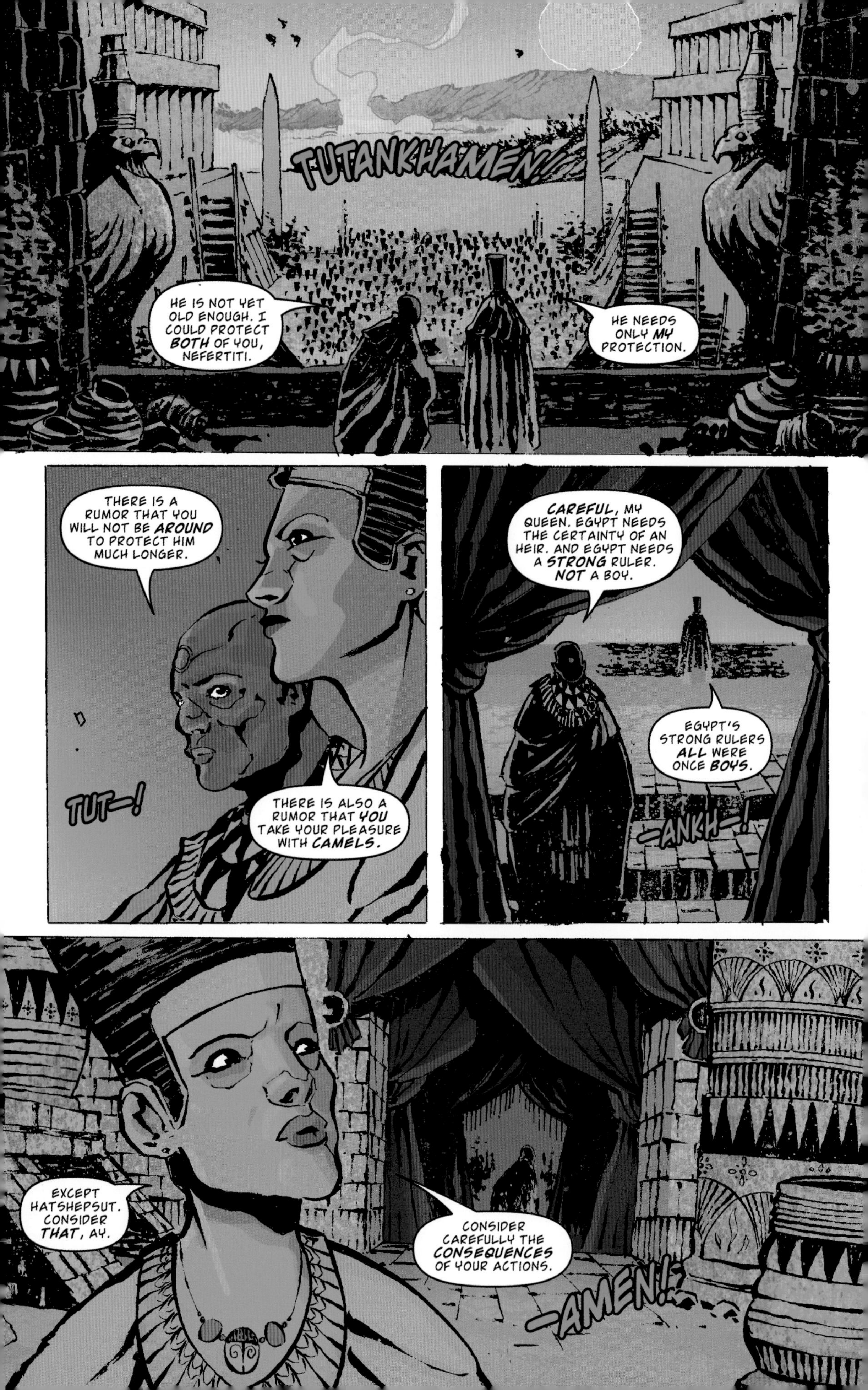

TUTANKHAMEN!
HE IS NOT YET OLD ENOUGH. I COULD PROTECT BOTH OF YOU, NEFERTITI.
HE NEEDS ONLY MY PROTECTION.
THERE IS A RUMOR THAT YOU WILL NOT BE AROUND TO PROTECT HIM MUCH LONGER.
TUT-!
THERE IS ALSO A RUMOR THAT YOU TAKE YOUR PLEASURE WITH CAMELS.
CAREFUL, MY QUEEN. EGYPT NEEDS THE CERTAINTY OF AN HEIR. AND EGYPT NEEDS A STRONG RULER. NOT A BOY.
EGYPT'S STRONG RULERS ALL WERE ONCE BOYS.
-ANKH-!
EXCEPT HATSHEPSUT. CONSIDER THAT, AY.
CONSIDER CAREFULLY THE CONSEQUENCES OF YOUR ACTIONS.
-AMEN!

I WILL BE MEETING OSIRIS SOON.

YOU MUST BE *CAREFUL* OF THE PRIESTHOOD. MANY OF THEM STILL WISH YOUR FATHER'S REFORMS HAD *NEVER* HAPPENED. OTHERS WILL *FIGHT* YOU IF YOU TRY TO REVERSE THEM. AND YOU MUST *NEVER* SHOW WEAKNESS AROUND HOREMHEB OR AY. *AY* ESPECIALLY. HE COULD NEVER HAVE ME, BUT HE WILL *ALWAYS LIVE* FOR THE IDEA THAT *HE* WILL BE PHARAOH SOMEDAY. SO YOU *MUST PROTECT* YOURSELF.

DO YOU UNDERSTAND WHAT I AM TELLING YOU?

YES, MOTHER.

PHARAOH MUST DO WHAT IS RIGHT *FOR EGYPT*. YOU WILL BE PHARAOH WHEN I AM GONE, PHARAOH WITH *NO REGENT*. SO YOU MUST PREPARE TO GIVE EGYPT AN HEIR. ANKHESENPAATEN IS THE *ONLY CHILD* IN EGYPT WHO IS FULLY OF ROYAL BLOOD.

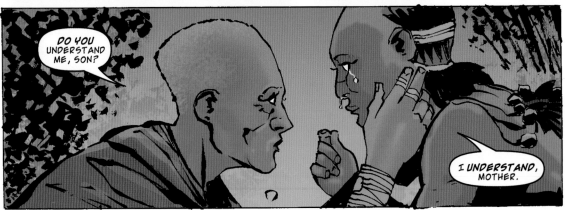

DO YOU UNDERSTAND ME, SON?

I UNDERSTAND, MOTHER.

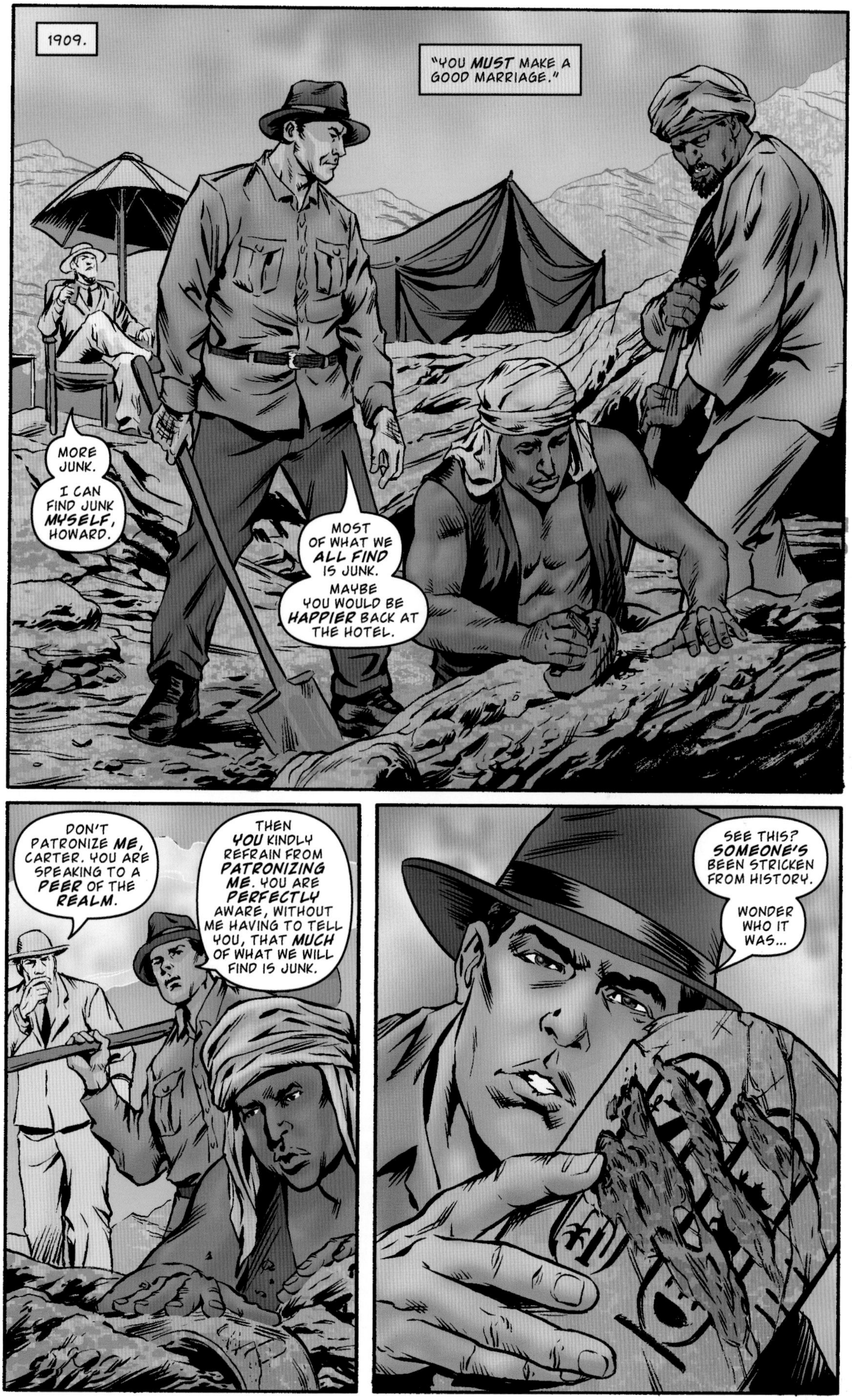
1909.
"YOU MUST MAKE A GOOD MARRIAGE."
MORE JUNK.
I CAN FIND JUNK MYSELF, HOWARD.
MOST OF WHAT WE ALL FIND IS JUNK.
MAYBE YOU WOULD BE HAPPIER BACK AT THE HOTEL.
DON'T PATRONIZE ME, CARTER. YOU ARE SPEAKING TO A PEER OF THE REALM.
THEN YOU KINDLY REFRAIN FROM PATRONIZING ME. YOU ARE PERFECTLY AWARE, WITHOUT ME HAVING TO TELL YOU, THAT MUCH OF WHAT WE WILL FIND IS JUNK.
SEE THIS? SOMEONE'S BEEN STRICKEN FROM HISTORY.
WONDER WHO IT WAS...

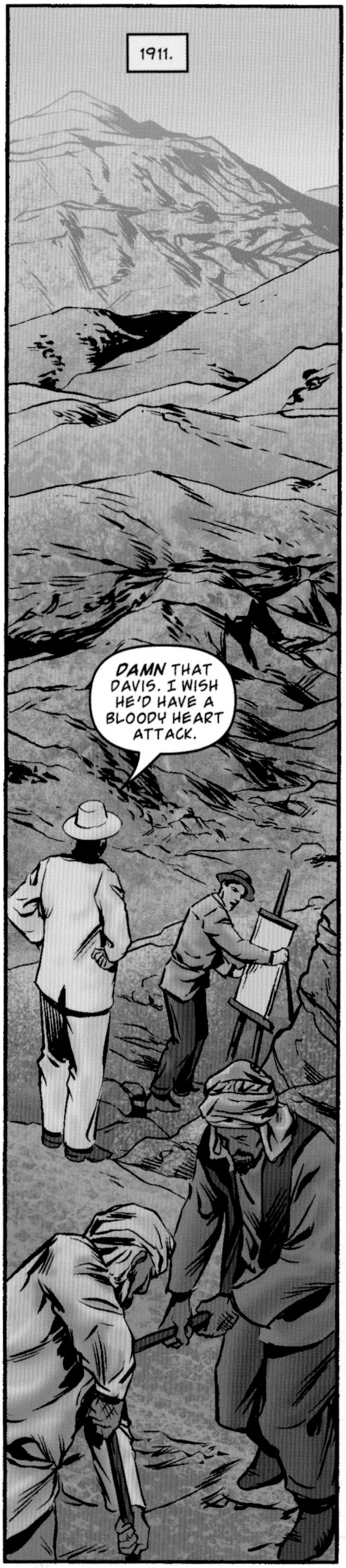
1911.
DAMN THAT DAVIS. I WISH HE'D HAVE A BLOODY HEART ATTACK.

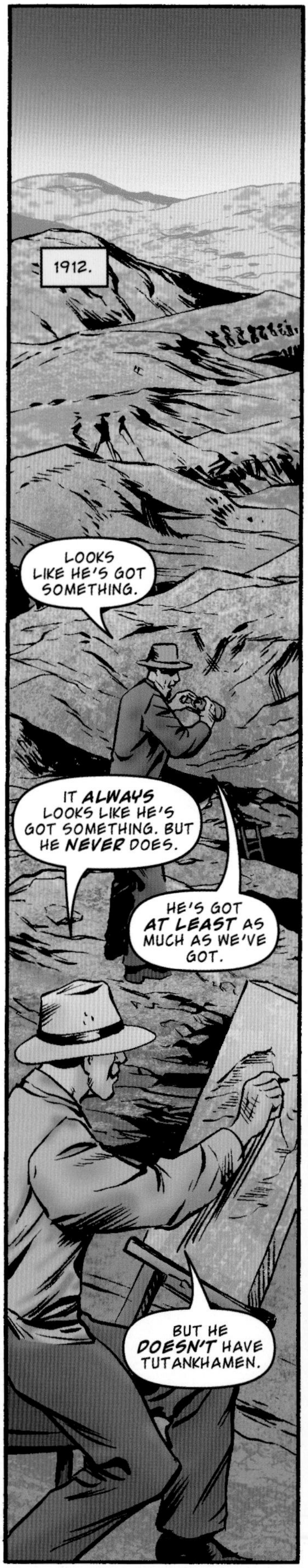
1912.
LOOKS LIKE HE'S GOT SOMETHING.
IT ALWAYS LOOKS LIKE HE'S GOT SOMETHING. BUT HE NEVER DOES.
HE'S GOT AT LEAST AS MUCH AS WE'VE GOT.
BUT HE DOESN'T HAVE TUTANKHAMEN.

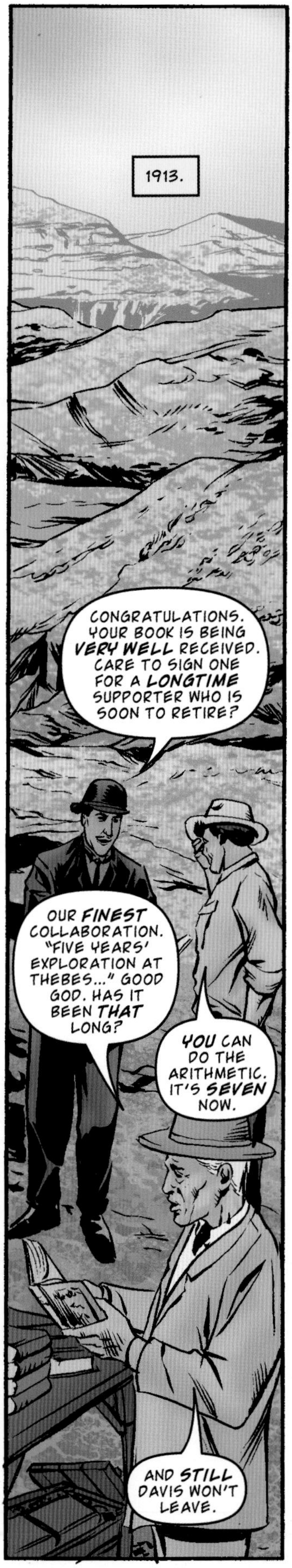
1913.
CONGRATULATIONS. YOUR BOOK IS BEING VERY WELL RECEIVED. CARE TO SIGN ONE FOR A LONGTIME SUPPORTER WHO IS SOON TO RETIRE?
OUR FINEST COLLABORATION. "FIVE YEARS' EXPLORATION AT THEBES..." GOOD GOD. HAS IT BEEN THAT LONG?
YOU CAN DO THE ARITHMETIC. IT'S SEVEN NOW.
AND STILL DAVIS WON'T LEAVE.

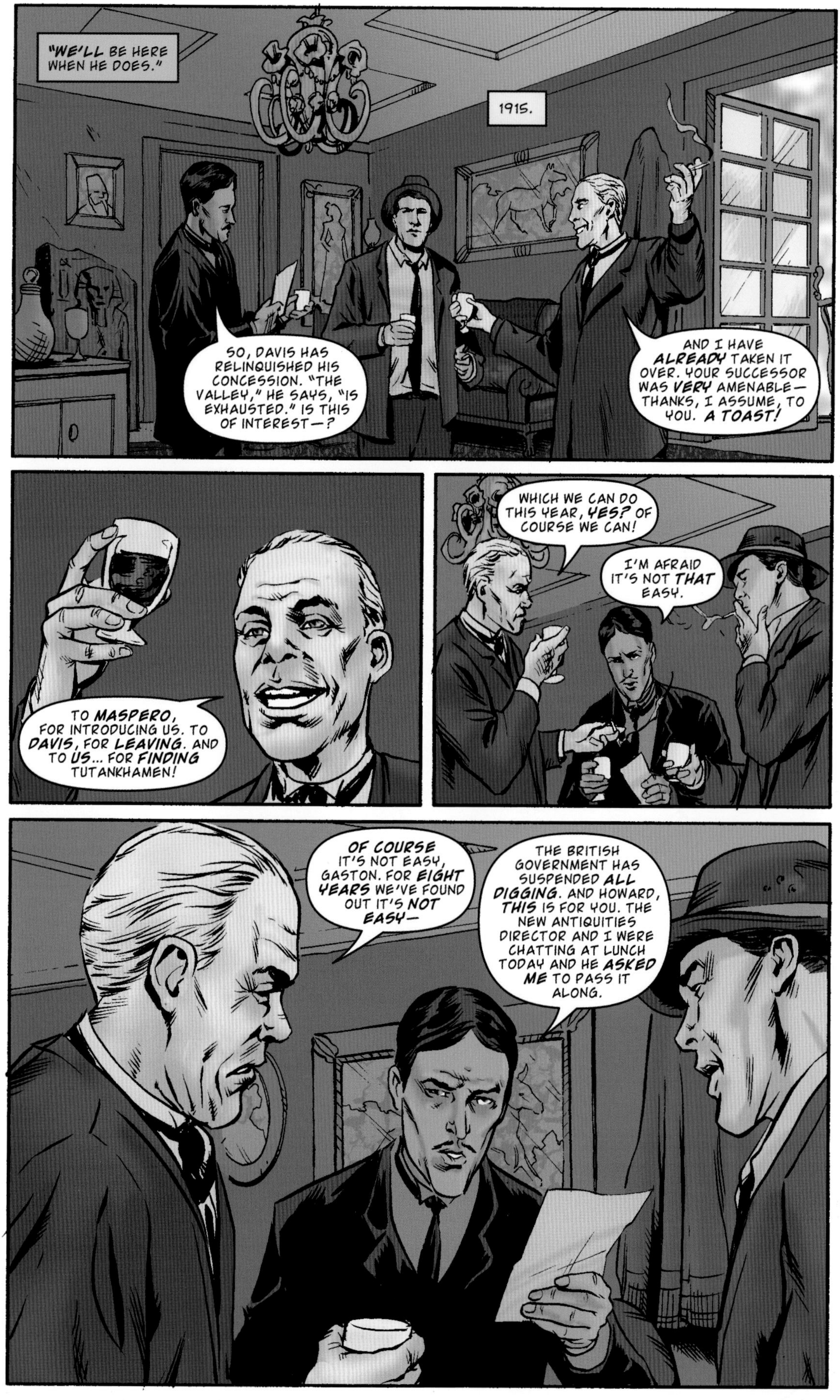
"WE'LL BE HERE WHEN HE DOES."
1915.
SO, DAVIS HAS RELINQUISHED HIS CONCESSION. "THE VALLEY," HE SAYS, "IS EXHAUSTED." IS THIS OF INTEREST—?
AND I HAVE ALREADY TAKEN IT OVER. YOUR SUCCESSOR WAS VERY AMENABLE—THANKS, I ASSUME, TO YOU. A TOAST!
TO MASPERO, FOR INTRODUCING US. TO DAVIS, FOR LEAVING. AND TO US... FOR FINDING TUTANKHAMEN!
WHICH WE CAN DO THIS YEAR, YES? OF COURSE WE CAN!
I'M AFRAID IT'S NOT THAT EASY.
OF COURSE IT'S NOT EASY, GASTON. FOR EIGHT YEARS WE'VE FOUND OUT IT'S NOT EASY—
THE BRITISH GOVERNMENT HAS SUSPENDED ALL DIGGING. AND HOWARD, THIS IS FOR YOU. THE NEW ANTIQUITIES DIRECTOR AND I WERE CHATTING AT LUNCH TODAY AND HE ASKED ME TO PASS IT ALONG.

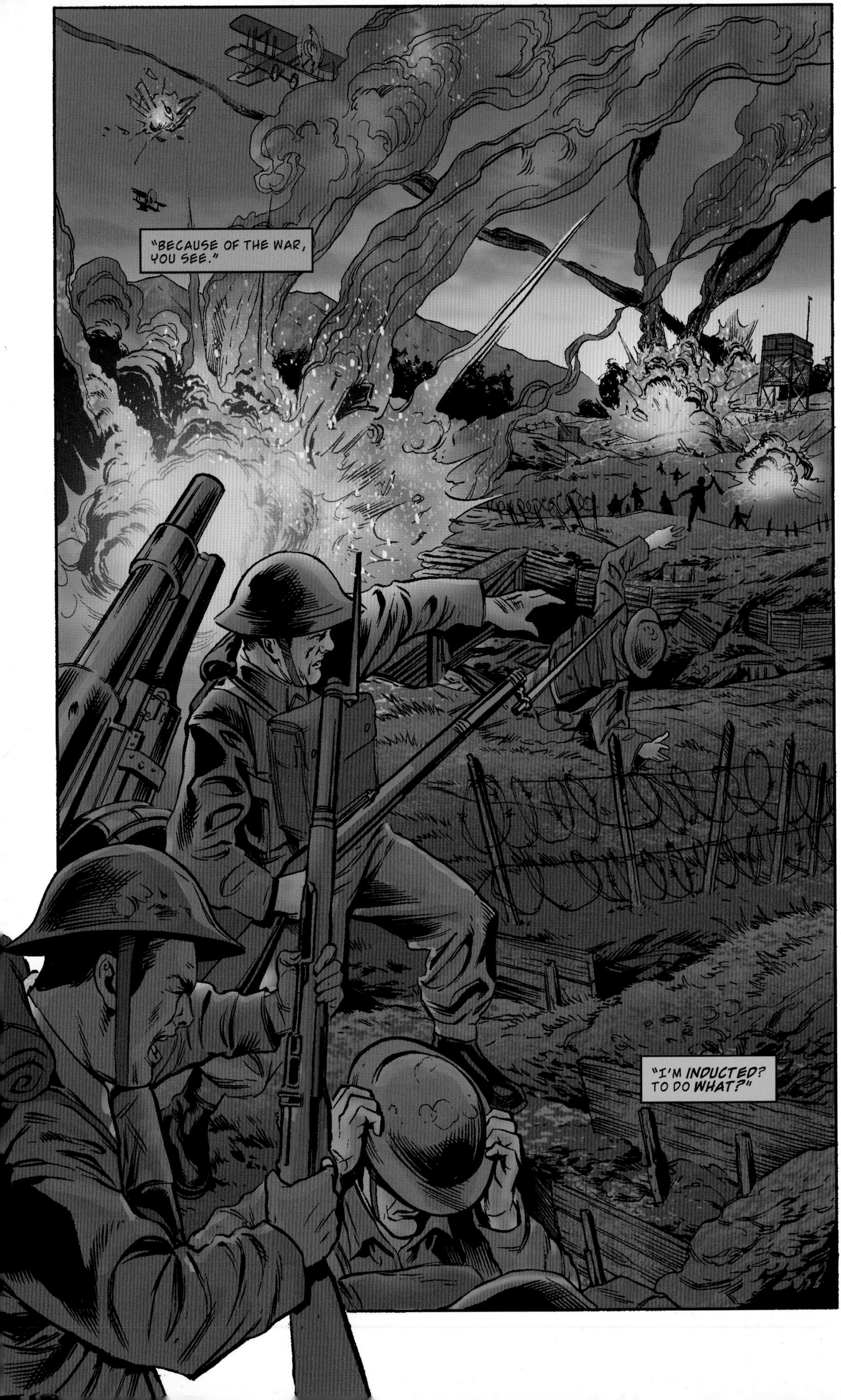
"BECAUSE OF THE WAR, YOU SEE."
"I'M INDUCTED? TO DO WHAT?"

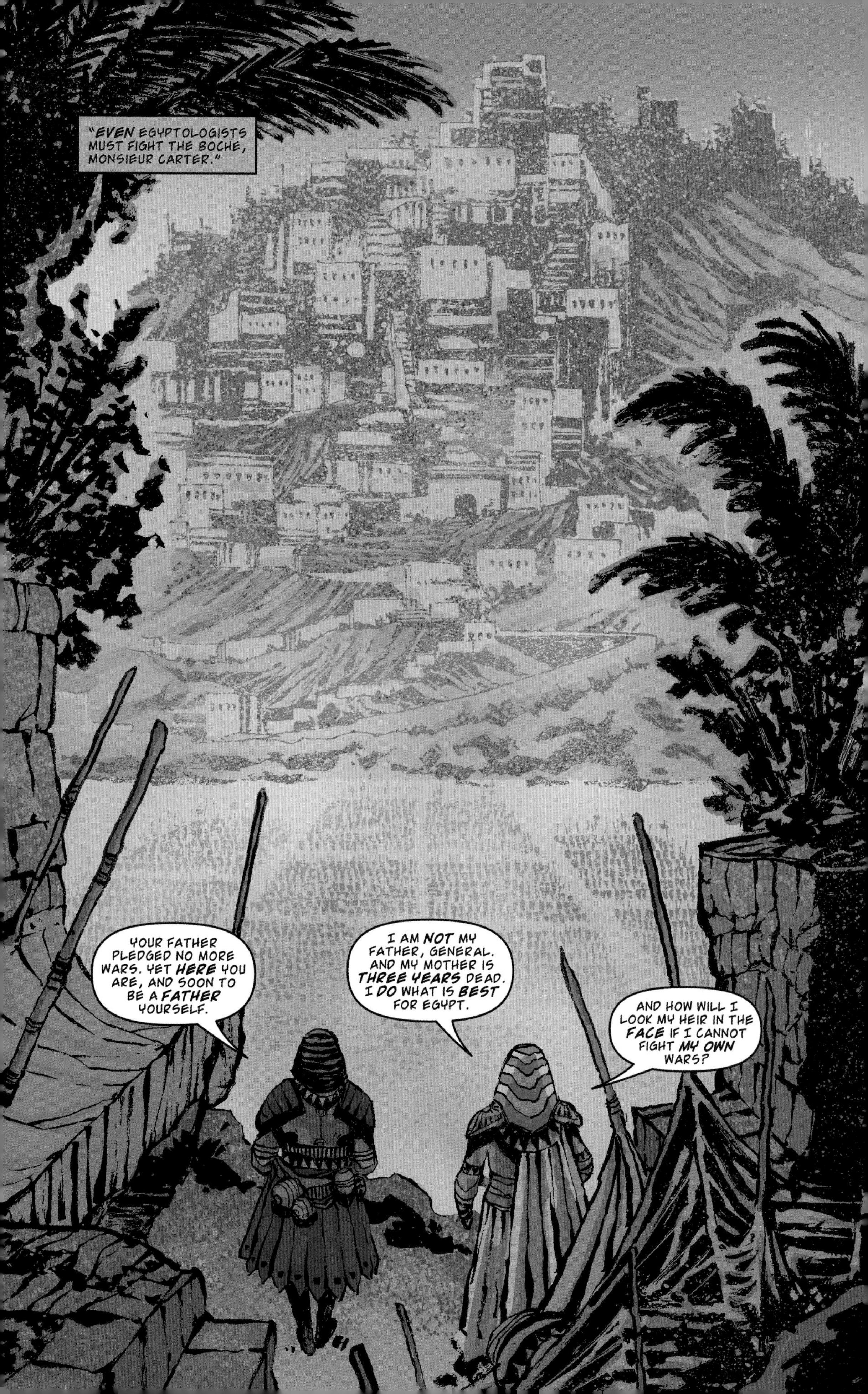
"EVEN EGYPTOLOGISTS MUST FIGHT THE BOCHE, MONSIEUR CARTER."
YOUR FATHER PLEDGED NO MORE WARS. YET HERE YOU ARE, AND SOON TO BE A FATHER YOURSELF.
I AM NOT MY FATHER, GENERAL. AND MY MOTHER IS THREE YEARS DEAD. I DO WHAT IS BEST FOR EGYPT.
AND HOW WILL I LOOK MY HEIR IN THE FACE IF I CANNOT FIGHT MY OWN WARS?

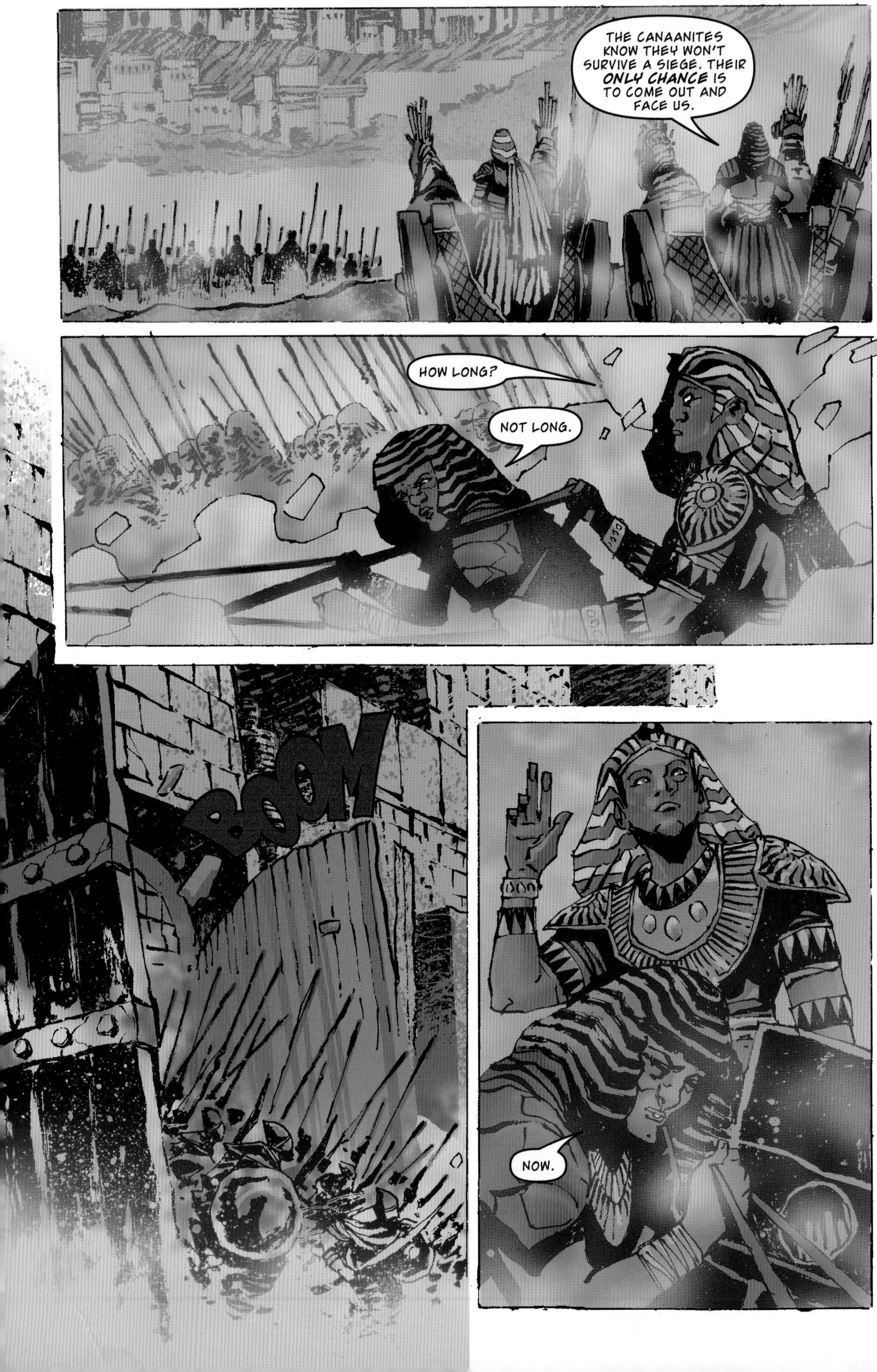
THE CANAANITES KNOW THEY WON'T SURVIVE A SIEGE. THEIR ONLY CHANCE IS TO COME OUT AND FACE US.
HOW LONG?
NOT LONG.
BOOM
NOW.

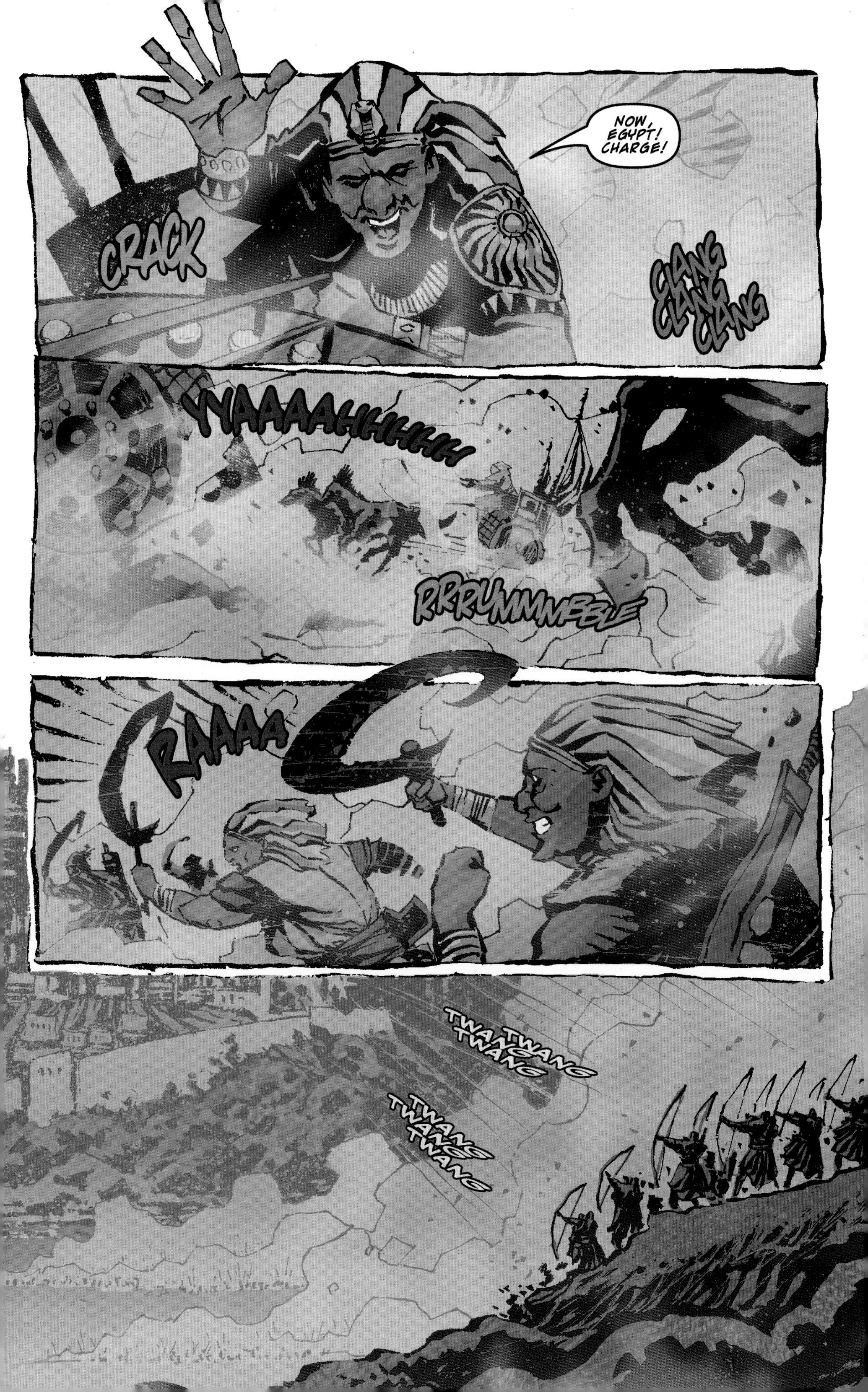
NOW, EGYPT! CHARGE!
CRACK
CLANG CLANG CLANG
YYAAAAAHHHHHH
RRRUMMMBBLE
RAAAA
TWANG TWANG TWANG
TWANG TWANG TWANG

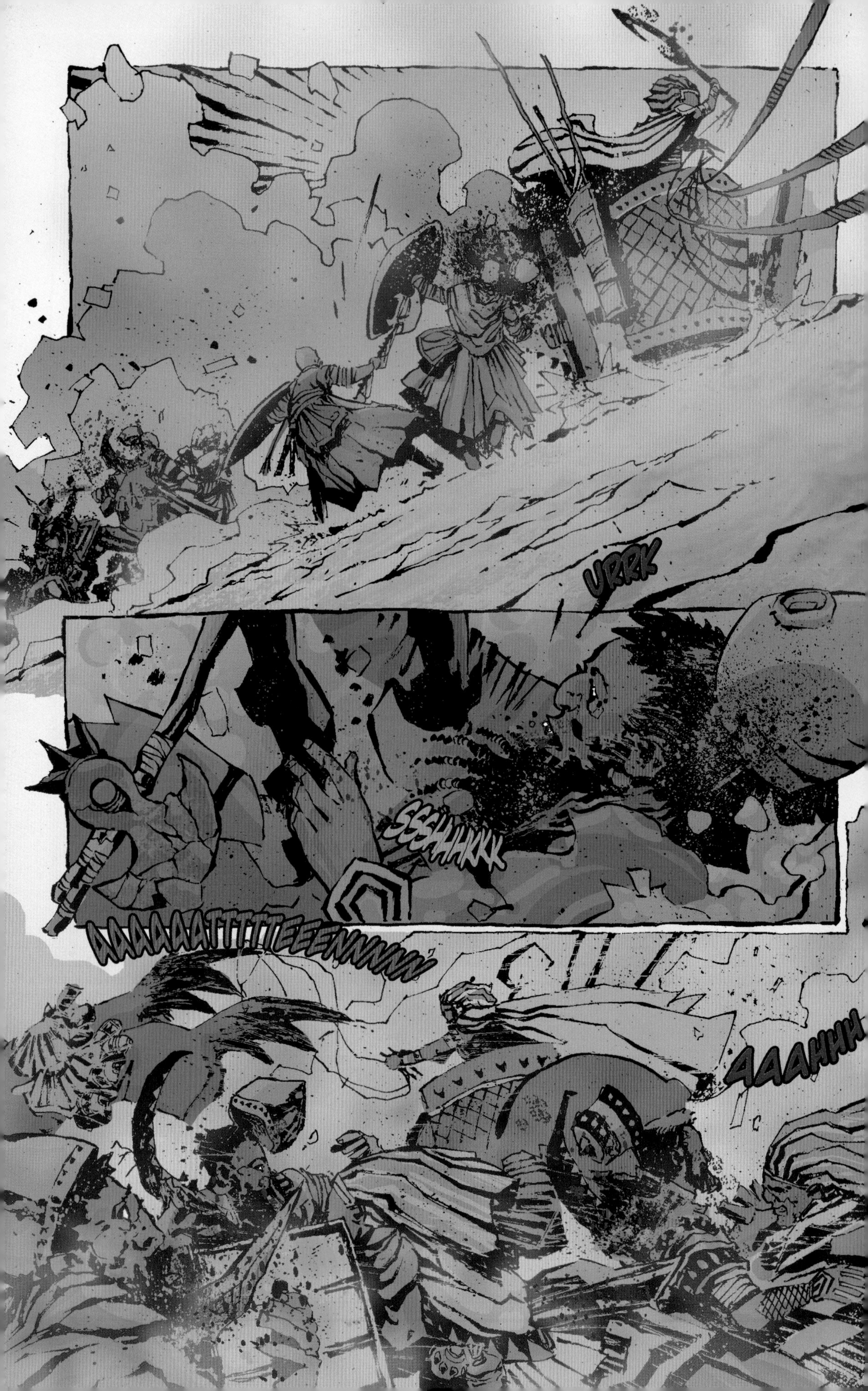
URRK
SSSHHHKKK
AAAAAATTTTTEEENNNNNN
AAAHHH

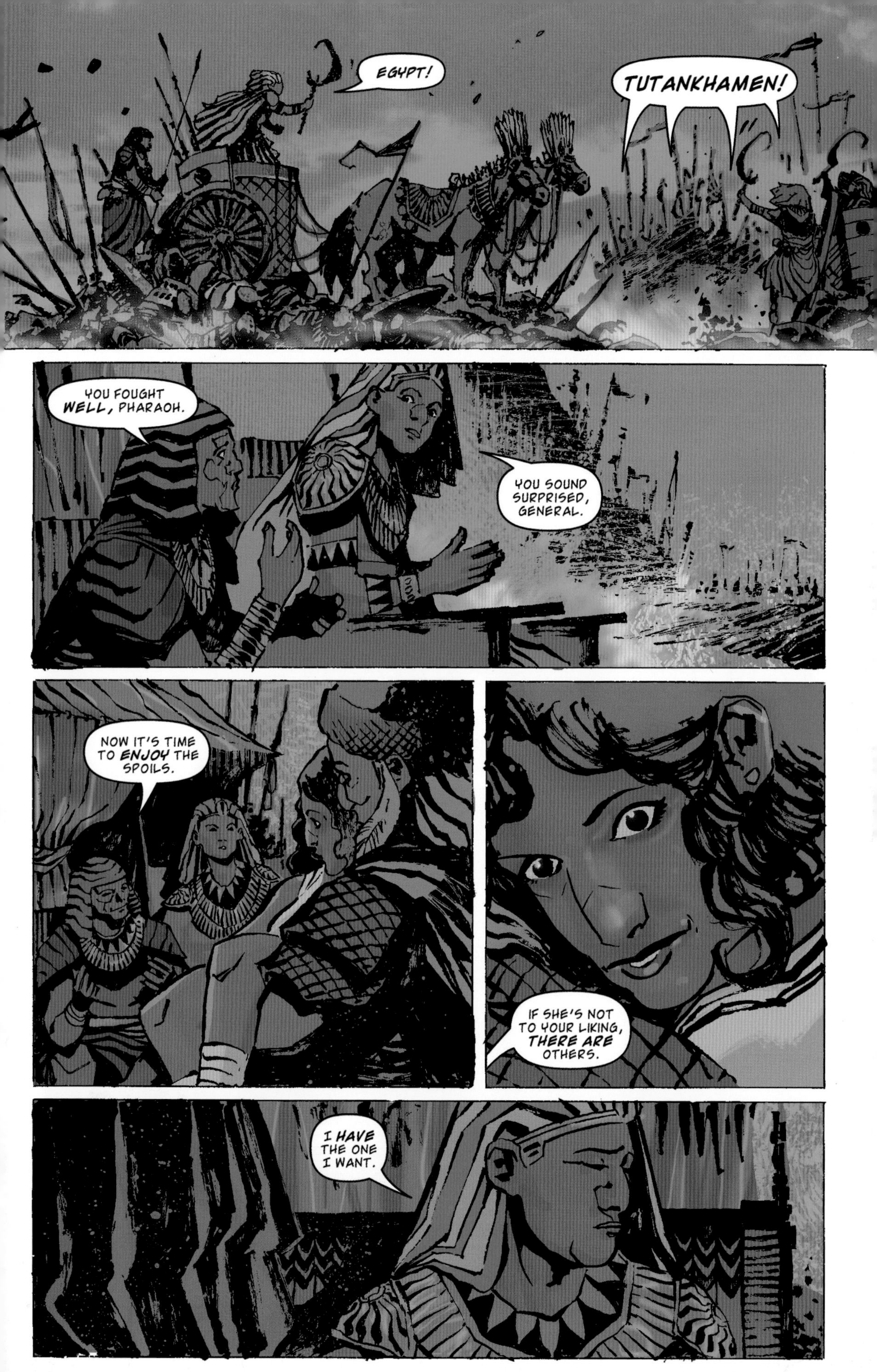
EGYPT!
TUTANKHAMEN!
YOU FOUGHT **WELL**, PHARAOH.
YOU SOUND SURPRISED, GENERAL.
NOW IT'S TIME TO **ENJOY** THE SPOILS.
IF SHE'S NOT TO YOUR LIKING, **THERE ARE** OTHERS.
I **HAVE** THE ONE I WANT.

YOUR MOTHER—*OUR* MOTHER—WOULD HAVE *LOVED* TO SEE HER.

I CAME SECOND, LIKE YOU. *BOTH* OF US HAD AN OLDER SIBLING WHO DIED. BUT ATEN WATCHES.

THE GODS WATCH.

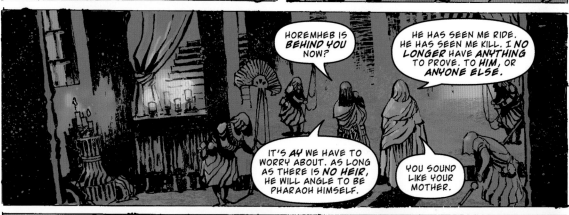

HOREMHEB IS *BEHIND YOU* NOW?

HE HAS SEEN ME RIDE. HE HAS SEEN ME KILL. I *NO LONGER* HAVE *ANYTHING* TO PROVE. TO *HIM,* OR *ANYONE ELSE.*

IT'S *AY* WE HAVE TO WORRY ABOUT. AS LONG AS THERE IS *NO HEIR,* HE WILL ANGLE TO BE PHARAOH HIMSELF.

YOU SOUND LIKE YOUR MOTHER.

IT'S TRUE, TUT.

YES. IT'S TRUE.

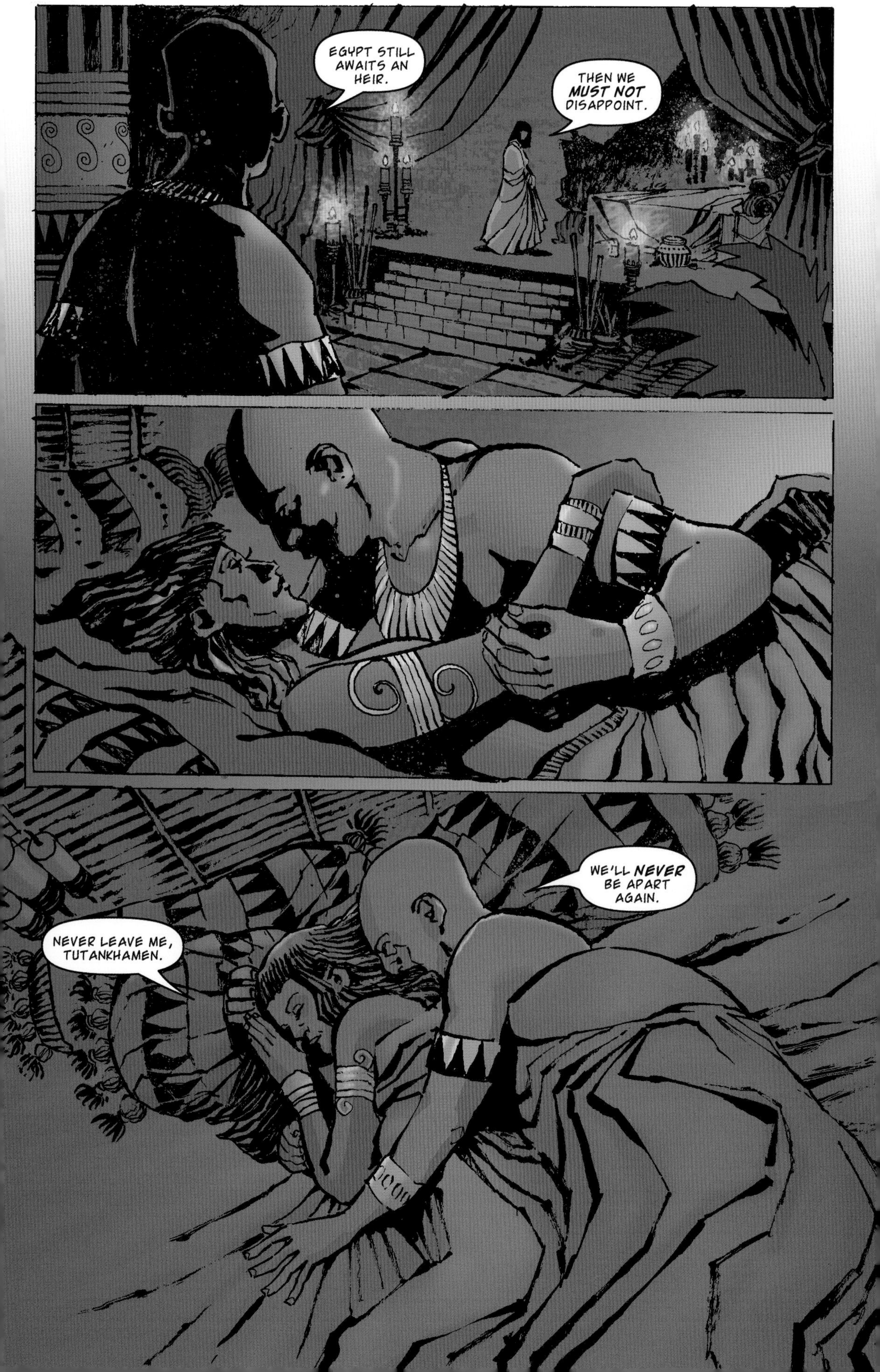
EGYPT STILL AWAITS AN HEIR.
THEN WE MUST NOT DISAPPOINT.
WE'LL NEVER BE APART AGAIN.
NEVER LEAVE ME, TUTANKHAMEN.

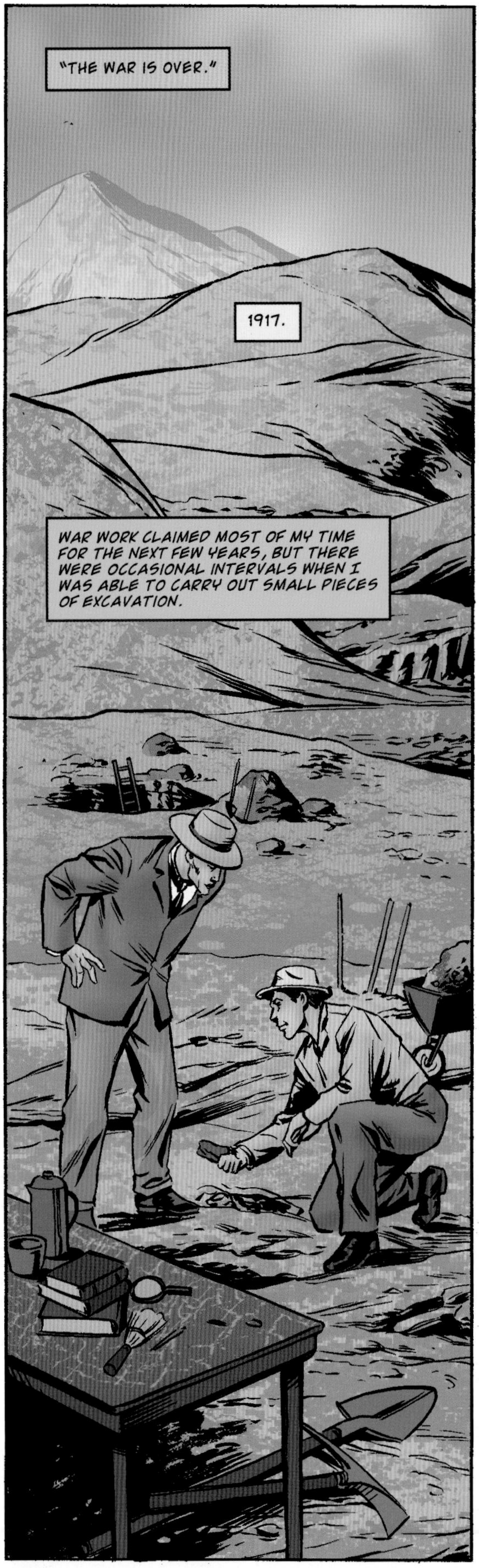
"THE WAR IS OVER."
1917.
WAR WORK CLAIMED MOST OF MY TIME FOR THE NEXT FEW YEARS, BUT THERE WERE OCCASIONAL INTERVALS WHEN I WAS ABLE TO CARRY OUT SMALL PIECES OF EXCAVATION.

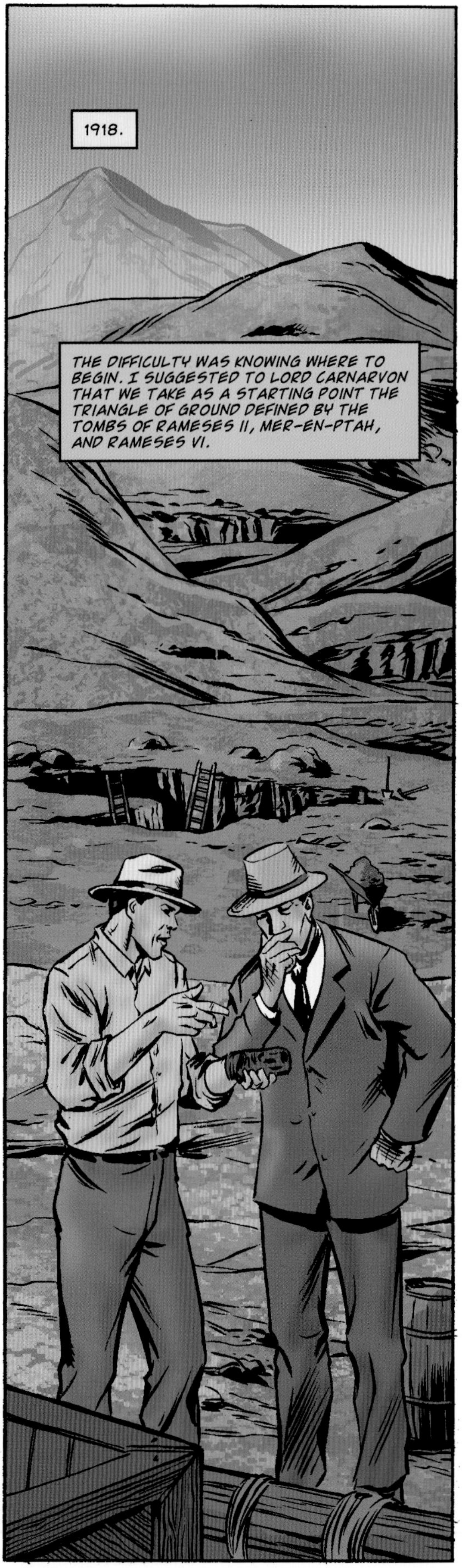
1918.
THE DIFFICULTY WAS KNOWING WHERE TO BEGIN. I SUGGESTED TO LORD CARNARVON THAT WE TAKE AS A STARTING POINT THE TRIANGLE OF GROUND DEFINED BY THE TOMBS OF RAMESES II, MER-EN-PTAH, AND RAMESES VI.

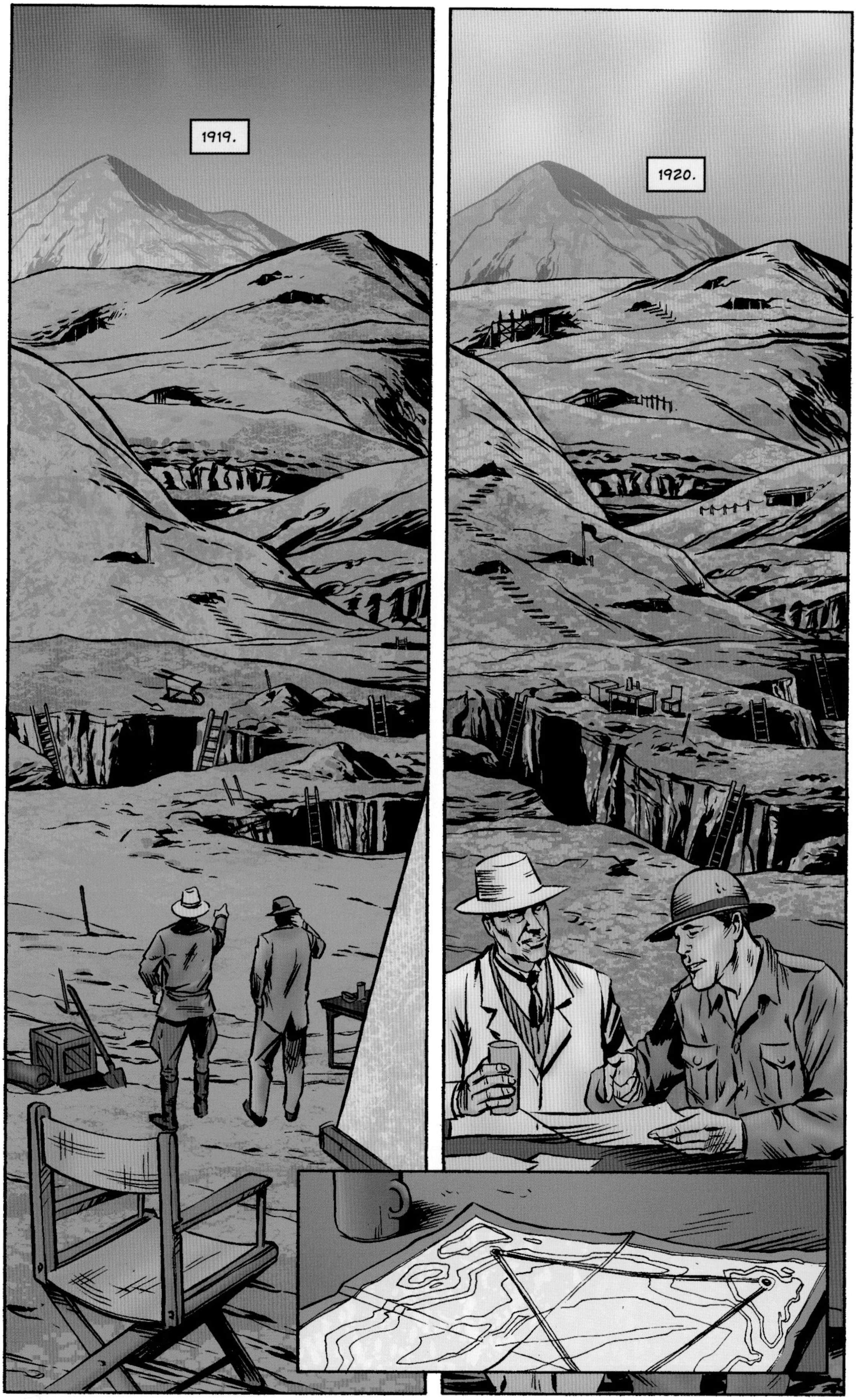
1919.
1920.

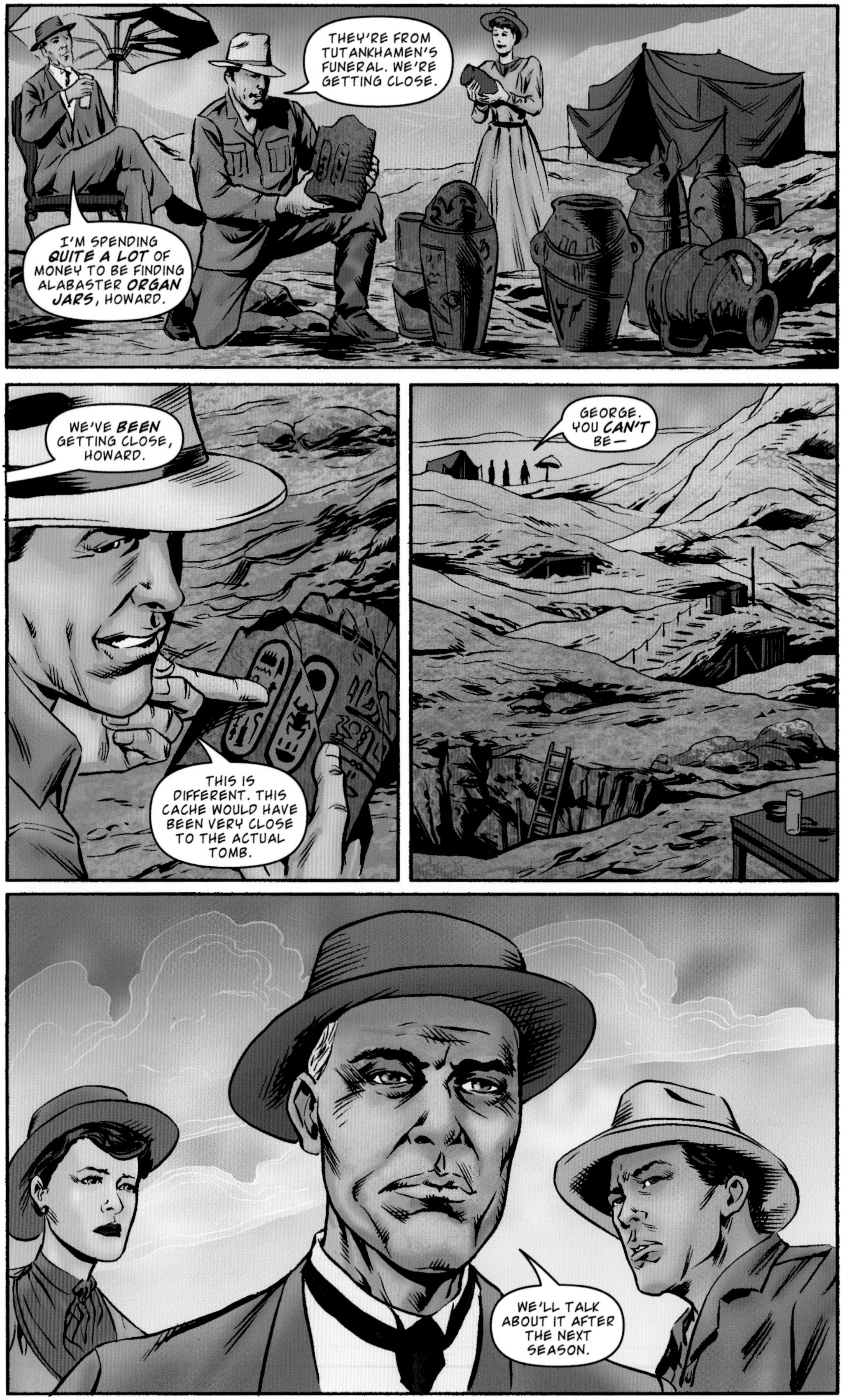
THEY'RE FROM TUTANKHAMEN'S FUNERAL. WE'RE GETTING CLOSE.
I'M SPENDING QUITE A LOT OF MONEY TO BE FINDING ALABASTER ORGAN JARS, HOWARD.
WE'VE BEEN GETTING CLOSE, HOWARD.
THIS IS DIFFERENT. THIS CACHE WOULD HAVE BEEN VERY CLOSE TO THE ACTUAL TOMB.
GEORGE. YOU CAN'T BE—
WE'LL TALK ABOUT IT AFTER THE NEXT SEASON.

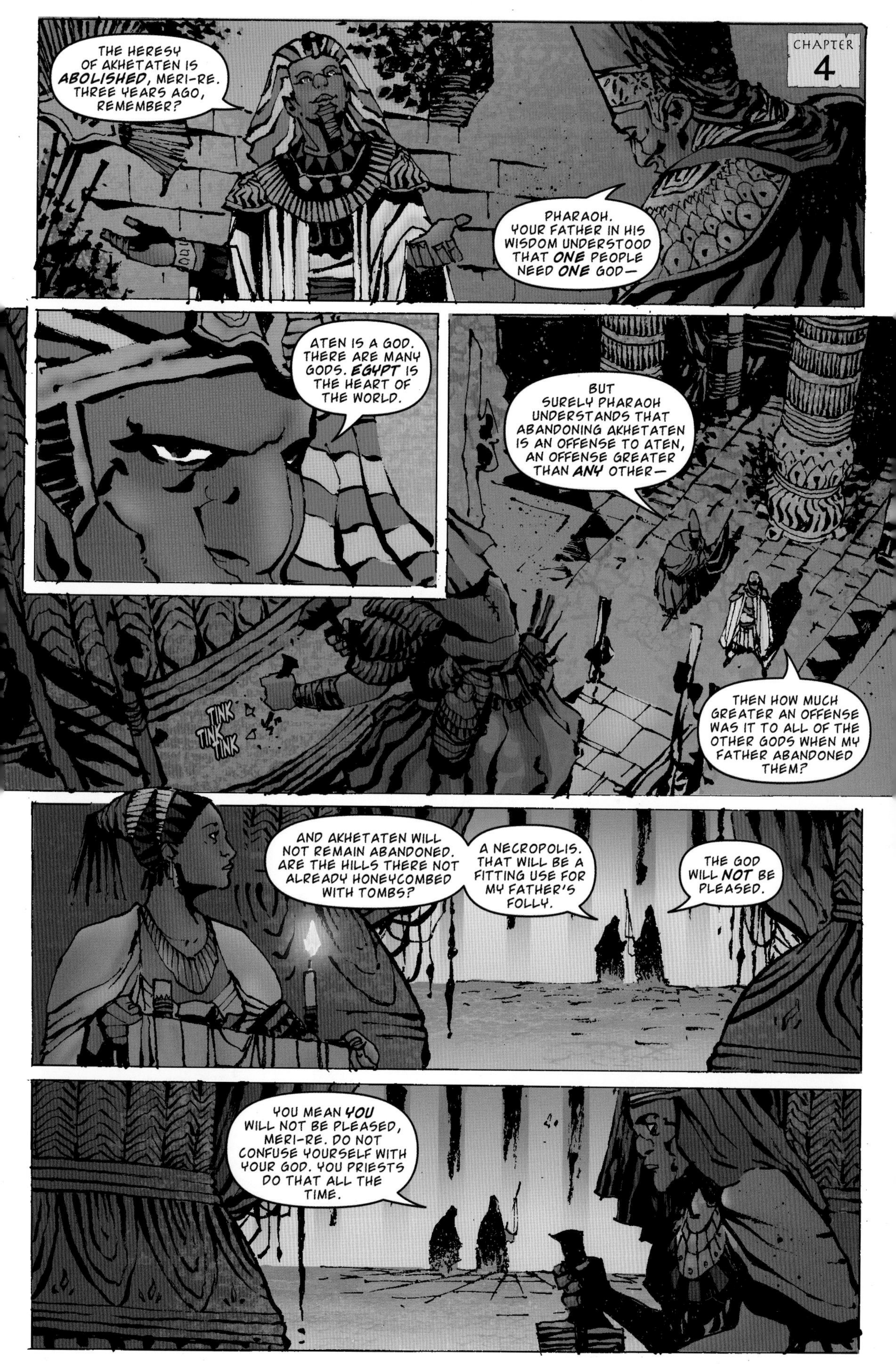
CHAPTER 4
THE HERESY OF AKHETATEN IS ABOLISHED, MERI-RE. THREE YEARS AGO, REMEMBER?
PHARAOH. YOUR FATHER IN HIS WISDOM UNDERSTOOD THAT ONE PEOPLE NEED ONE GOD—
ATEN IS A GOD. THERE ARE MANY GODS. EGYPT IS THE HEART OF THE WORLD.
BUT SURELY PHARAOH UNDERSTANDS THAT ABANDONING AKHETATEN IS AN OFFENSE TO ATEN, AN OFFENSE GREATER THAN ANY OTHER—
TINK TINK TINK
THEN HOW MUCH GREATER AN OFFENSE WAS IT TO ALL OF THE OTHER GODS WHEN MY FATHER ABANDONED THEM?
AND AKHETATEN WILL NOT REMAIN ABANDONED. ARE THE HILLS THERE NOT ALREADY HONEYCOMBED WITH TOMBS?
A NECROPOLIS. THAT WILL BE A FITTING USE FOR MY FATHER'S FOLLY.
THE GOD WILL NOT BE PLEASED.
YOU MEAN YOU WILL NOT BE PLEASED, MERI-RE. DO NOT CONFUSE YOURSELF WITH YOUR GOD. YOU PRIESTS DO THAT ALL THE TIME.

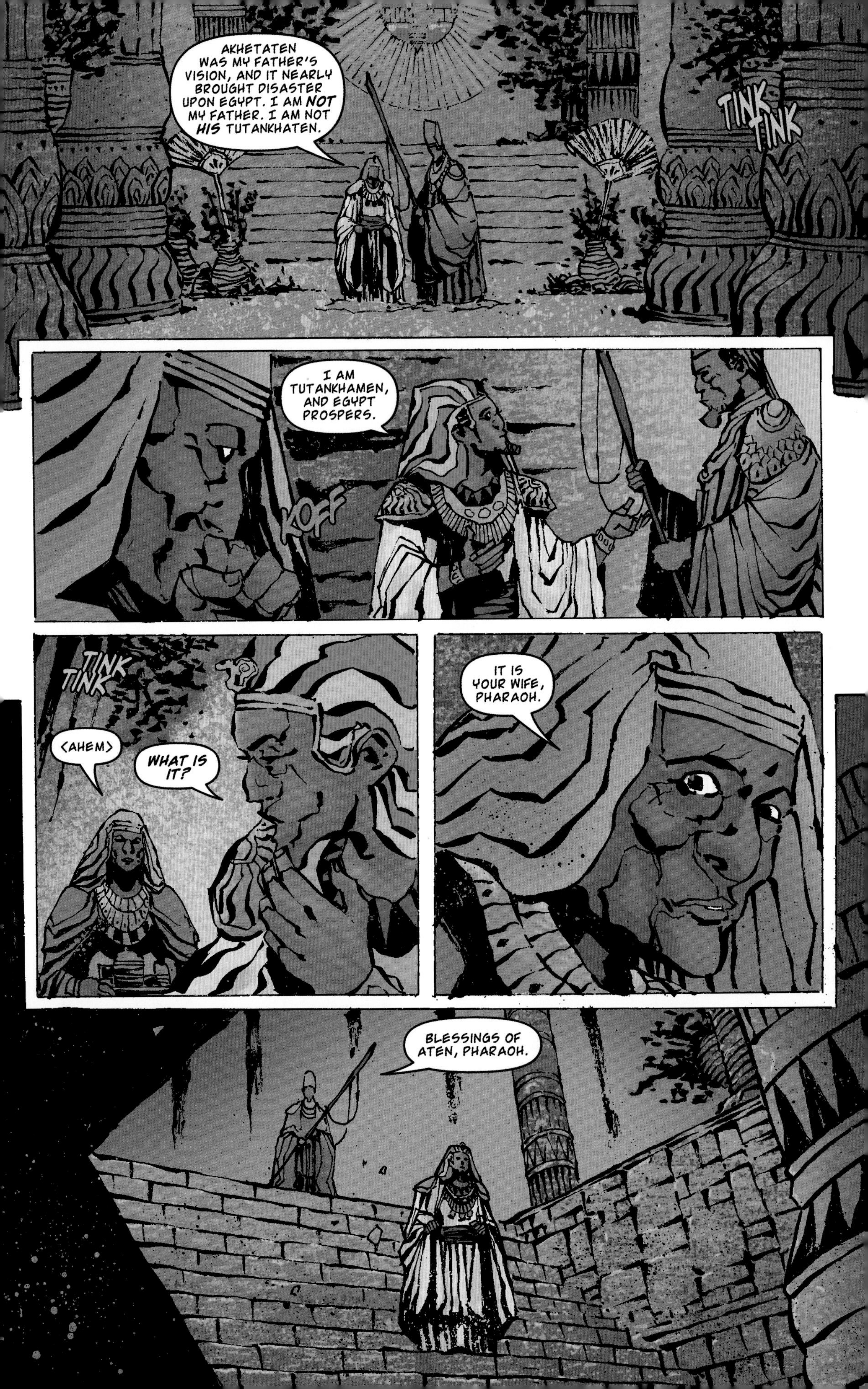
AKHETATEN WAS MY FATHER'S VISION, AND IT NEARLY BROUGHT DISASTER UPON EGYPT. I AM NOT MY FATHER. I AM NOT HIS TUTANKHATEN.
TINK TINK
I AM TUTANKHAMEN, AND EGYPT PROSPERS.
KOFF
TINK TINK
<AHEM>
WHAT IS IT?
IT IS YOUR WIFE, PHARAOH.
BLESSINGS OF ATEN, PHARAOH.

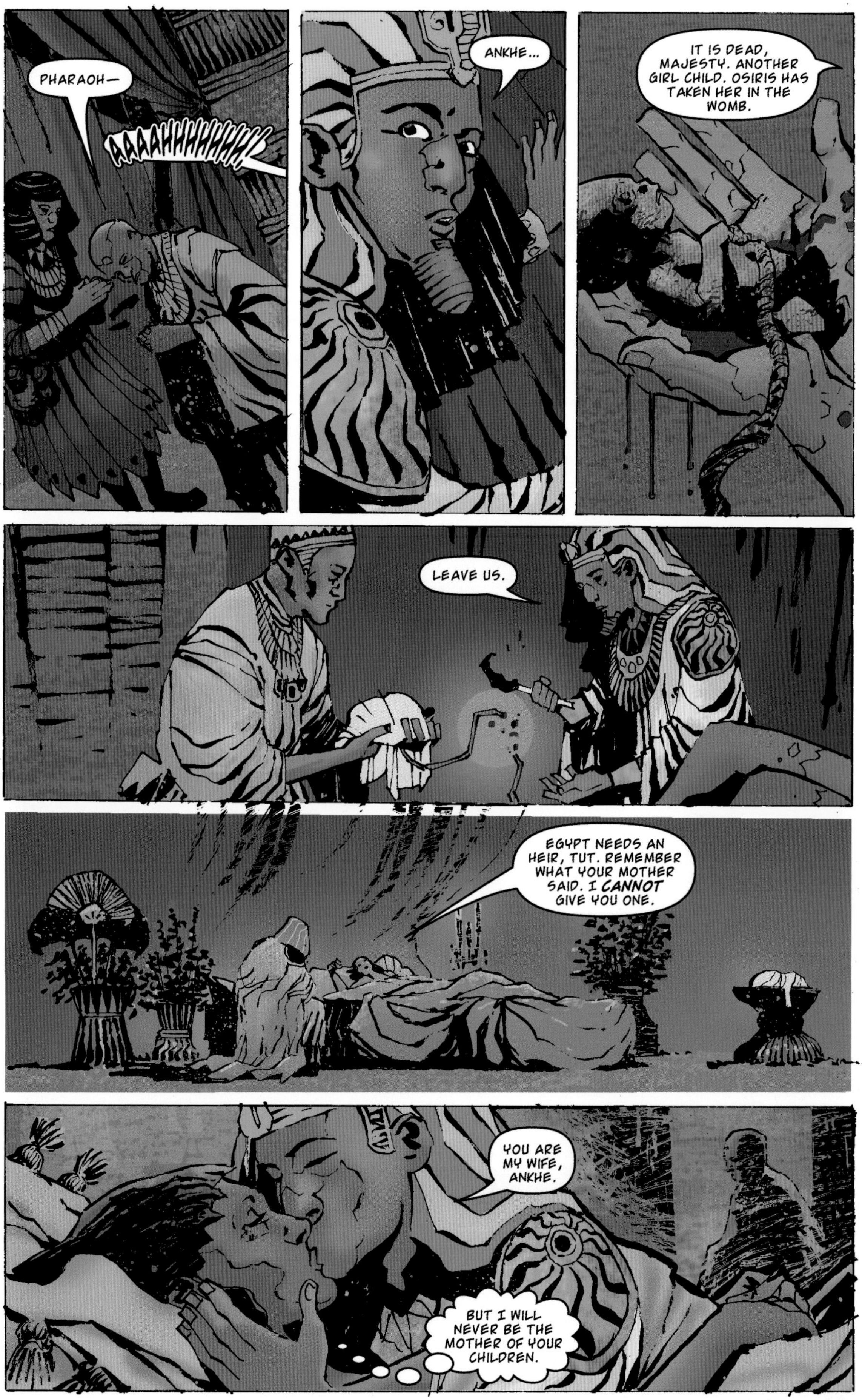
PHARAOH—
AAAAHHHHHHH!
ANKHE...
IT IS DEAD, MAJESTY. ANOTHER GIRL CHILD. OSIRIS HAS TAKEN HER IN THE WOMB.
LEAVE US.
EGYPT NEEDS AN HEIR, TUT. REMEMBER WHAT YOUR MOTHER SAID. I CANNOT GIVE YOU ONE.
YOU ARE MY WIFE, ANKHE.
BUT I WILL NEVER BE THE MOTHER OF YOUR CHILDREN.

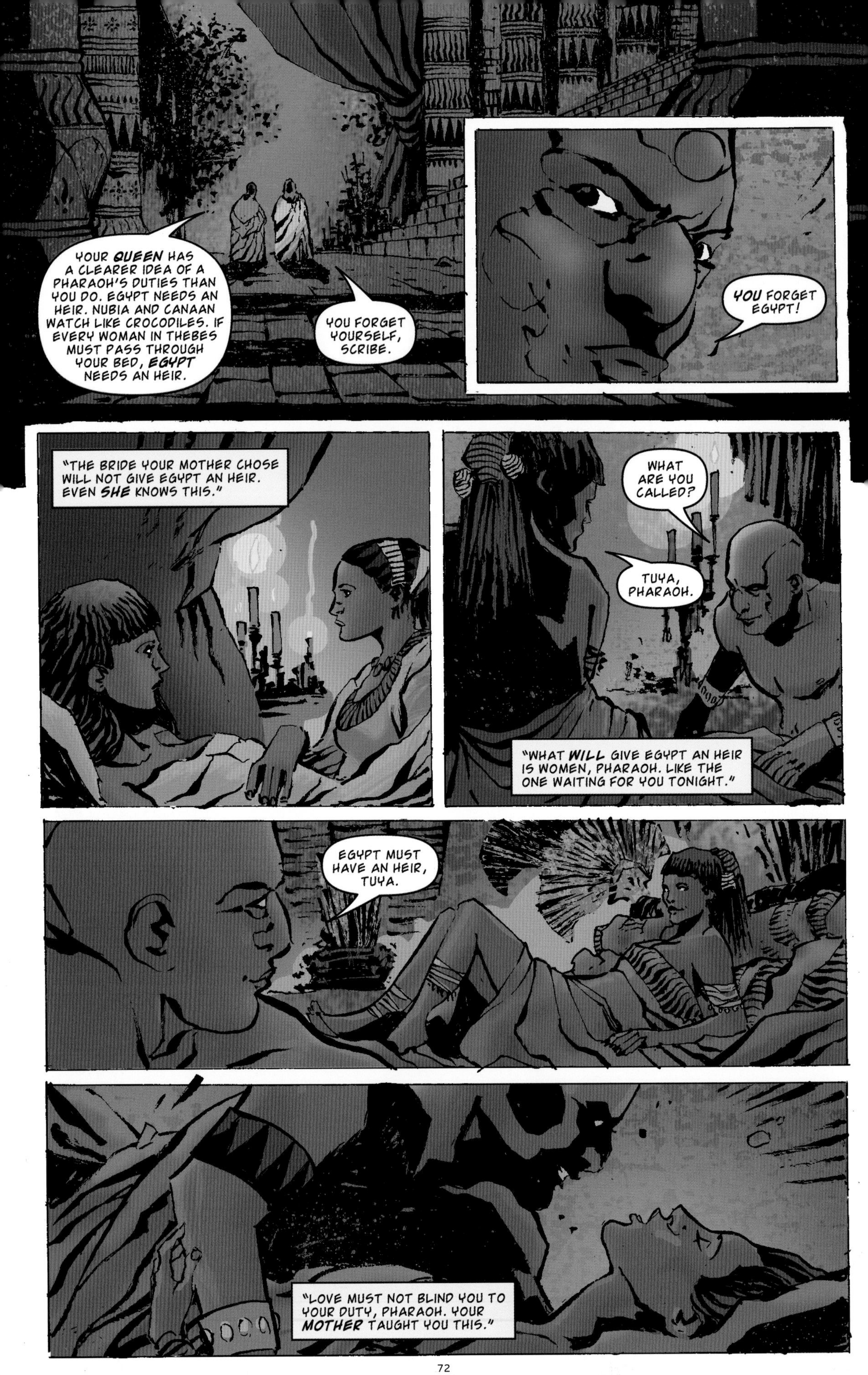
YOUR QUEEN HAS A CLEARER IDEA OF A PHARAOH'S DUTIES THAN YOU DO. EGYPT NEEDS AN HEIR. NUBIA AND CANAAN WATCH LIKE CROCODILES. IF EVERY WOMAN IN THEBES MUST PASS THROUGH YOUR BED, EGYPT NEEDS AN HEIR.
YOU FORGET YOURSELF, SCRIBE.
YOU FORGET EGYPT!
"THE BRIDE YOUR MOTHER CHOSE WILL NOT GIVE EGYPT AN HEIR. EVEN SHE KNOWS THIS."
WHAT ARE YOU CALLED?
TUYA, PHARAOH.
"WHAT WILL GIVE EGYPT AN HEIR IS WOMEN, PHARAOH. LIKE THE ONE WAITING FOR YOU TONIGHT."
EGYPT MUST HAVE AN HEIR, TUYA.
"LOVE MUST NOT BLIND YOU TO YOUR DUTY, PHARAOH. YOUR MOTHER TAUGHT YOU THIS."

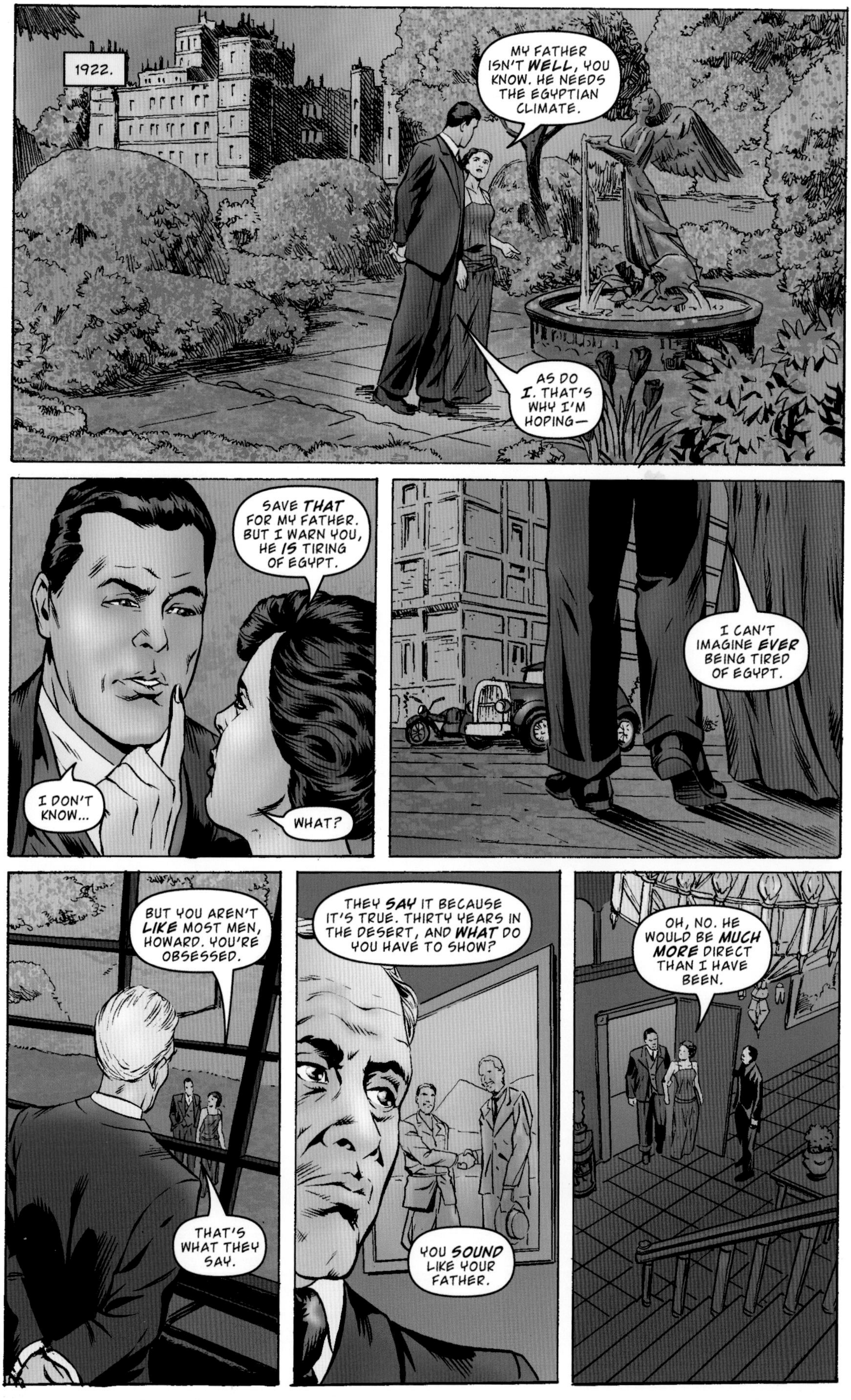
1922.
MY FATHER ISN'T WELL, YOU KNOW. HE NEEDS THE EGYPTIAN CLIMATE.
AS DO I. THAT'S WHY I'M HOPING—
SAVE THAT FOR MY FATHER. BUT I WARN YOU, HE IS TIRING OF EGYPT.
I DON'T KNOW...
WHAT?
I CAN'T IMAGINE EVER BEING TIRED OF EGYPT.
BUT YOU AREN'T LIKE MOST MEN, HOWARD. YOU'RE OBSESSED.
THAT'S WHAT THEY SAY.
THEY SAY IT BECAUSE IT'S TRUE. THIRTY YEARS IN THE DESERT, AND WHAT DO YOU HAVE TO SHOW?
YOU SOUND LIKE YOUR FATHER.
OH, NO. HE WOULD BE MUCH MORE DIRECT THAN I HAVE BEEN.

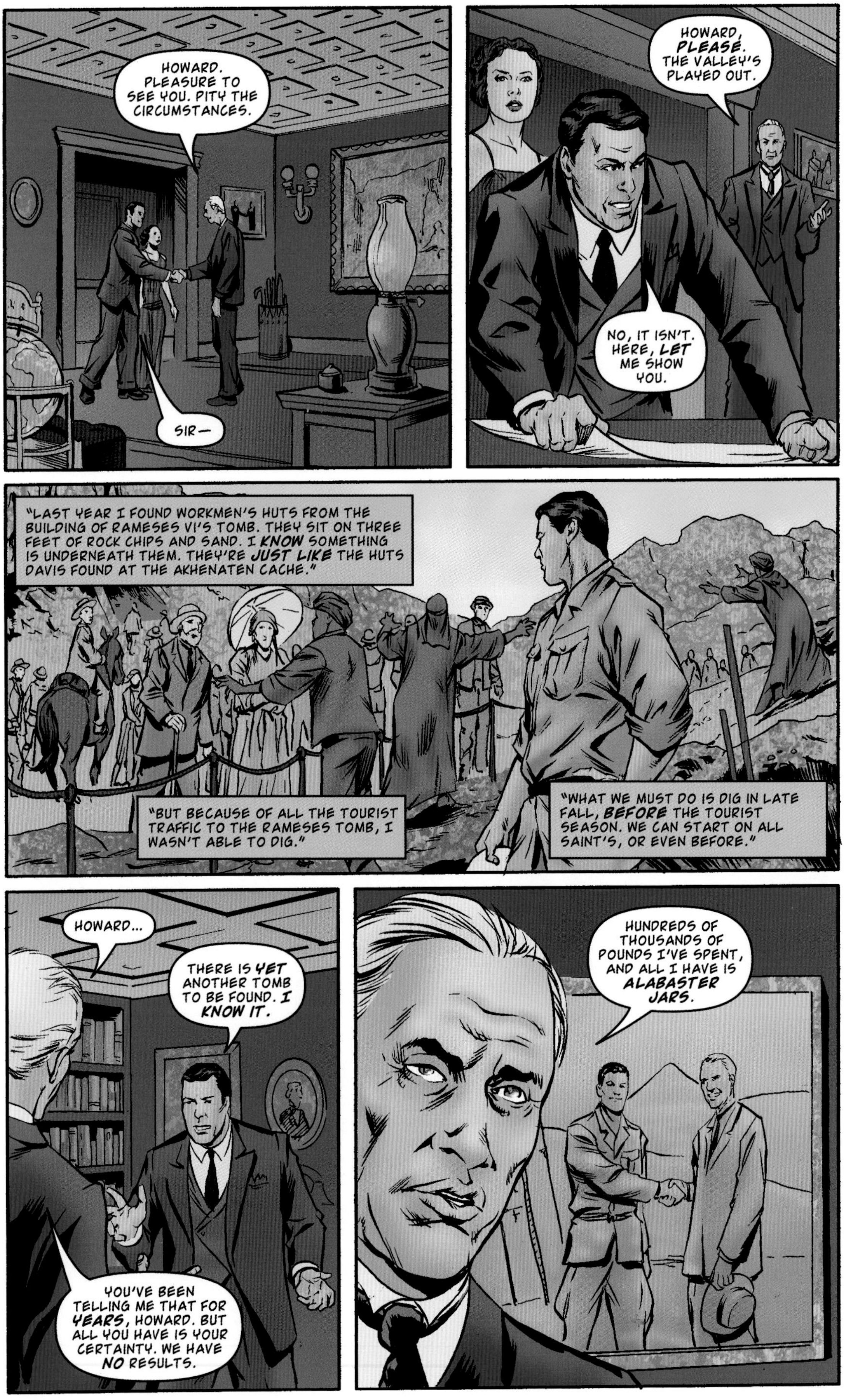
HOWARD. PLEASURE TO SEE YOU. PITY THE CIRCUMSTANCES.
SIR—
HOWARD, PLEASE. THE VALLEY'S PLAYED OUT.
NO, IT ISN'T. HERE, LET ME SHOW YOU.
"LAST YEAR I FOUND WORKMEN'S HUTS FROM THE BUILDING OF RAMESES VI'S TOMB. THEY SIT ON THREE FEET OF ROCK CHIPS AND SAND. I KNOW SOMETHING IS UNDERNEATH THEM. THEY'RE JUST LIKE THE HUTS DAVIS FOUND AT THE AKHENATEN CACHE."
"BUT BECAUSE OF ALL THE TOURIST TRAFFIC TO THE RAMESES TOMB, I WASN'T ABLE TO DIG."
"WHAT WE MUST DO IS DIG IN LATE FALL, BEFORE THE TOURIST SEASON. WE CAN START ON ALL SAINT'S, OR EVEN BEFORE."
HOWARD...
THERE IS YET ANOTHER TOMB TO BE FOUND. I KNOW IT.
YOU'VE BEEN TELLING ME THAT FOR YEARS, HOWARD. BUT ALL YOU HAVE IS YOUR CERTAINTY. WE HAVE NO RESULTS.
HUNDREDS OF THOUSANDS OF POUNDS I'VE SPENT, AND ALL I HAVE IS ALABASTER JARS.

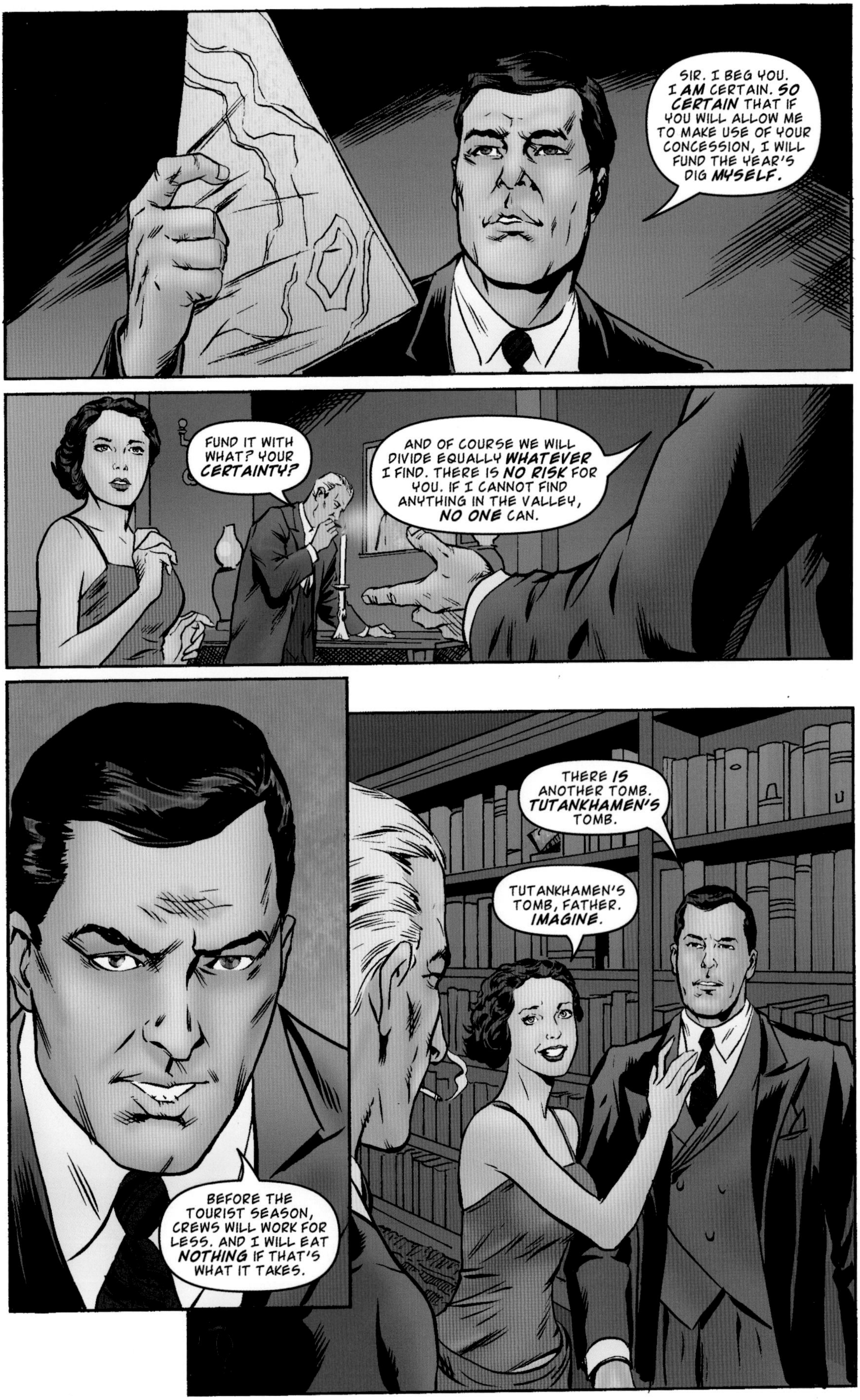
SIR. I BEG YOU. I AM CERTAIN. SO CERTAIN THAT IF YOU WILL ALLOW ME TO MAKE USE OF YOUR CONCESSION, I WILL FUND THE YEAR'S DIG MYSELF.
FUND IT WITH WHAT? YOUR CERTAINTY?
AND OF COURSE WE WILL DIVIDE EQUALLY WHATEVER I FIND. THERE IS NO RISK FOR YOU. IF I CANNOT FIND ANYTHING IN THE VALLEY, NO ONE CAN.
BEFORE THE TOURIST SEASON, CREWS WILL WORK FOR LESS. AND I WILL EAT NOTHING IF THAT'S WHAT IT TAKES.
THERE IS ANOTHER TOMB. TUTANKHAMEN'S TOMB.
TUTANKHAMEN'S TOMB, FATHER. IMAGINE.

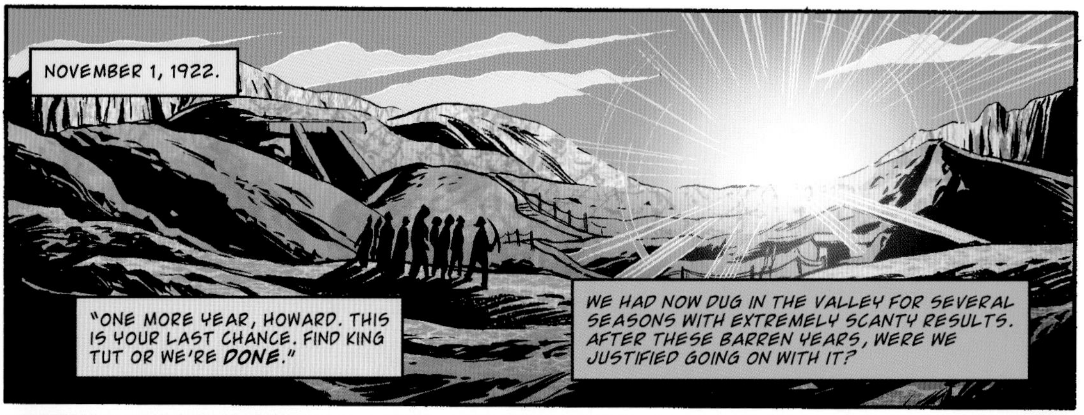
NOVEMBER 1, 1922.
"ONE MORE YEAR, HOWARD. THIS IS YOUR LAST CHANCE. FIND KING TUT OR WE'RE **DONE**."
WE HAD NOW DUG IN THE VALLEY FOR SEVERAL SEASONS WITH EXTREMELY SCANTY RESULTS. AFTER THESE BARREN YEARS, WERE WE JUSTIFIED GOING ON WITH IT?

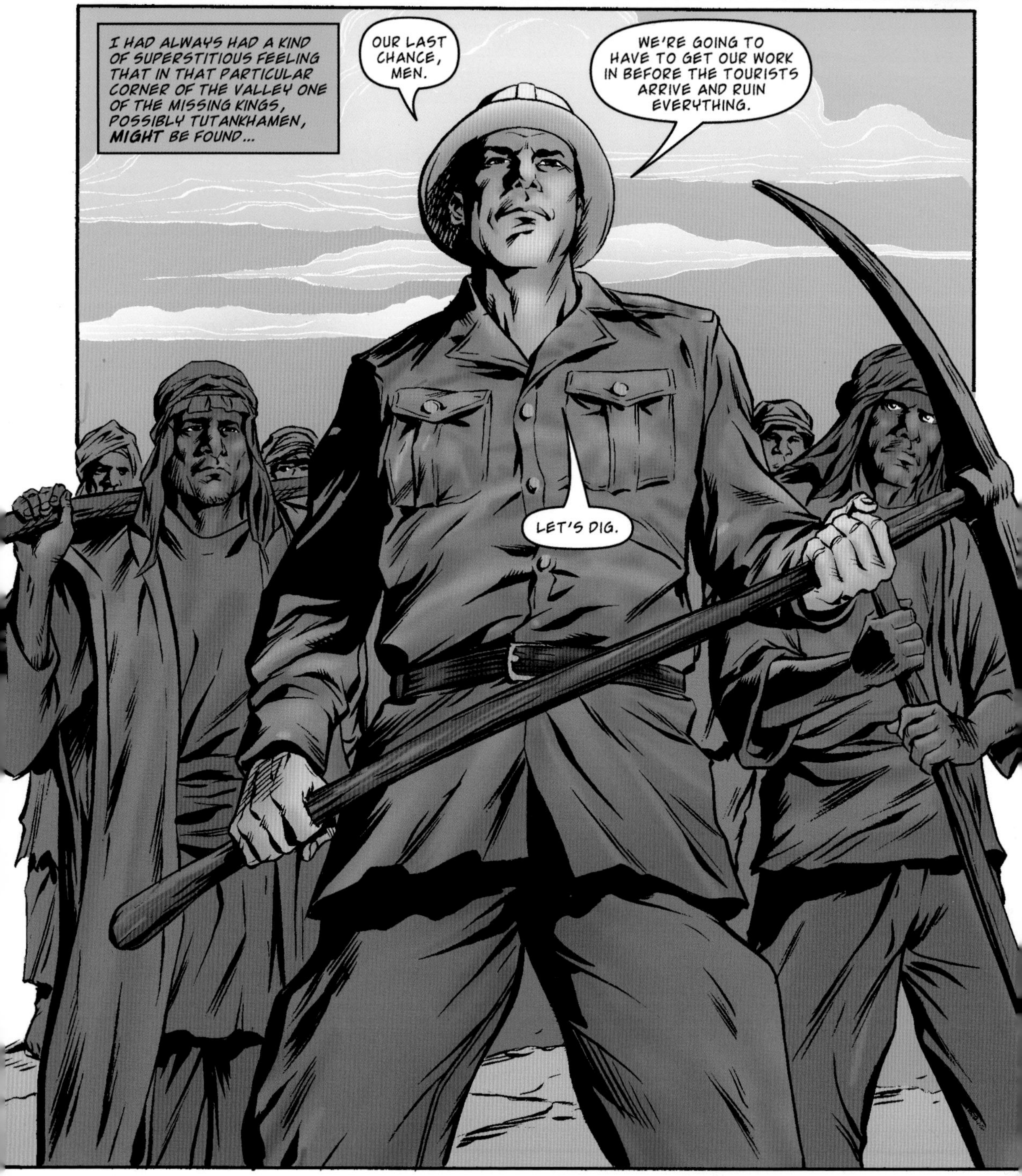
I HAD ALWAYS HAD A KIND OF SUPERSTITIOUS FEELING THAT IN THAT PARTICULAR CORNER OF THE VALLEY ONE OF THE MISSING KINGS, POSSIBLY TUTANKHAMEN, **MIGHT** BE FOUND...
OUR LAST CHANCE, MEN.
WE'RE GOING TO HAVE TO GET OUR WORK IN BEFORE THE TOURISTS ARRIVE AND RUIN EVERYTHING.
LET'S DIG.

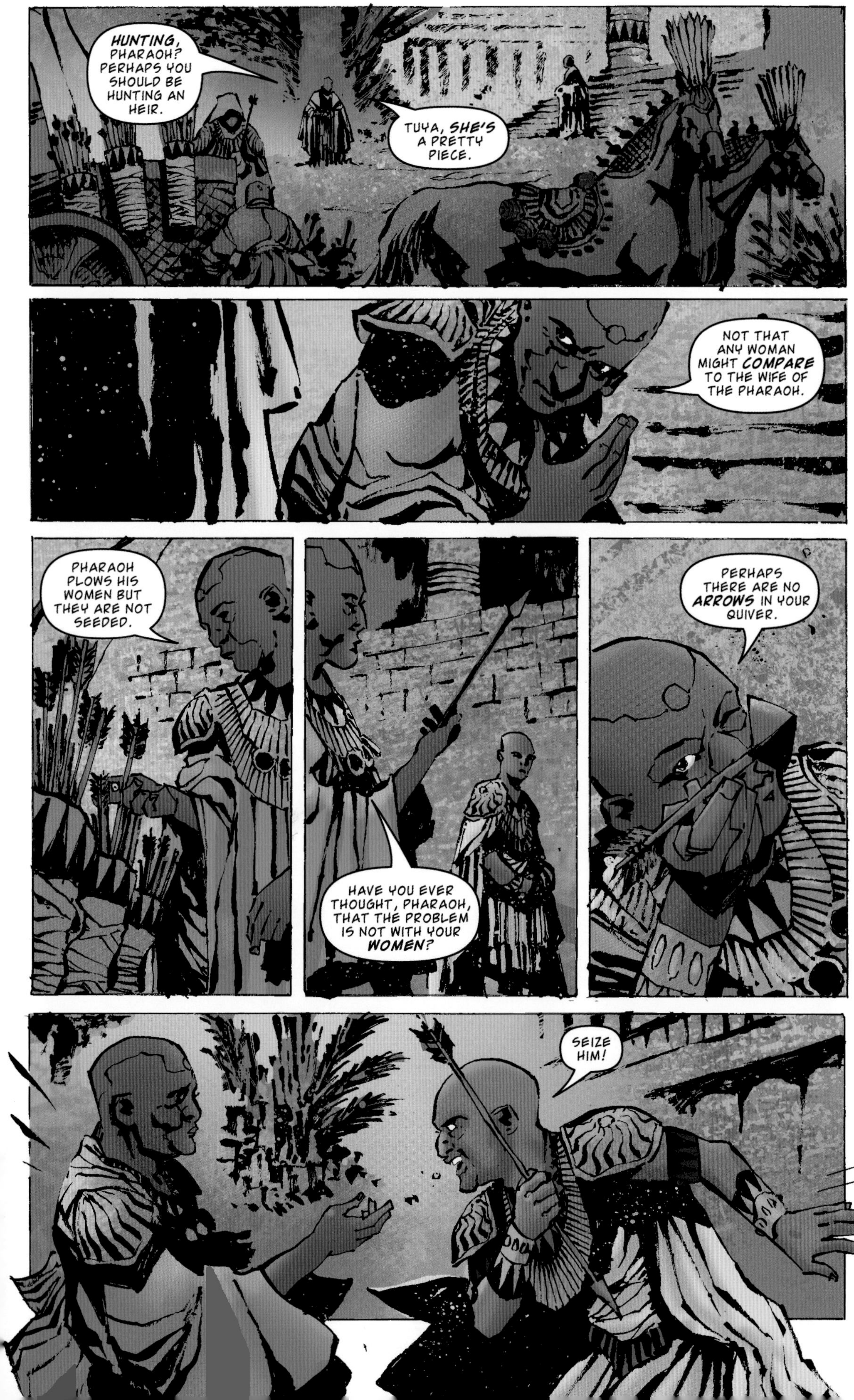
HUNTING, PHARAOH? PERHAPS YOU SHOULD BE HUNTING AN HEIR.
TUYA, SHE'S A PRETTY PIECE.
NOT THAT ANY WOMAN MIGHT COMPARE TO THE WIFE OF THE PHARAOH.
PHARAOH PLOWS HIS WOMEN BUT THEY ARE NOT SEEDED.
HAVE YOU EVER THOUGHT, PHARAOH, THAT THE PROBLEM IS NOT WITH YOUR WOMEN?
PERHAPS THERE ARE NO ARROWS IN YOUR QUIVER.
SEIZE HIM!

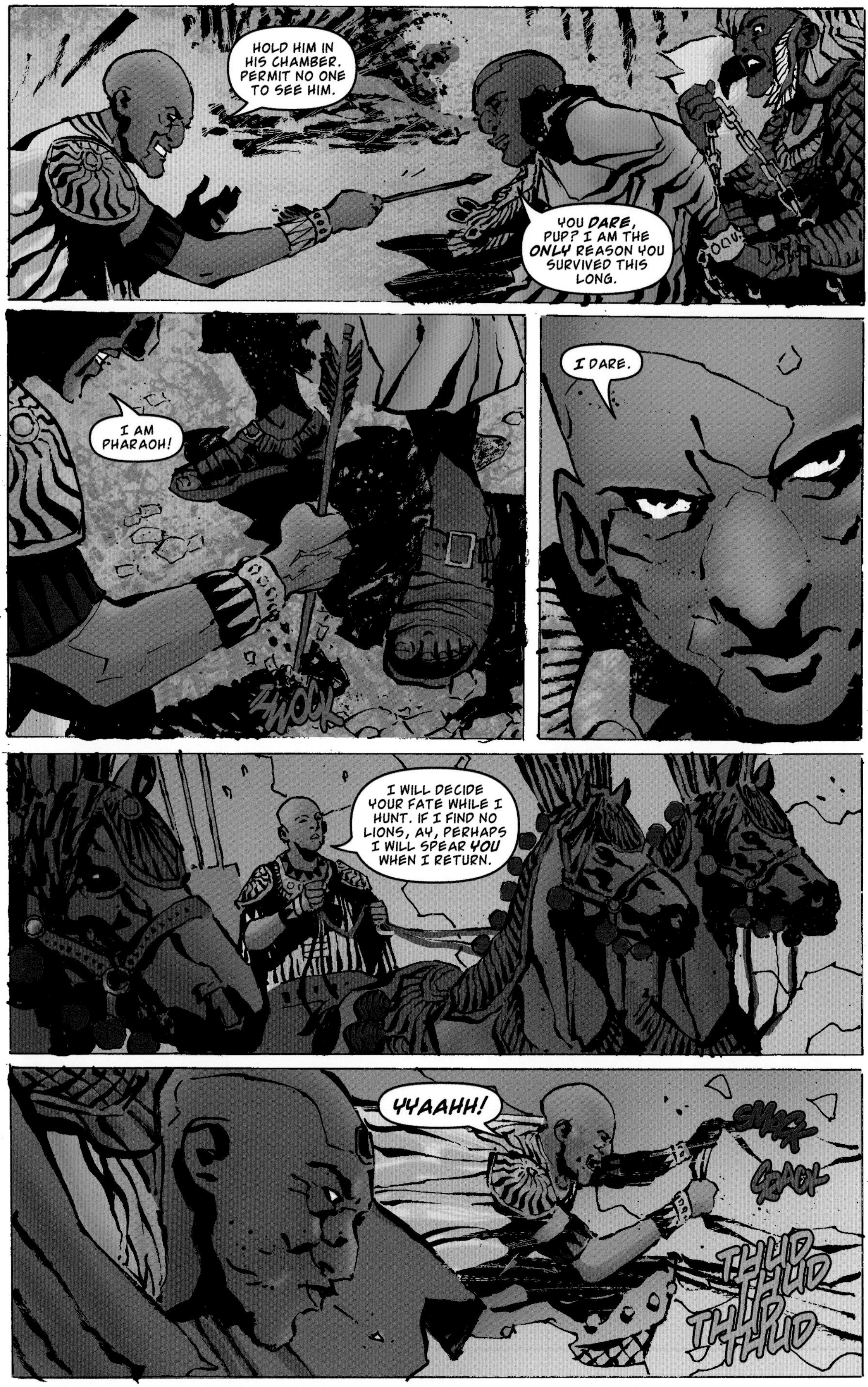
HOLD HIM IN HIS CHAMBER. PERMIT NO ONE TO SEE HIM.
YOU DARE, PUP? I AM THE ONLY REASON YOU SURVIVED THIS LONG.
I AM PHARAOH!
SWOCK
I DARE.
I WILL DECIDE YOUR FATE WHILE I HUNT. IF I FIND NO LIONS, AY, PERHAPS I WILL SPEAR YOU WHEN I RETURN.
YYAAHH!
CRACK
THUD
THUD
THUD
THUD

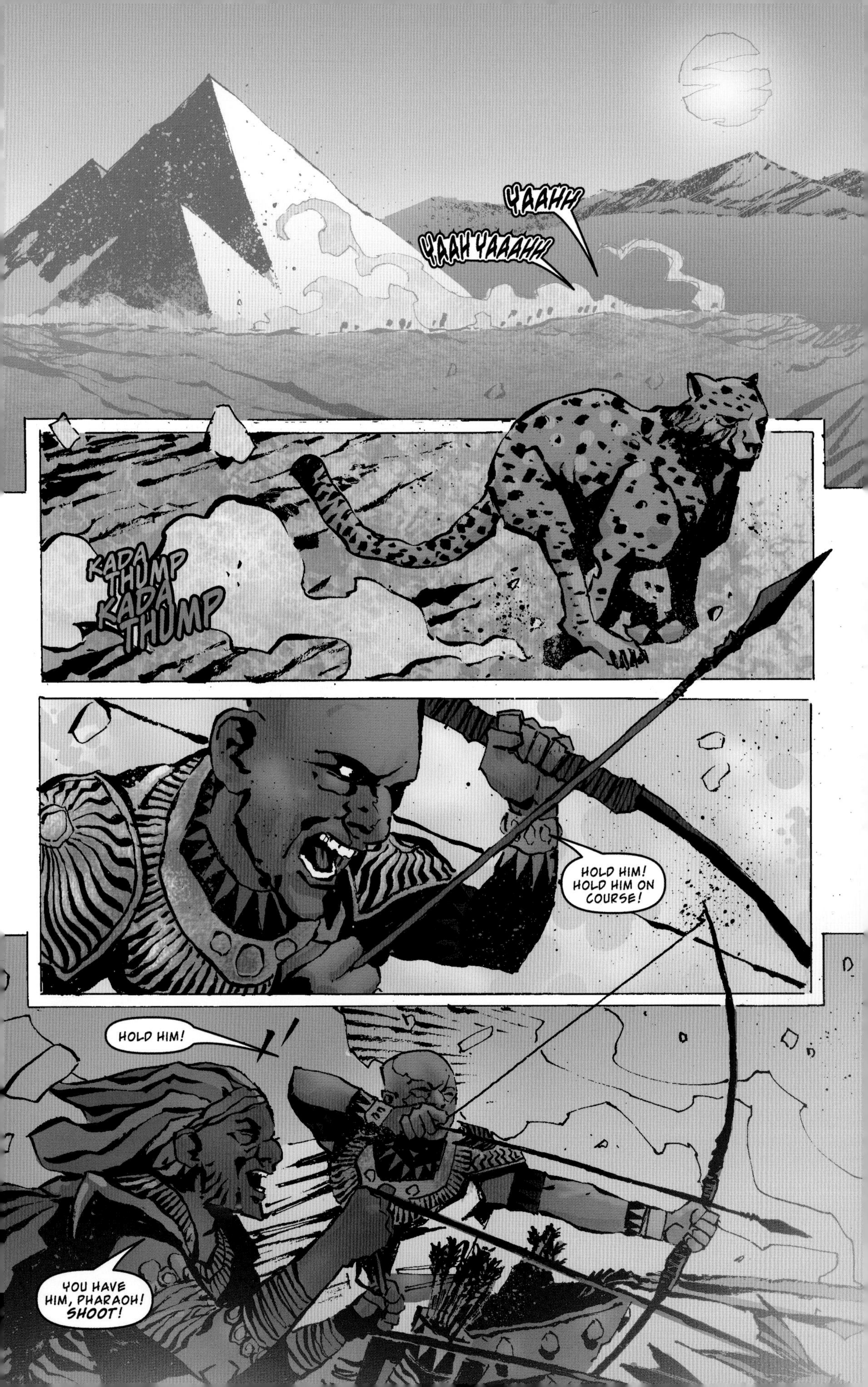
YAAHH
YAAH YAAAHH
KADA THUMP KADA THUMP
HOLD HIM! HOLD HIM ON COURSE!
HOLD HIM!
YOU HAVE HIM, PHARAOH! SHOOT!

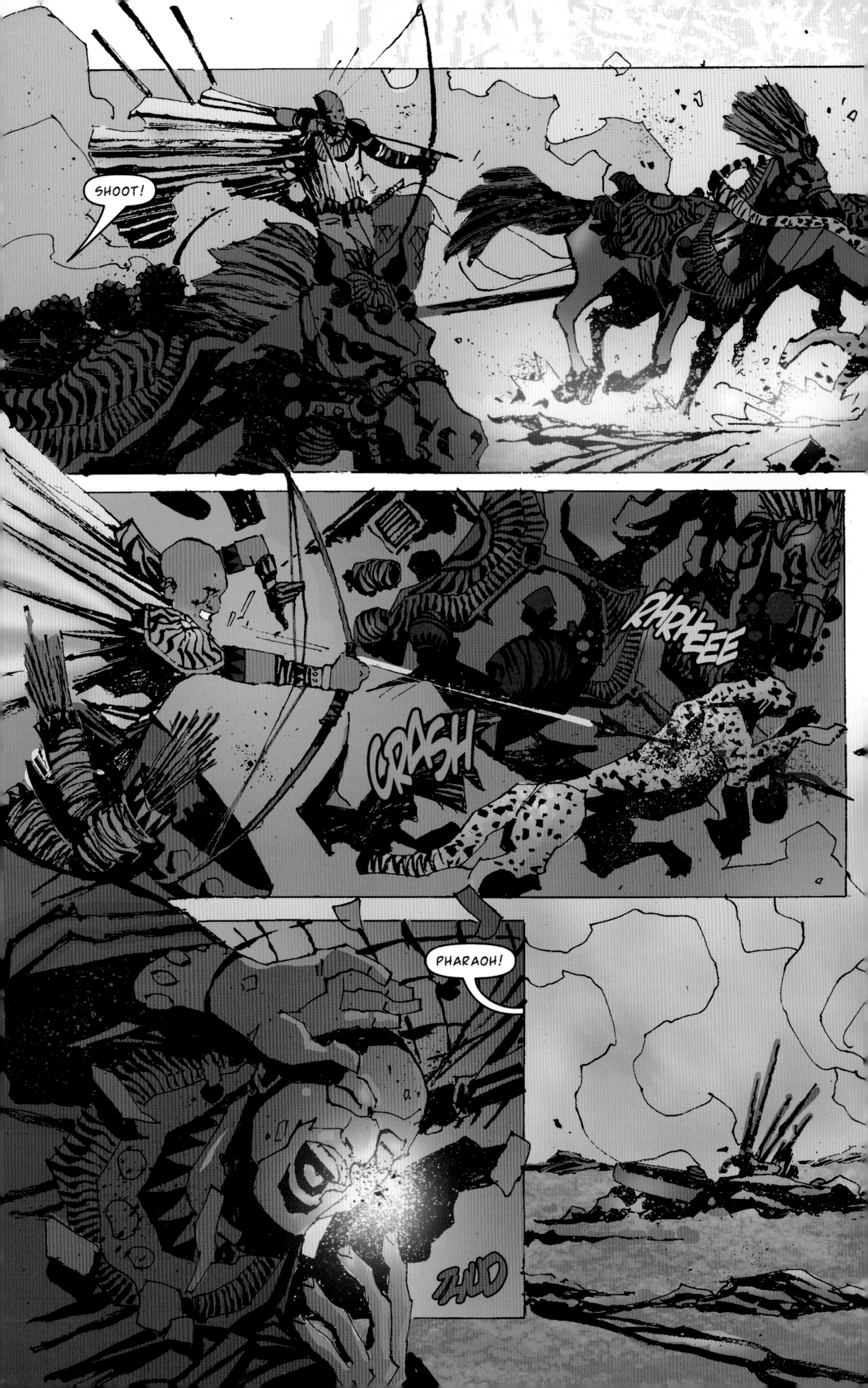
SHOOT!
RHRHEEE
CRASH
PHARAOH!
THUD

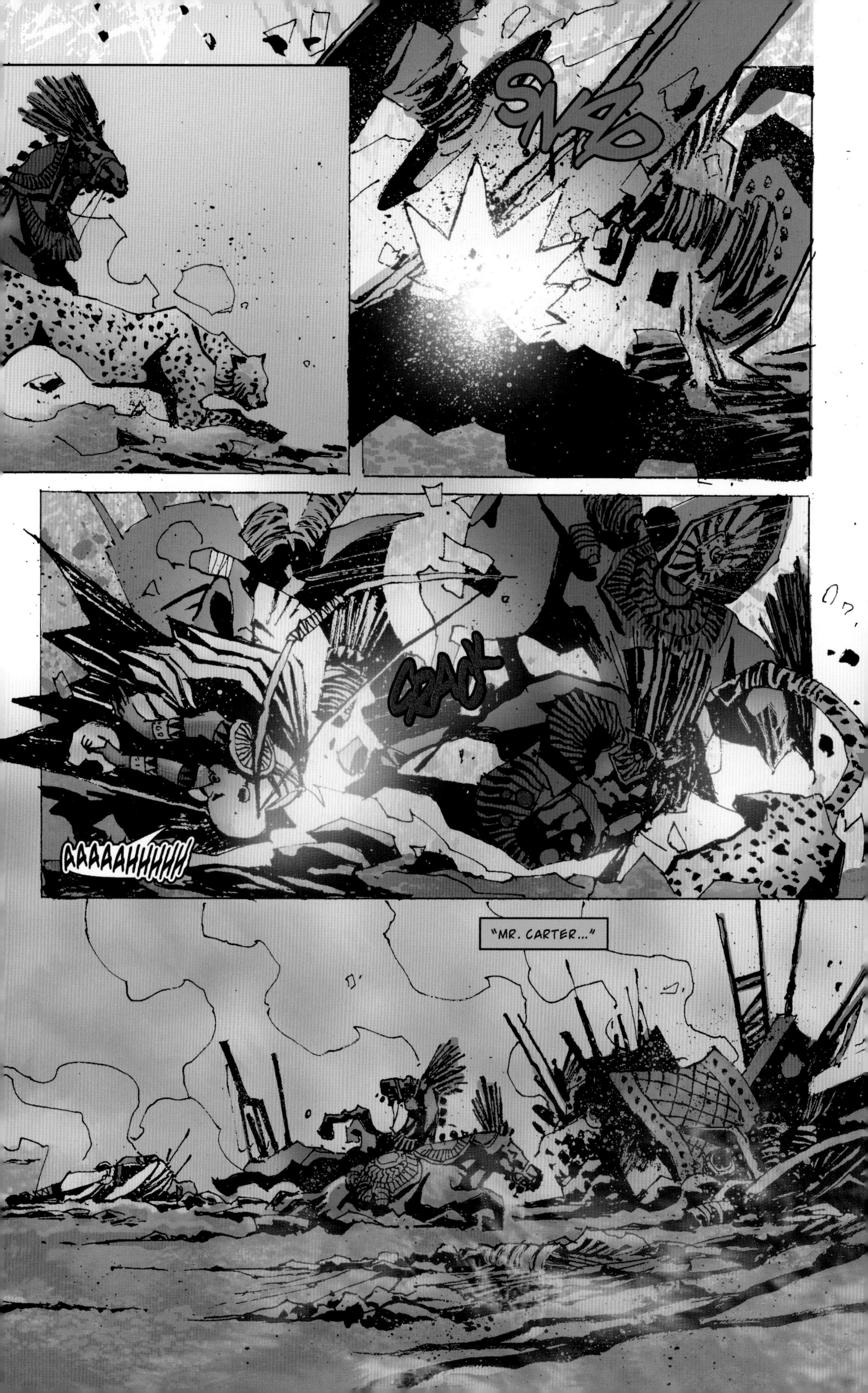
SNAP
CRACK
AAAAAHHHHH
"MR. CARTER..."

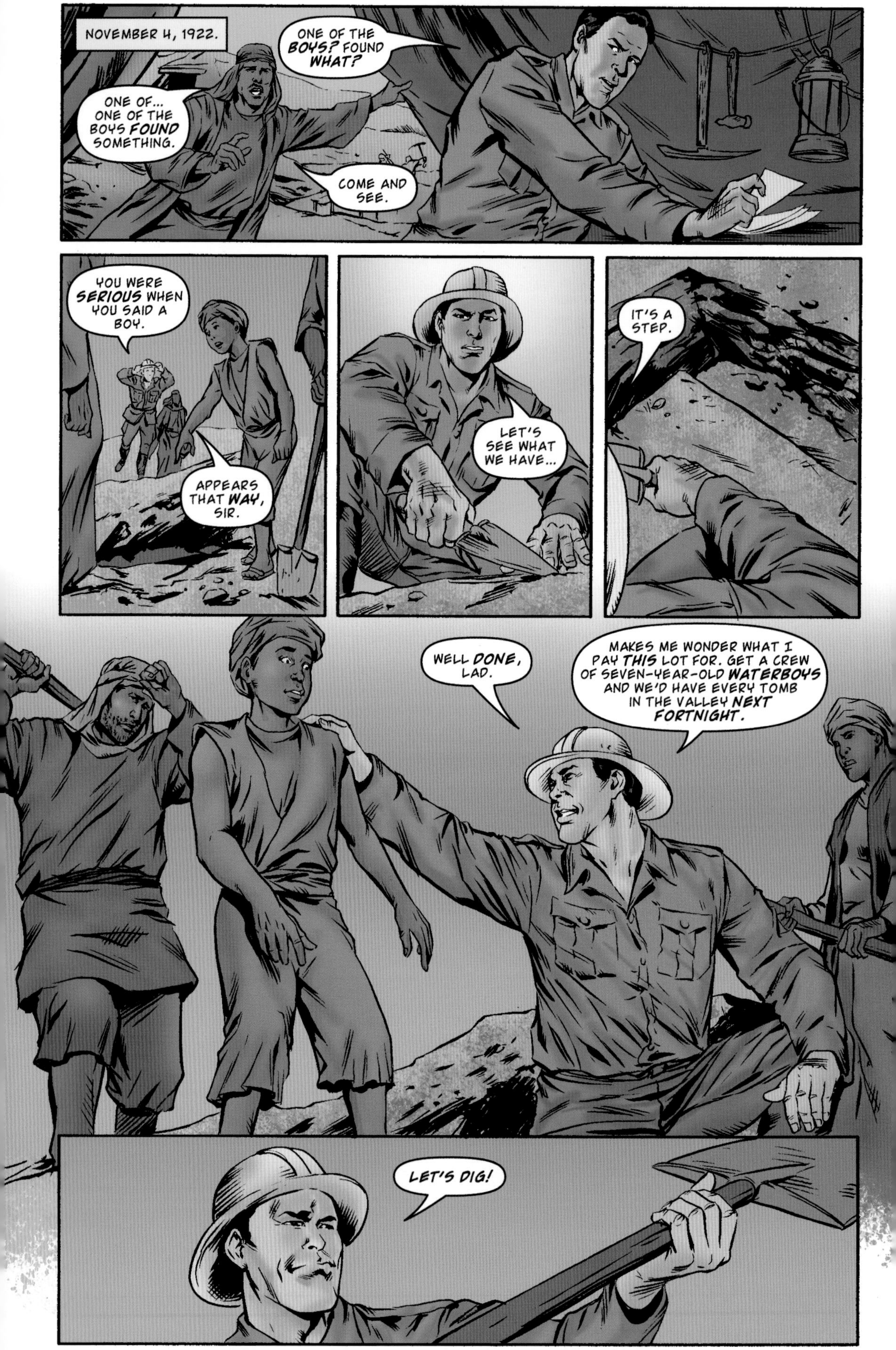
NOVEMBER 4, 1922.
ONE OF... ONE OF THE BOYS FOUND SOMETHING.
ONE OF THE BOYS? FOUND WHAT?
COME AND SEE.
YOU WERE SERIOUS WHEN YOU SAID A BOY.
APPEARS THAT WAY, SIR.
LET'S SEE WHAT WE HAVE...
IT'S A STEP.
WELL DONE, LAD.
MAKES ME WONDER WHAT I PAY THIS LOT FOR. GET A CREW OF SEVEN-YEAR-OLD WATERBOYS AND WE'D HAVE EVERY TOMB IN THE VALLEY NEXT FORTNIGHT.
LET'S DIG!

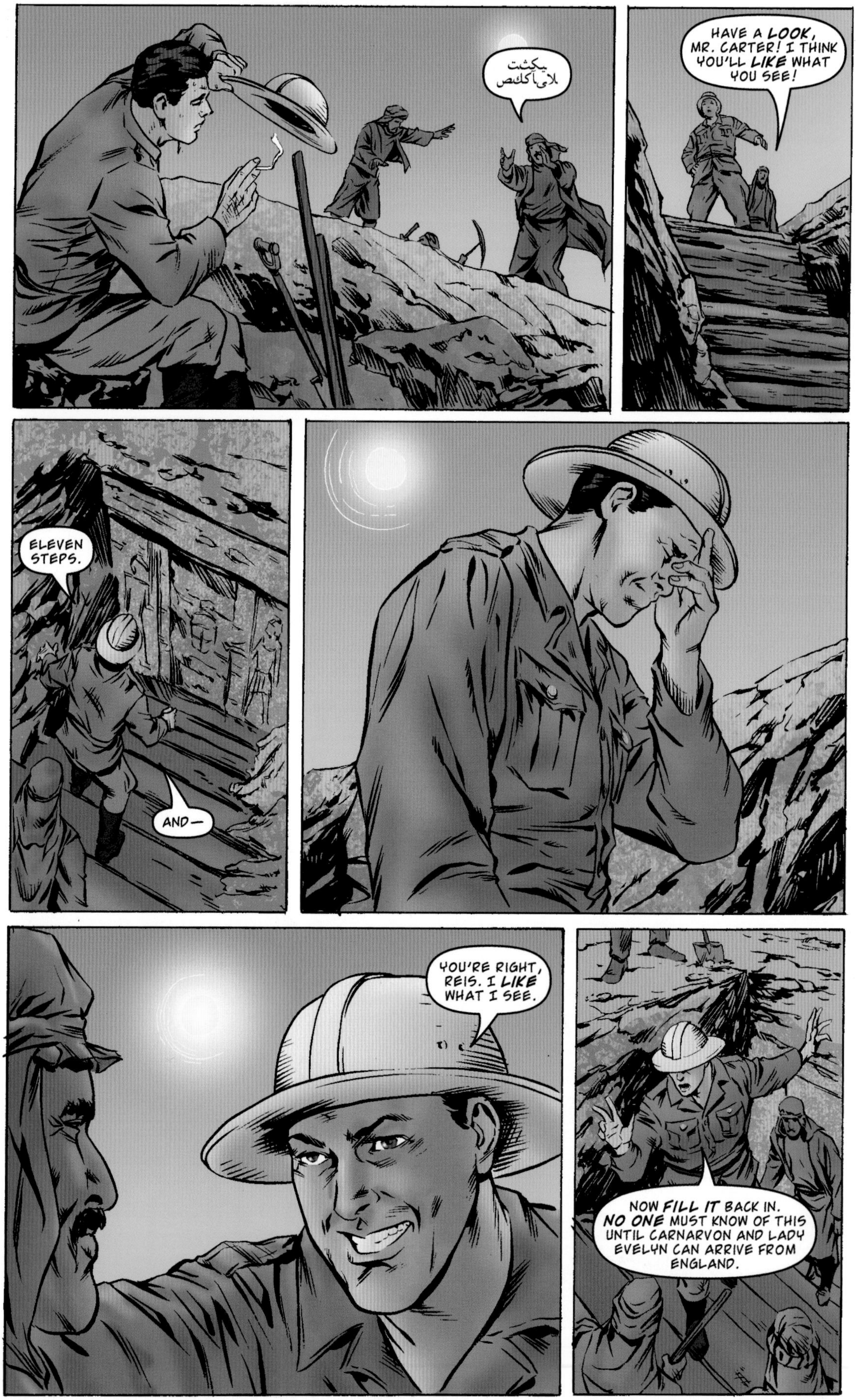
HAVE A LOOK, MR. CARTER! I THINK YOU'LL LIKE WHAT YOU SEE!
ELEVEN STEPS.
AND—
YOU'RE RIGHT, REIS. I LIKE WHAT I SEE.
NOW FILL IT BACK IN. NO ONE MUST KNOW OF THIS UNTIL CARNARVON AND LADY EVELYN CAN ARRIVE FROM ENGLAND.

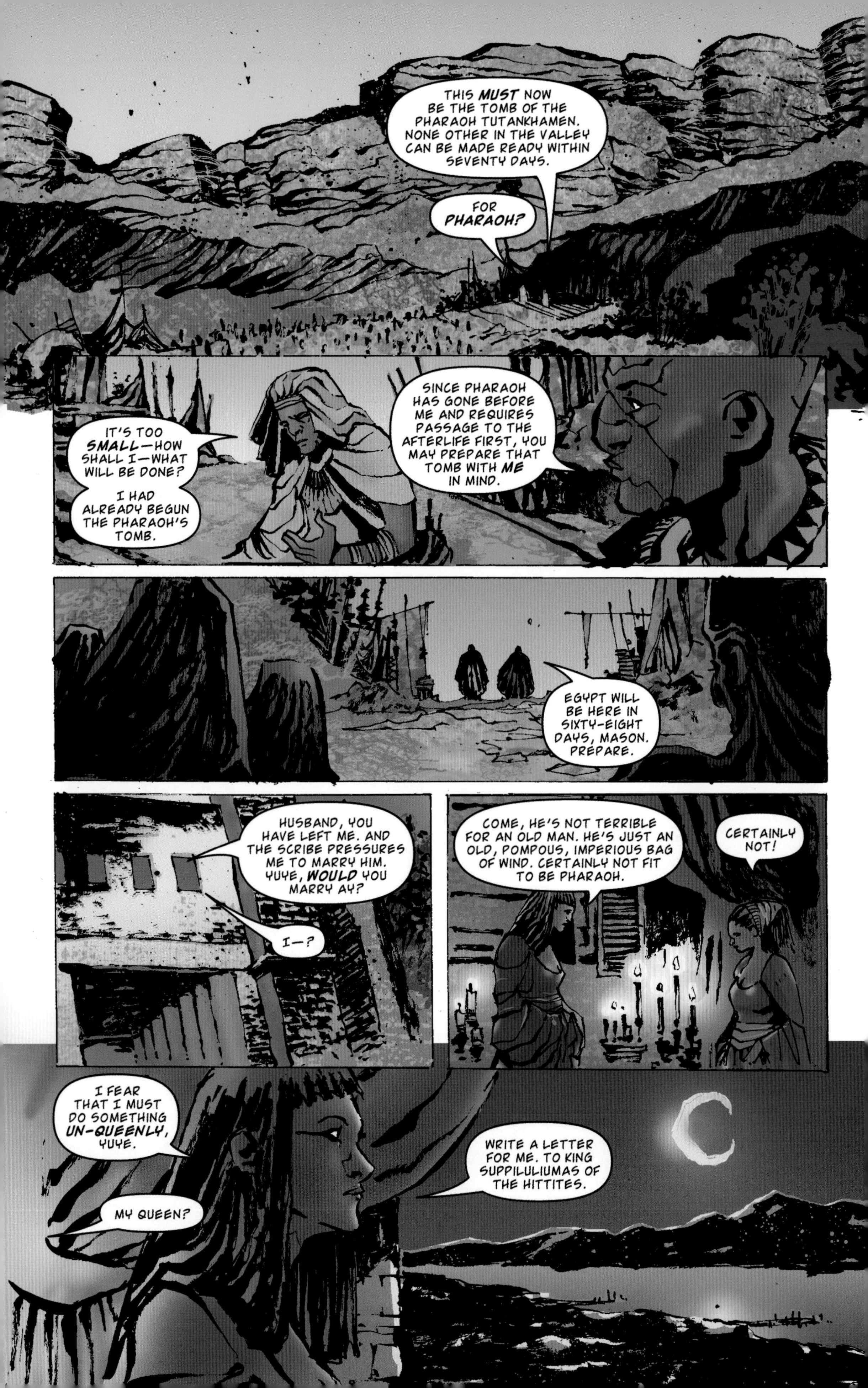
THIS MUST NOW BE THE TOMB OF THE PHARAOH TUTANKHAMEN. NONE OTHER IN THE VALLEY CAN BE MADE READY WITHIN SEVENTY DAYS.
FOR PHARAOH?
IT'S TOO SMALL—HOW SHALL I—WHAT WILL BE DONE?
I HAD ALREADY BEGUN THE PHARAOH'S TOMB.
SINCE PHARAOH HAS GONE BEFORE ME AND REQUIRES PASSAGE TO THE AFTERLIFE FIRST, YOU MAY PREPARE THAT TOMB WITH ME IN MIND.
EGYPT WILL BE HERE IN SIXTY-EIGHT DAYS, MASON. PREPARE.
HUSBAND, YOU HAVE LEFT ME. AND THE SCRIBE PRESSURES ME TO MARRY HIM. YUYE, WOULD YOU MARRY AY?
I—?
COME, HE'S NOT TERRIBLE FOR AN OLD MAN. HE'S JUST AN OLD, POMPOUS, IMPERIOUS BAG OF WIND. CERTAINLY NOT FIT TO BE PHARAOH.
CERTAINLY NOT!
I FEAR THAT I MUST DO SOMETHING UN-QUEENLY, YUYE.
MY QUEEN?
WRITE A LETTER FOR ME. TO KING SUPPILULIUMAS OF THE HITTITES.

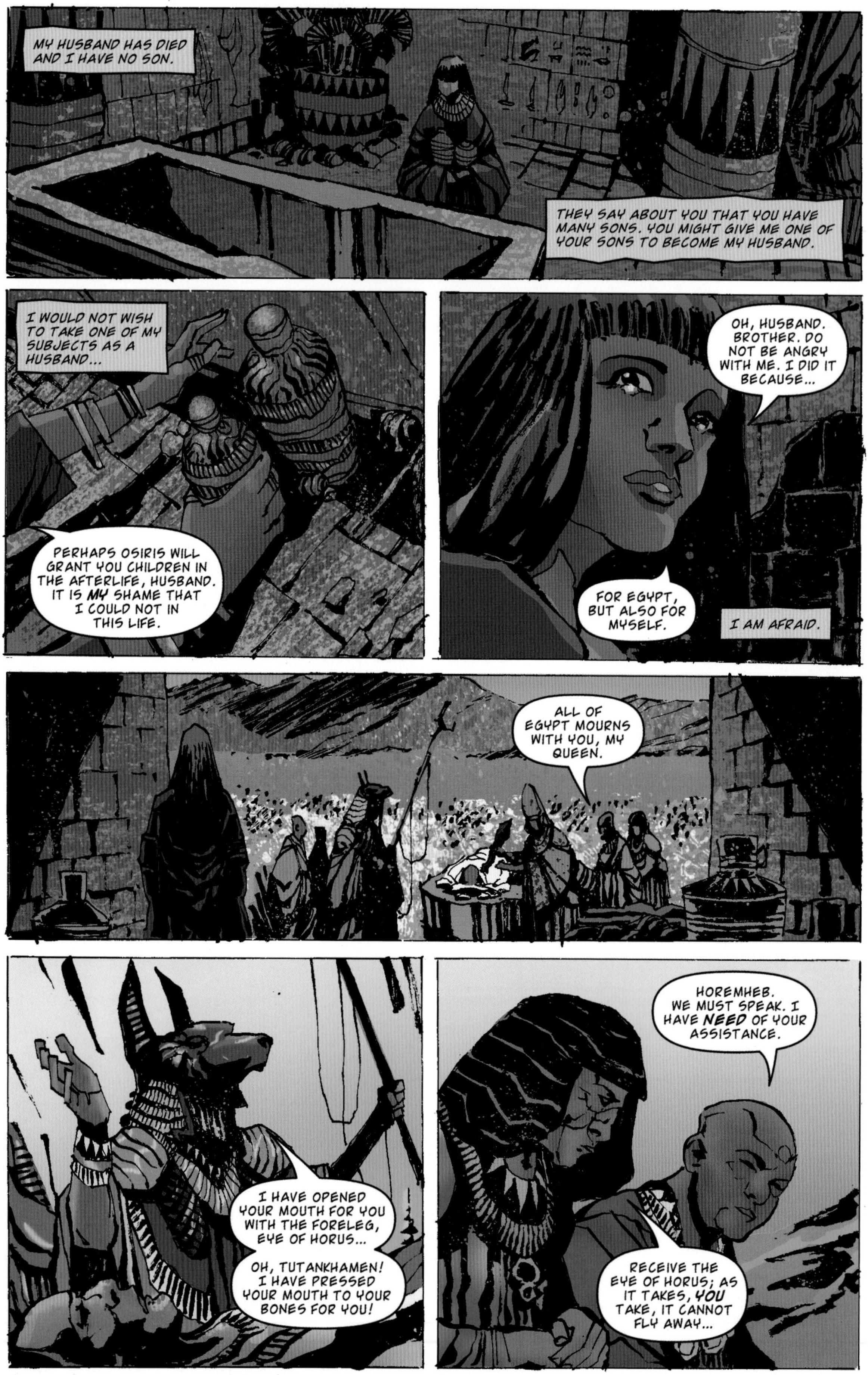
MY HUSBAND HAS DIED AND I HAVE NO SON.
THEY SAY ABOUT YOU THAT YOU HAVE MANY SONS. YOU MIGHT GIVE ME ONE OF YOUR SONS TO BECOME MY HUSBAND.
I WOULD NOT WISH TO TAKE ONE OF MY SUBJECTS AS A HUSBAND...
PERHAPS OSIRIS WILL GRANT YOU CHILDREN IN THE AFTERLIFE, HUSBAND. IT IS MY SHAME THAT I COULD NOT IN THIS LIFE.
OH, HUSBAND. BROTHER. DO NOT BE ANGRY WITH ME. I DID IT BECAUSE...
FOR EGYPT, BUT ALSO FOR MYSELF.
I AM AFRAID.
ALL OF EGYPT MOURNS WITH YOU, MY QUEEN.
I HAVE OPENED YOUR MOUTH FOR YOU WITH THE FORELEG, EYE OF HORUS...
OH, TUTANKHAMEN! I HAVE PRESSED YOUR MOUTH TO YOUR BONES FOR YOU!
HOREMHEB. WE MUST SPEAK. I HAVE NEED OF YOUR ASSISTANCE.
RECEIVE THE EYE OF HORUS; AS IT TAKES, YOU TAKE, IT CANNOT FLY AWAY...

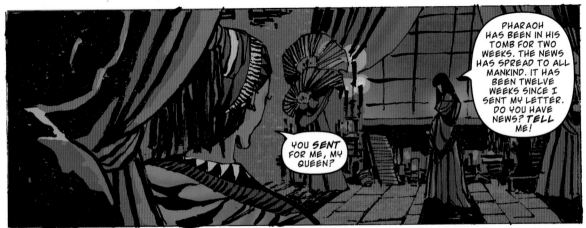

PHARAOH HAS BEEN IN HIS TOMB FOR TWO WEEKS. THE NEWS HAS SPREAD TO ALL MANKIND. IT HAS BEEN TWELVE WEEKS SINCE I SENT MY LETTER. DO YOU HAVE NEWS? TELL ME!

YOU SENT FOR ME, MY QUEEN?

"A PRINCE OF THE HITTITES, ZENNANZA, WAS MOVED BY YOUR LETTER, MY QUEEN. BUT I KNOW THIS ONLY FROM GOSSIP."

OH, BUT YOU HAVE MORE THAN THAT, YUYE. DO YOU NOT?

YOU HAVE NEWS.

TELL THE QUEEN THE NEWS, YUYE. TELL HER.

YUYE?

AND AFTER HER NEWS, I SHALL TELL YOU THE NEWS I HAVE BROUGHT.

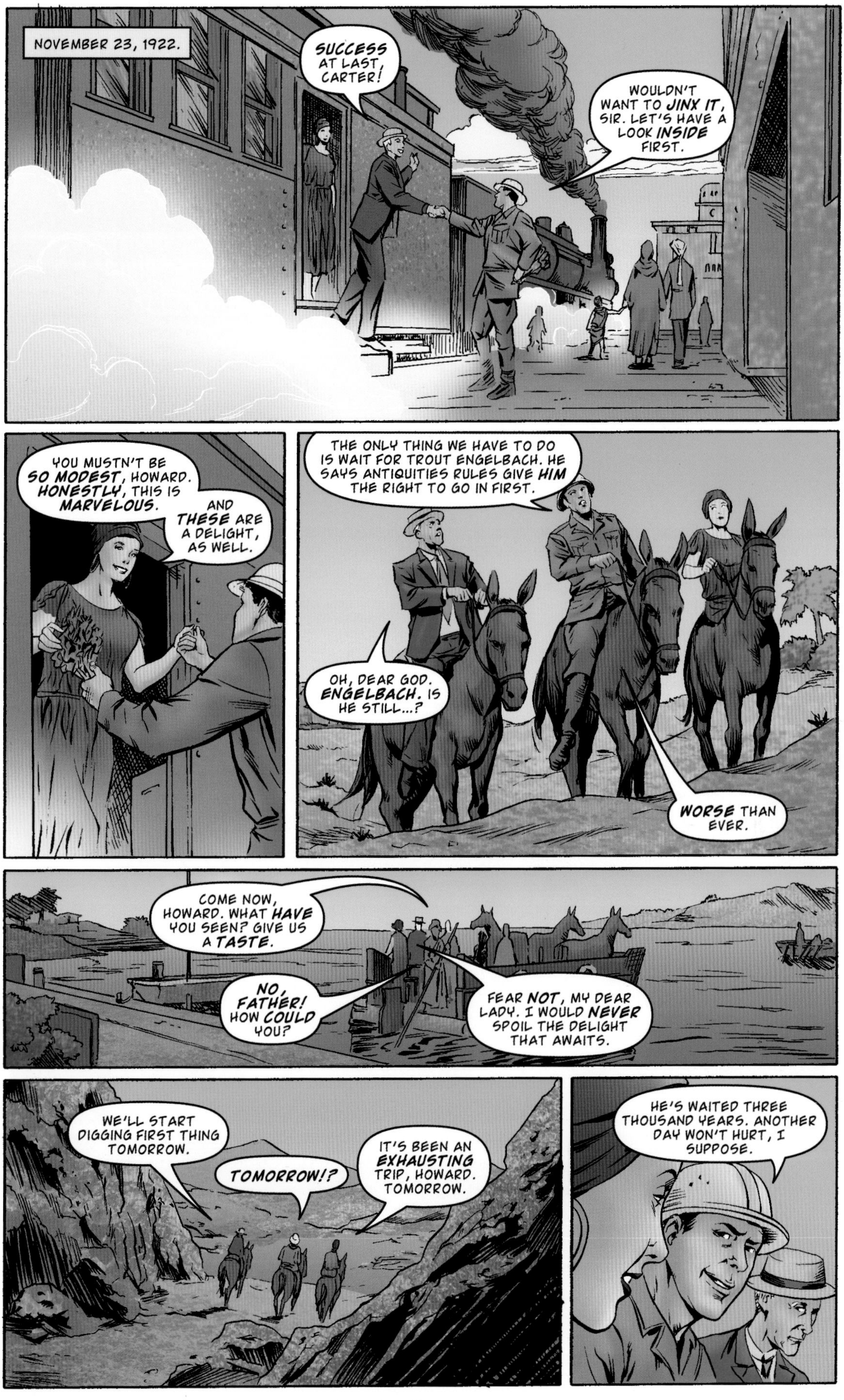
NOVEMBER 23, 1922.
SUCCESS AT LAST, CARTER!
WOULDN'T WANT TO JINX IT, SIR. LET'S HAVE A LOOK INSIDE FIRST.
YOU MUSTN'T BE SO MODEST, HOWARD. HONESTLY, THIS IS MARVELOUS.
AND THESE ARE A DELIGHT, AS WELL.
THE ONLY THING WE HAVE TO DO IS WAIT FOR TROUT ENGELBACH. HE SAYS ANTIQUITIES RULES GIVE HIM THE RIGHT TO GO IN FIRST.
OH, DEAR GOD. ENGELBACH. IS HE STILL...?
WORSE THAN EVER.
COME NOW, HOWARD. WHAT HAVE YOU SEEN? GIVE US A TASTE.
NO, FATHER! HOW COULD YOU?
FEAR NOT, MY DEAR LADY. I WOULD NEVER SPOIL THE DELIGHT THAT AWAITS.
WE'LL START DIGGING FIRST THING TOMORROW.
TOMORROW!?
IT'S BEEN AN EXHAUSTING TRIP, HOWARD. TOMORROW.
HE'S WAITED THREE THOUSAND YEARS. ANOTHER DAY WON'T HURT, I SUPPOSE.

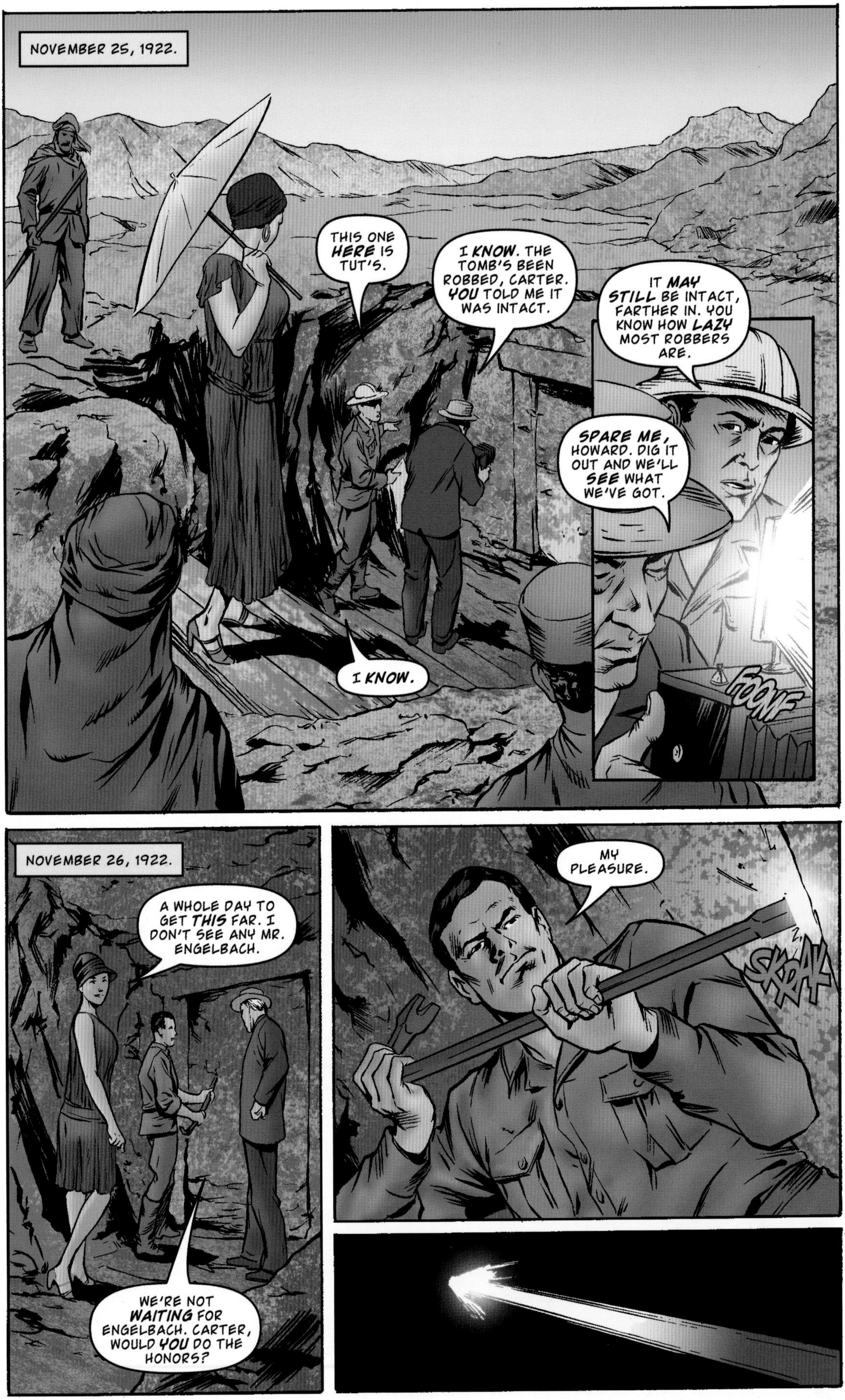
NOVEMBER 25, 1922.
THIS ONE HERE IS TUT'S.
I KNOW. THE TOMB'S BEEN ROBBED, CARTER. YOU TOLD ME IT WAS INTACT.
IT MAY STILL BE INTACT, FARTHER IN. YOU KNOW HOW LAZY MOST ROBBERS ARE.
SPARE ME, HOWARD. DIG IT OUT AND WE'LL SEE WHAT WE'VE GOT.
I KNOW.
FOOMF
NOVEMBER 26, 1922.
A WHOLE DAY TO GET THIS FAR. I DON'T SEE ANY MR. ENGELBACH.
WE'RE NOT WAITING FOR ENGELBACH. CARTER, WOULD YOU DO THE HONORS?
MY PLEASURE.
SKRAK

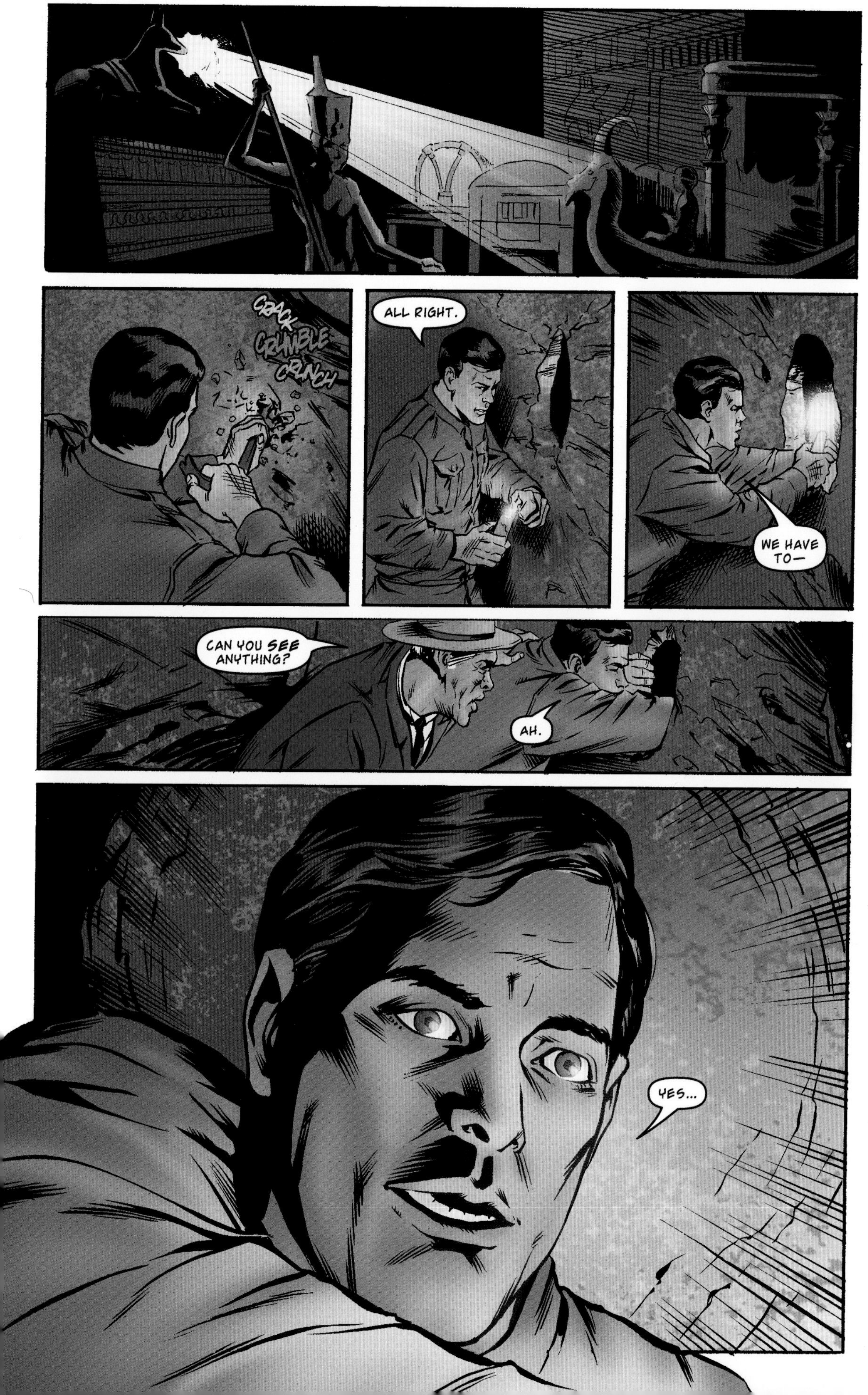
CRACK
CRUMBLE
CRUNCH
ALL RIGHT.
WE HAVE TO—
CAN YOU SEE ANYTHING?
AH.
YES...

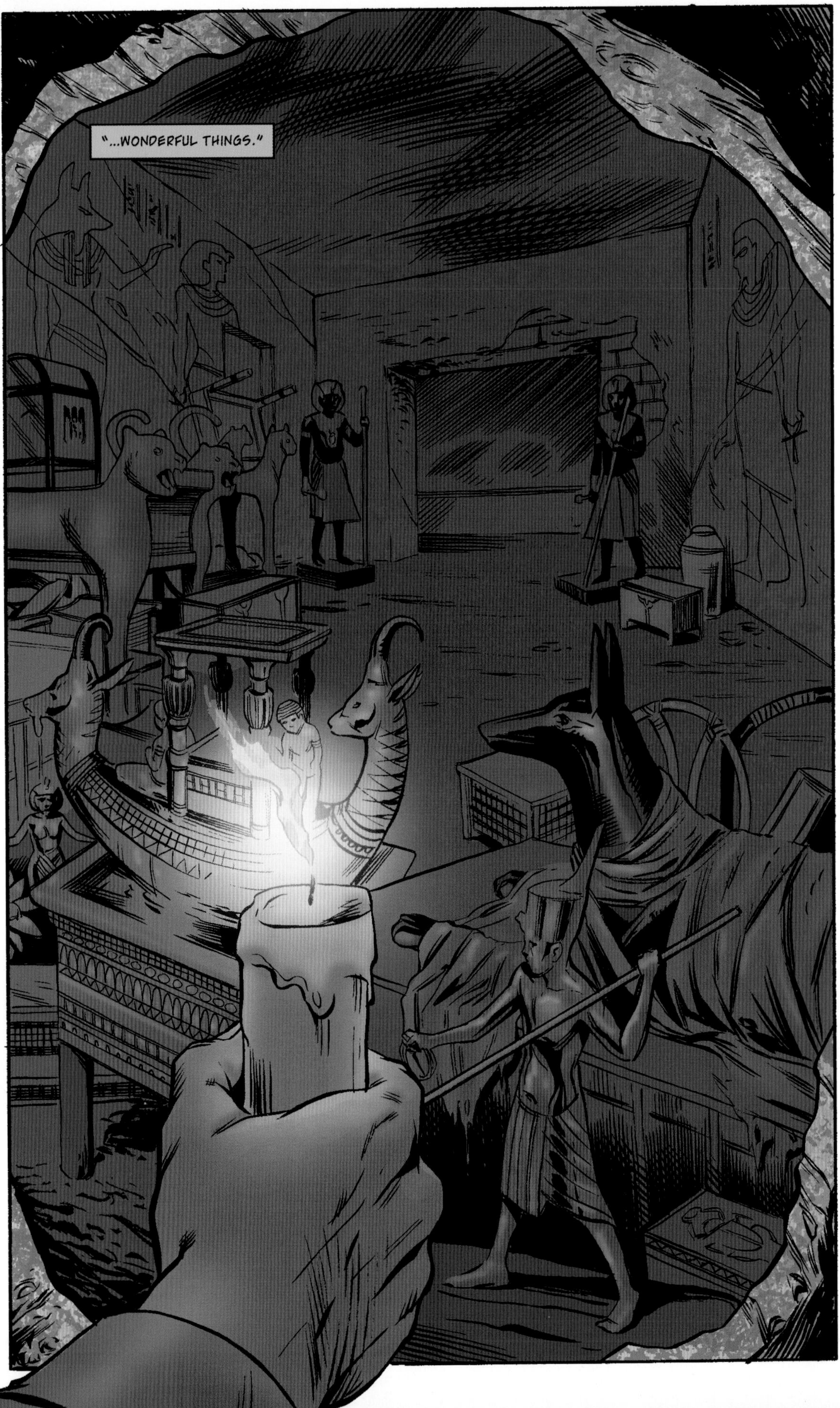
"...WONDERFUL THINGS."

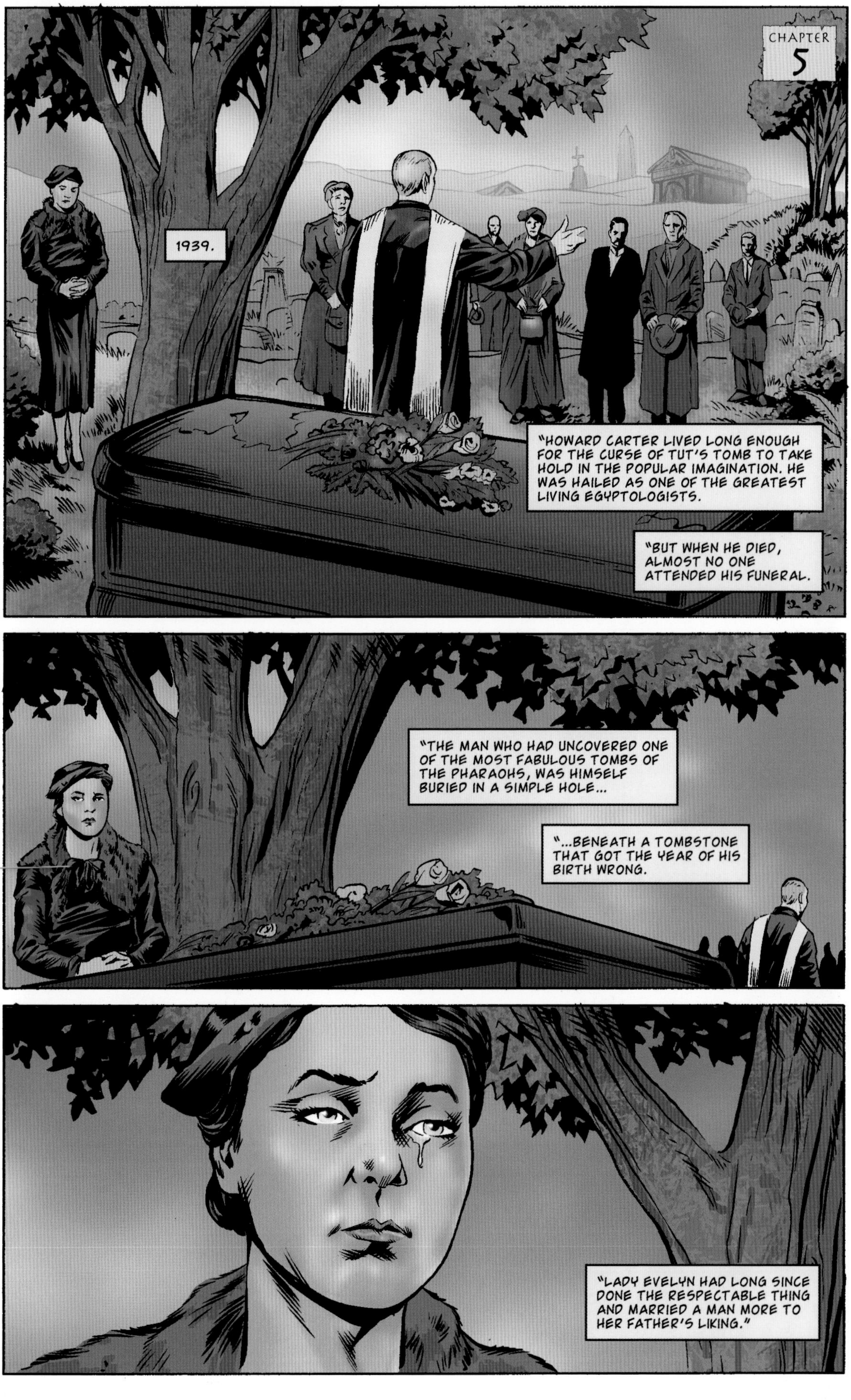
CHAPTER 5
1939.
"HOWARD CARTER LIVED LONG ENOUGH FOR THE CURSE OF TUT'S TOMB TO TAKE HOLD IN THE POPULAR IMAGINATION. HE WAS HAILED AS ONE OF THE GREATEST LIVING EGYPTOLOGISTS.
"BUT WHEN HE DIED, ALMOST NO ONE ATTENDED HIS FUNERAL.
"THE MAN WHO HAD UNCOVERED ONE OF THE MOST FABULOUS TOMBS OF THE PHARAOHS, WAS HIMSELF BURIED IN A SIMPLE HOLE...
"...BENEATH A TOMBSTONE THAT GOT THE YEAR OF HIS BIRTH WRONG.
"LADY EVELYN HAD LONG SINCE DONE THE RESPECTABLE THING AND MARRIED A MAN MORE TO HER FATHER'S LIKING."

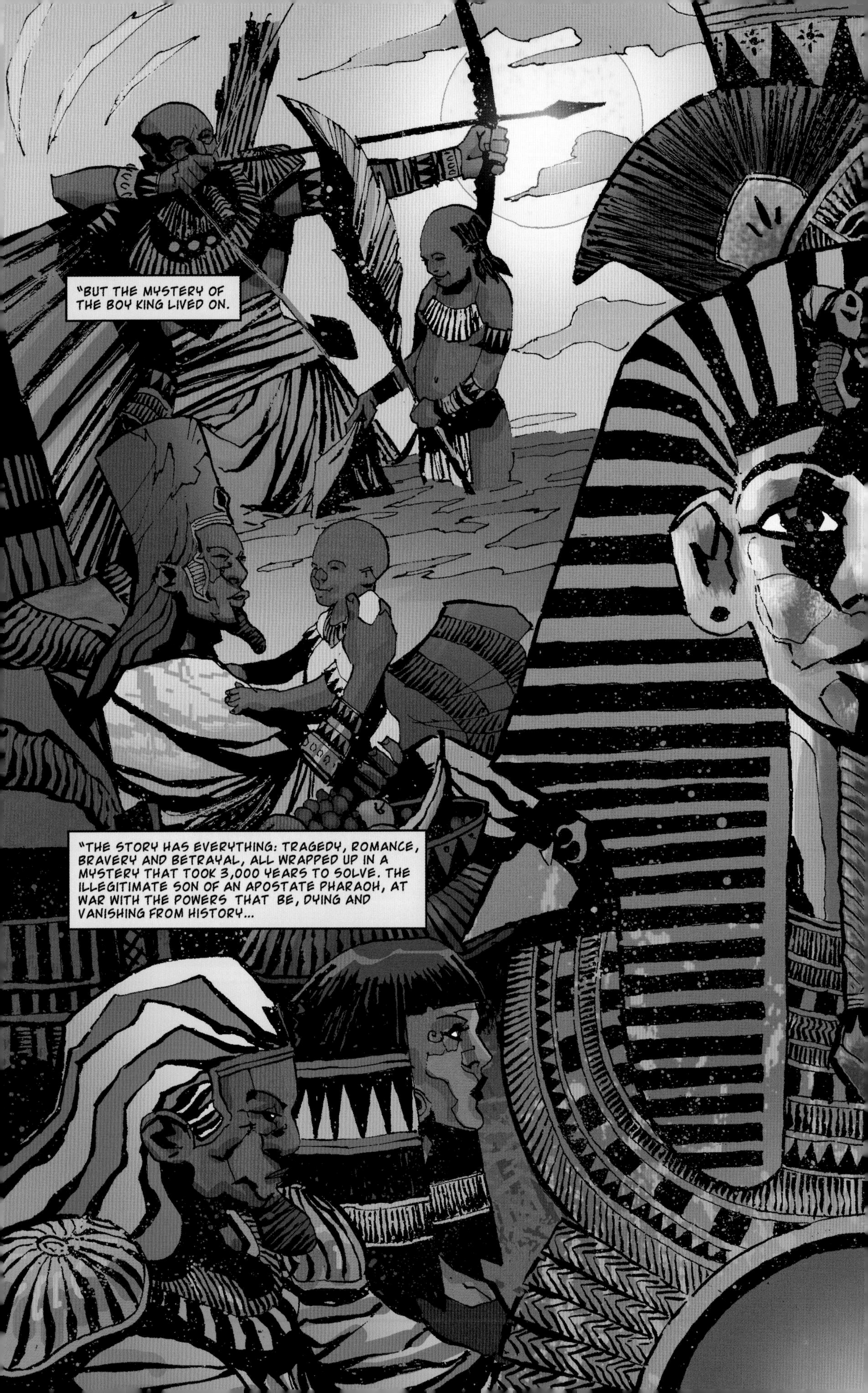
"BUT THE MYSTERY OF THE BOY KING LIVED ON.
"THE STORY HAS EVERYTHING: TRAGEDY, ROMANCE, BRAVERY AND BETRAYAL, ALL WRAPPED UP IN A MYSTERY THAT TOOK 3,000 YEARS TO SOLVE. THE ILLEGITIMATE SON OF AN APOSTATE PHARAOH, AT WAR WITH THE POWERS THAT BE, DYING AND VANISHING FROM HISTORY...

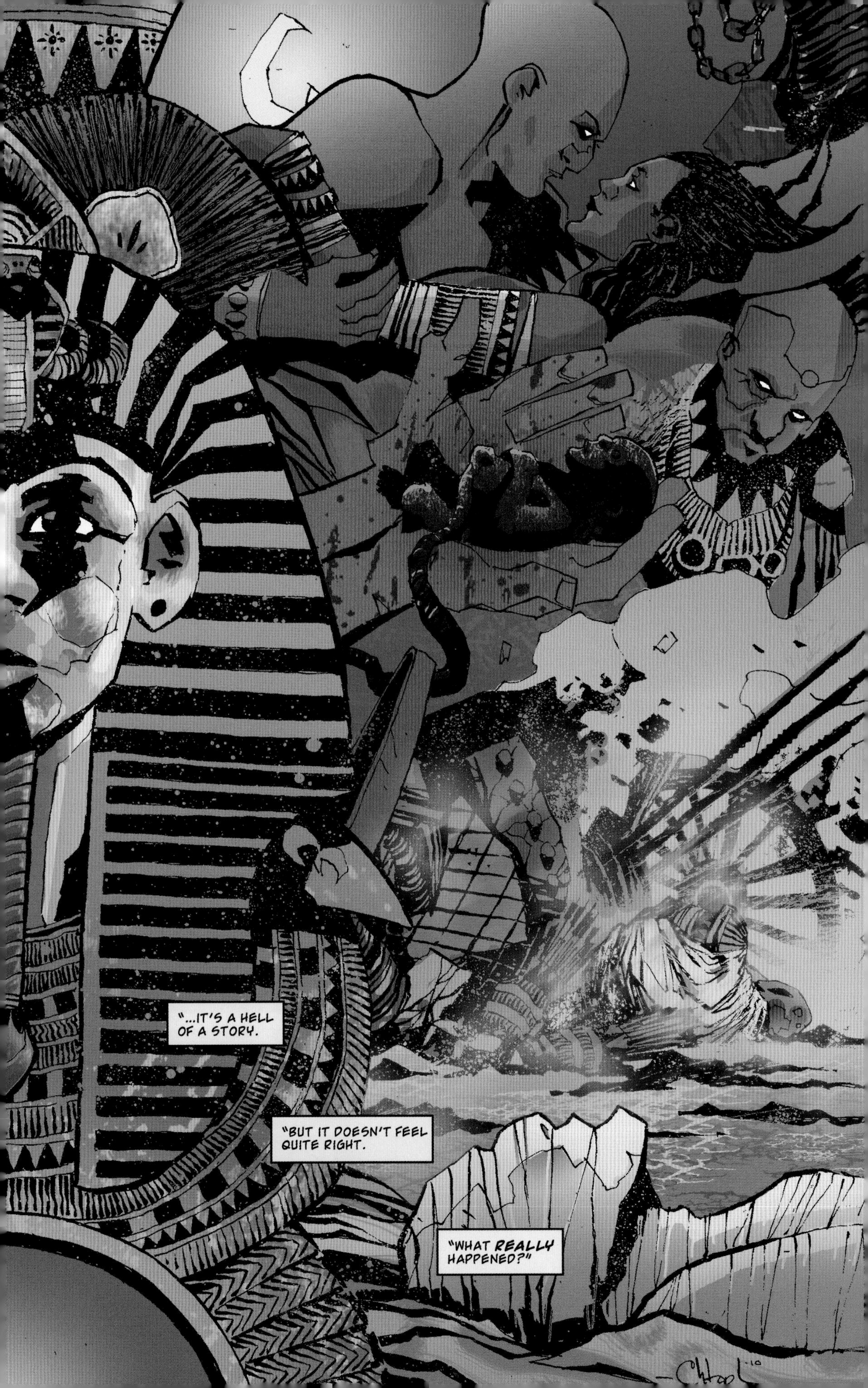
"...IT'S A HELL OF A STORY.
"BUT IT DOESN'T FEEL QUITE RIGHT.
"WHAT *REALLY* HAPPENED?"

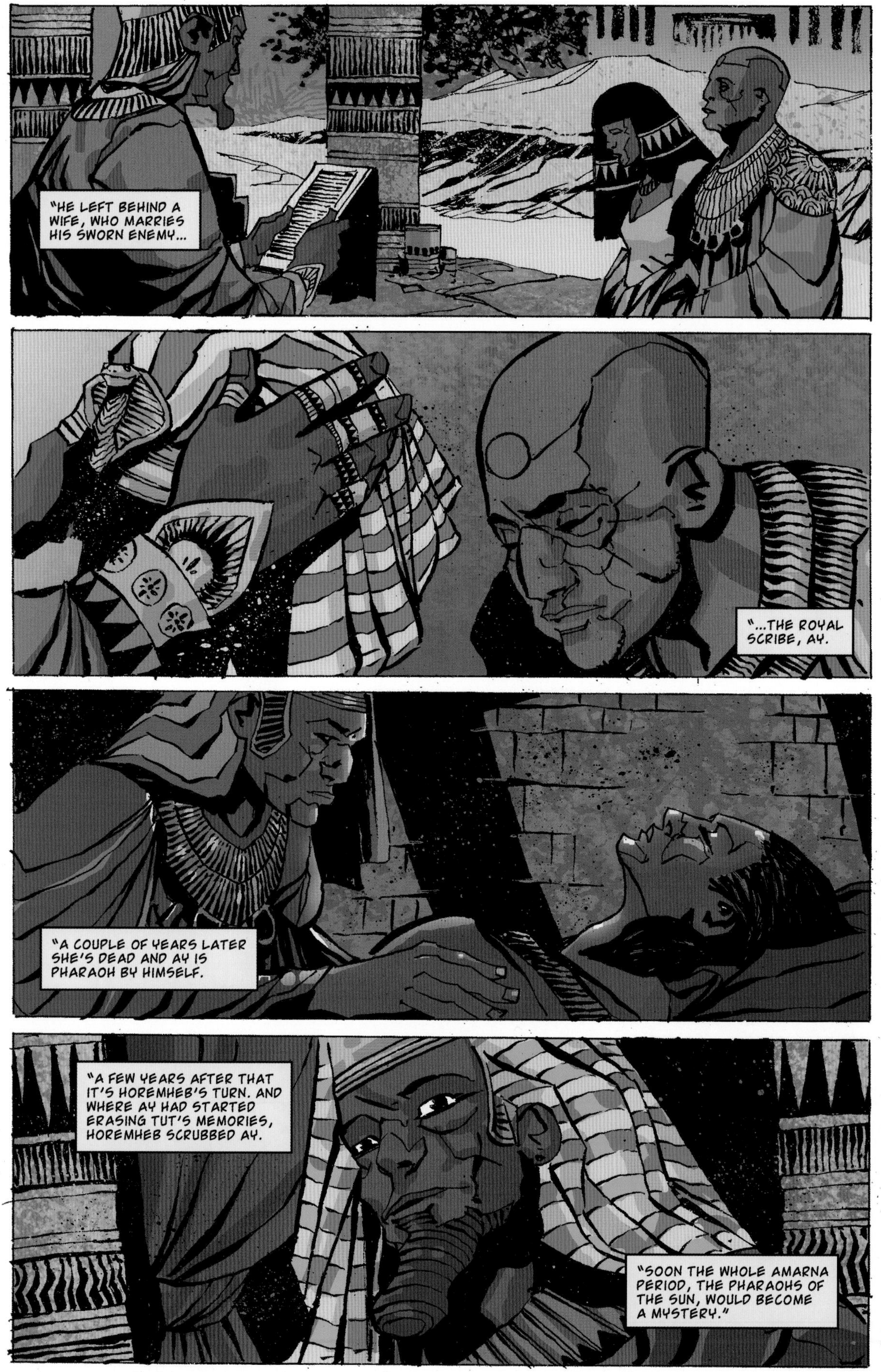
"HE LEFT BEHIND A WIFE, WHO MARRIES HIS SWORN ENEMY...
"...THE ROYAL SCRIBE, AY.
"A COUPLE OF YEARS LATER SHE'S DEAD AND AY IS PHARAOH BY HIMSELF.
"A FEW YEARS AFTER THAT IT'S HOREMHEB'S TURN. AND WHERE AY HAD STARTED ERASING TUT'S MEMORIES, HOREMHEB SCRUBBED AY.
"SOON THE WHOLE AMARNA PERIOD, THE PHARAOHS OF THE SUN, WOULD BECOME A MYSTERY."

"AND BY THE TIME ALL OF THOSE SUCCESSIONS HAD PASSED, IT'S AS IF TUT HAD NEVER EXISTED.

"EGYPTIANS REVERED THEIR PHARAOHS. DEIFIED THEM IN SOME CASES. WHO MADE TUT DISAPPEAR?

"THERE'S REALLY ONLY ONE POSSIBILITY. AY.

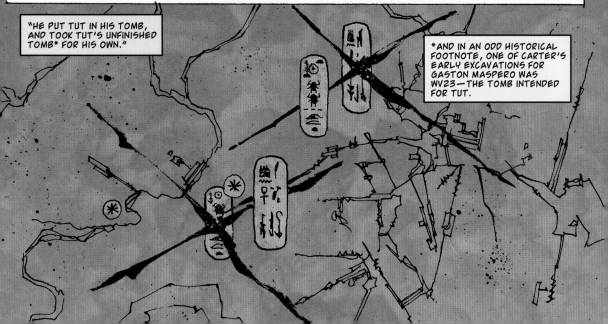

"HE PUT TUT IN HIS TOMB, AND TOOK TUT'S UNFINISHED TOMB* FOR HIS OWN."

*AND IN AN ODD HISTORICAL FOOTNOTE, ONE OF CARTER'S EARLY EXCAVATIONS FOR GASTON MASPERO WAS WV23—THE TOMB INTENDED FOR TUT.

"AY HAD BEEN AFTER POWER SINCE HE TRIED TO SEDUCE NEFERTITI, PRACTICALLY THE MINUTE AKHENATEN TOOK THE THRONE AND MARRIED HER.

"BUT NEFERTITI CALLED HIS BLUFF AND WARNED HIM AWAY.

...FEED YOUR HEART TO THE CROCODILES.

"FOR A WHILE, AY TRIED TO ACT INDIRECTLY, TO MAKE OTHER PEOPLE DO HIS DIRTY WORK."

TAKE HIM TO WAR.

HE'S NOT READY.

ALL THE MORE REASON.

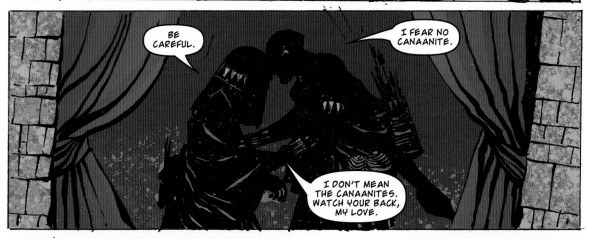

BE CAREFUL.

I FEAR NO CANAANITE.

I DON'T MEAN THE CANAANITES. WATCH YOUR BACK, MY LOVE.

WITHOUT YOU I AM LOST.

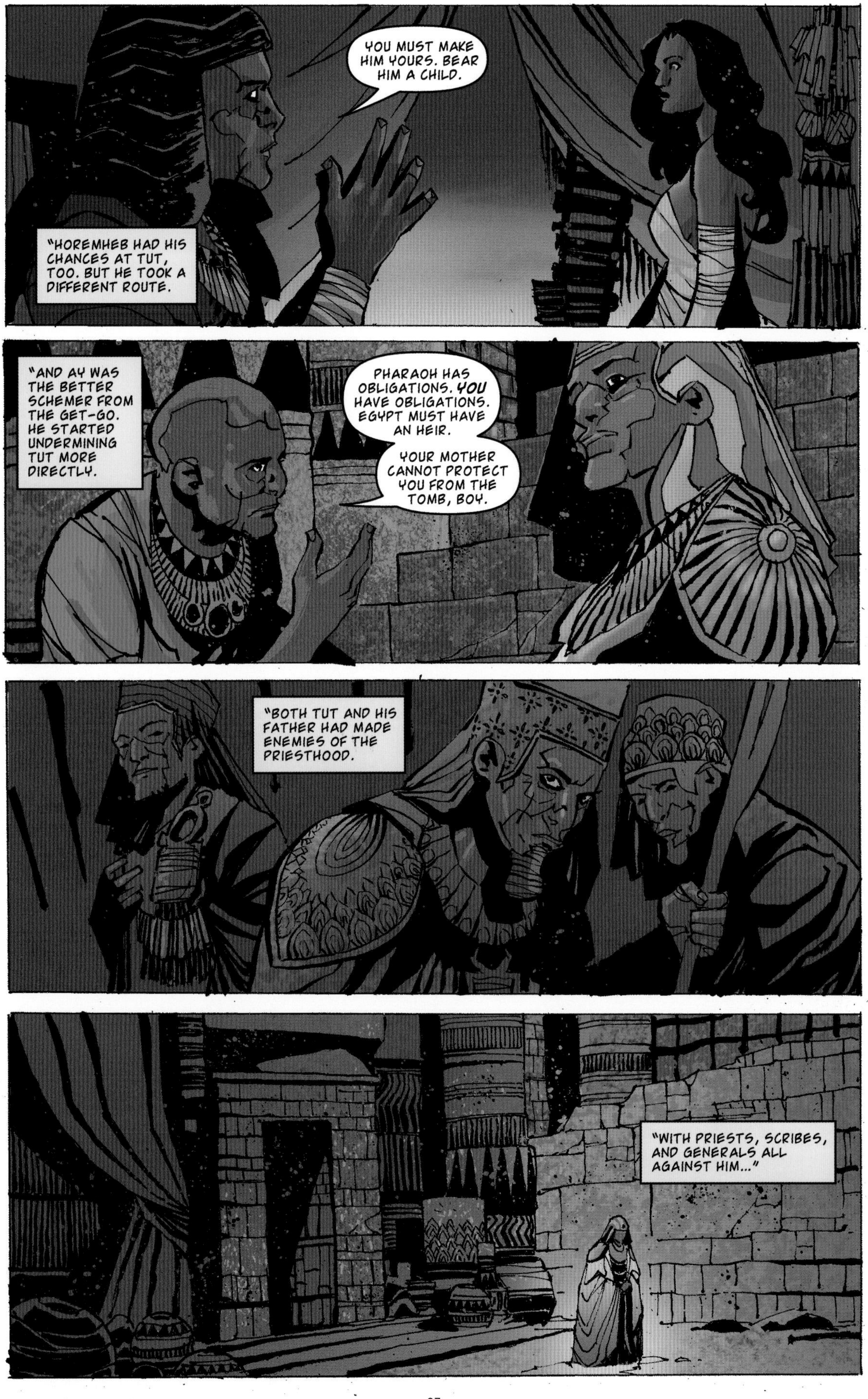
YOU MUST MAKE HIM YOURS. BEAR HIM A CHILD.
"HOREMHEB HAD HIS CHANCES AT TUT, TOO. BUT HE TOOK A DIFFERENT ROUTE.
"AND AY WAS THE BETTER SCHEMER FROM THE GET-GO. HE STARTED UNDERMINING TUT MORE DIRECTLY.
PHARAOH HAS OBLIGATIONS. YOU HAVE OBLIGATIONS. EGYPT MUST HAVE AN HEIR.
YOUR MOTHER CANNOT PROTECT YOU FROM THE TOMB, BOY.
"BOTH TUT AND HIS FATHER HAD MADE ENEMIES OF THE PRIESTHOOD.
"WITH PRIESTS, SCRIBES, AND GENERALS ALL AGAINST HIM..."

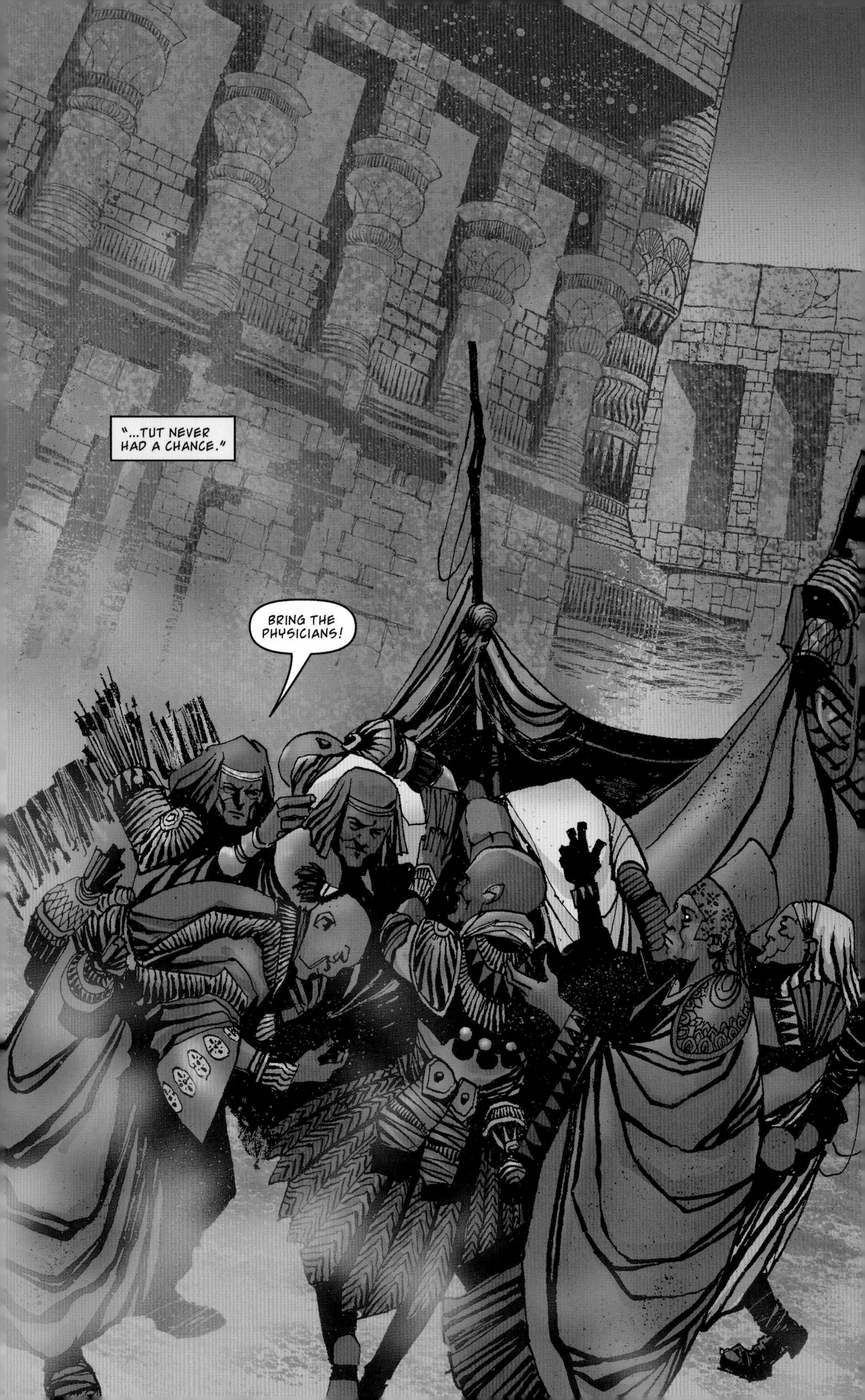
"...TUT NEVER HAD A CHANCE."
BRING THE PHYSICIANS!

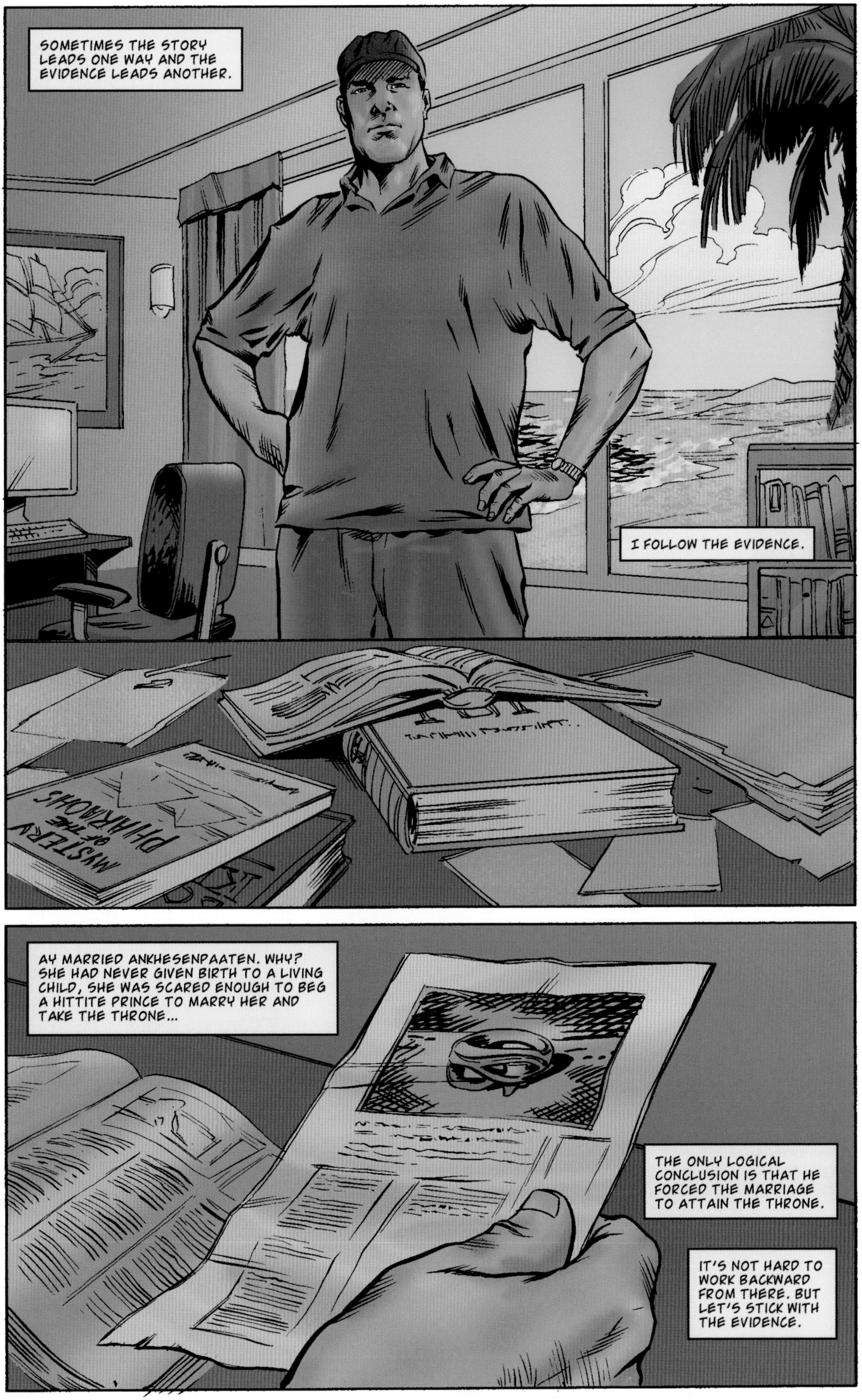
SOMETIMES THE STORY LEADS ONE WAY AND THE EVIDENCE LEADS ANOTHER.
I FOLLOW THE EVIDENCE.
MYSTERY OF THE PHARAOHS
AY MARRIED ANKHESENPAATEN. WHY? SHE HAD NEVER GIVEN BIRTH TO A LIVING CHILD, SHE WAS SCARED ENOUGH TO BEG A HITTITE PRINCE TO MARRY HER AND TAKE THE THRONE...
THE ONLY LOGICAL CONCLUSION IS THAT HE FORCED THE MARRIAGE TO ATTAIN THE THRONE.
IT'S NOT HARD TO WORK BACKWARD FROM THERE. BUT LET'S STICK WITH THE EVIDENCE.

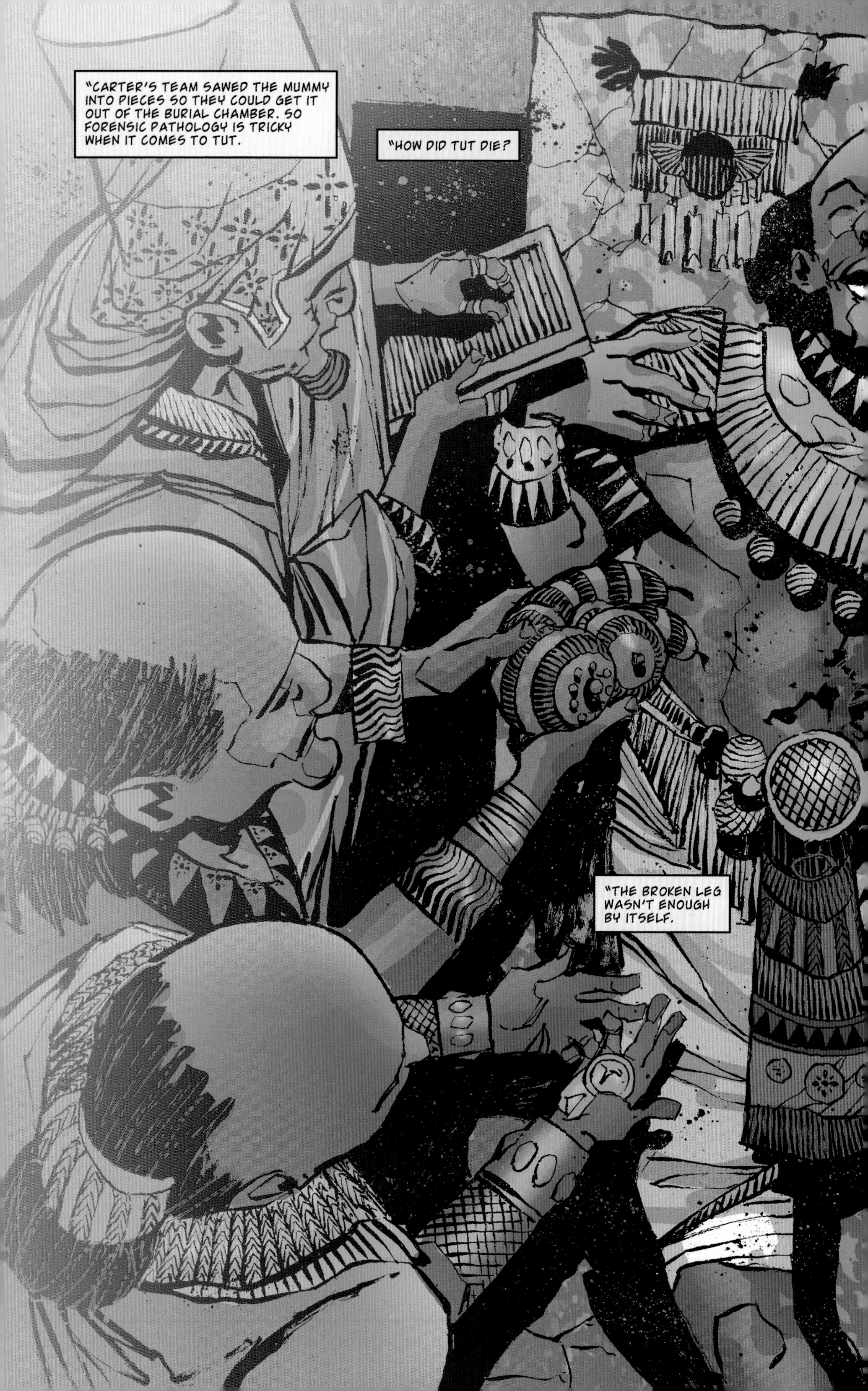
"CARTER'S TEAM SAWED THE MUMMY INTO PIECES SO THEY COULD GET IT OUT OF THE BURIAL CHAMBER. SO FORENSIC PATHOLOGY IS TRICKY WHEN IT COMES TO TUT.
"HOW DID TUT DIE?
"THE BROKEN LEG WASN'T ENOUGH BY ITSELF.

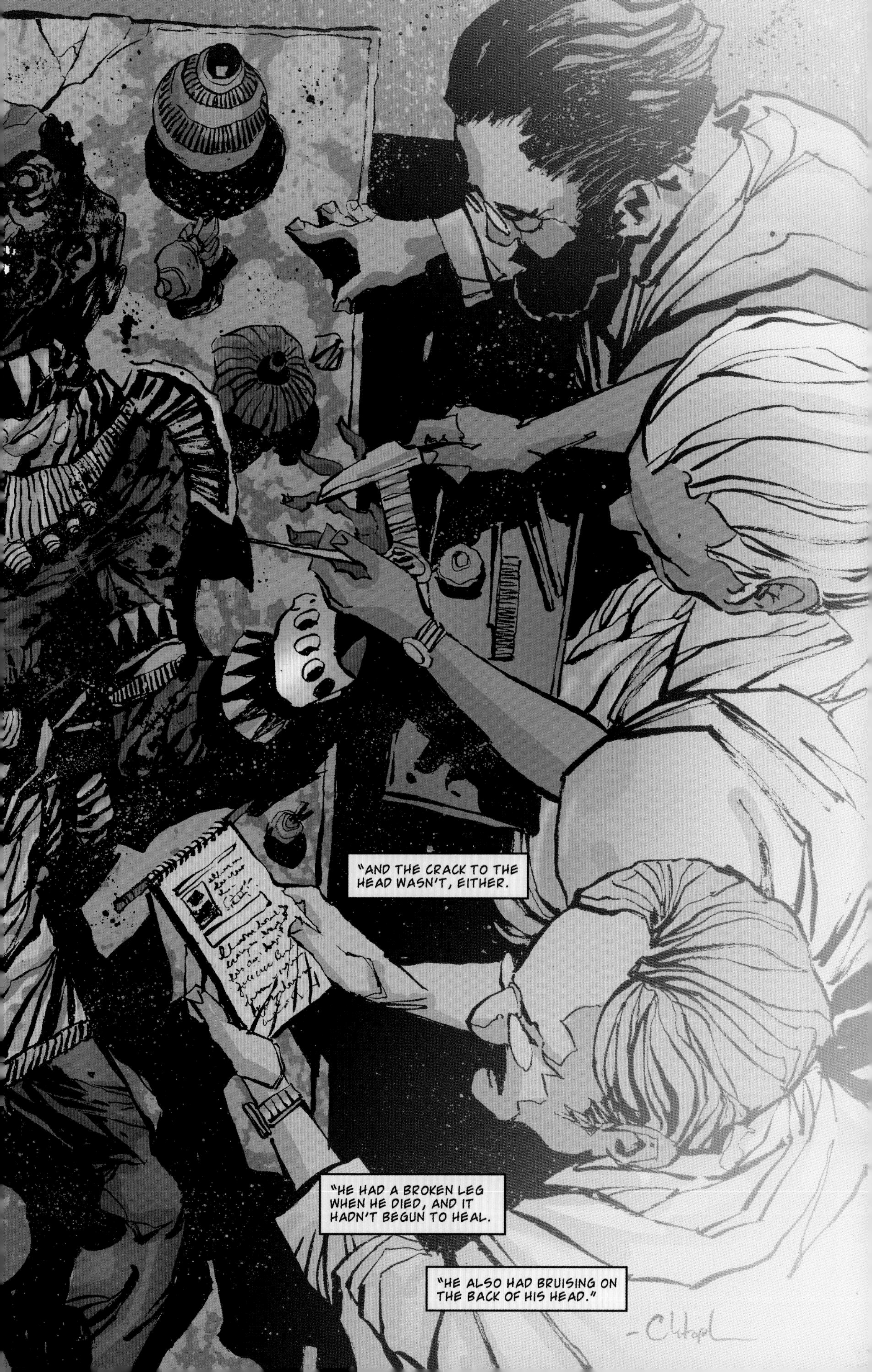
"AND THE CRACK TO THE HEAD WASN'T, EITHER.
"HE HAD A BROKEN LEG WHEN HE DIED, AND IT HADN'T BEGUN TO HEAL.
"HE ALSO HAD BRUISING ON THE BACK OF HIS HEAD."

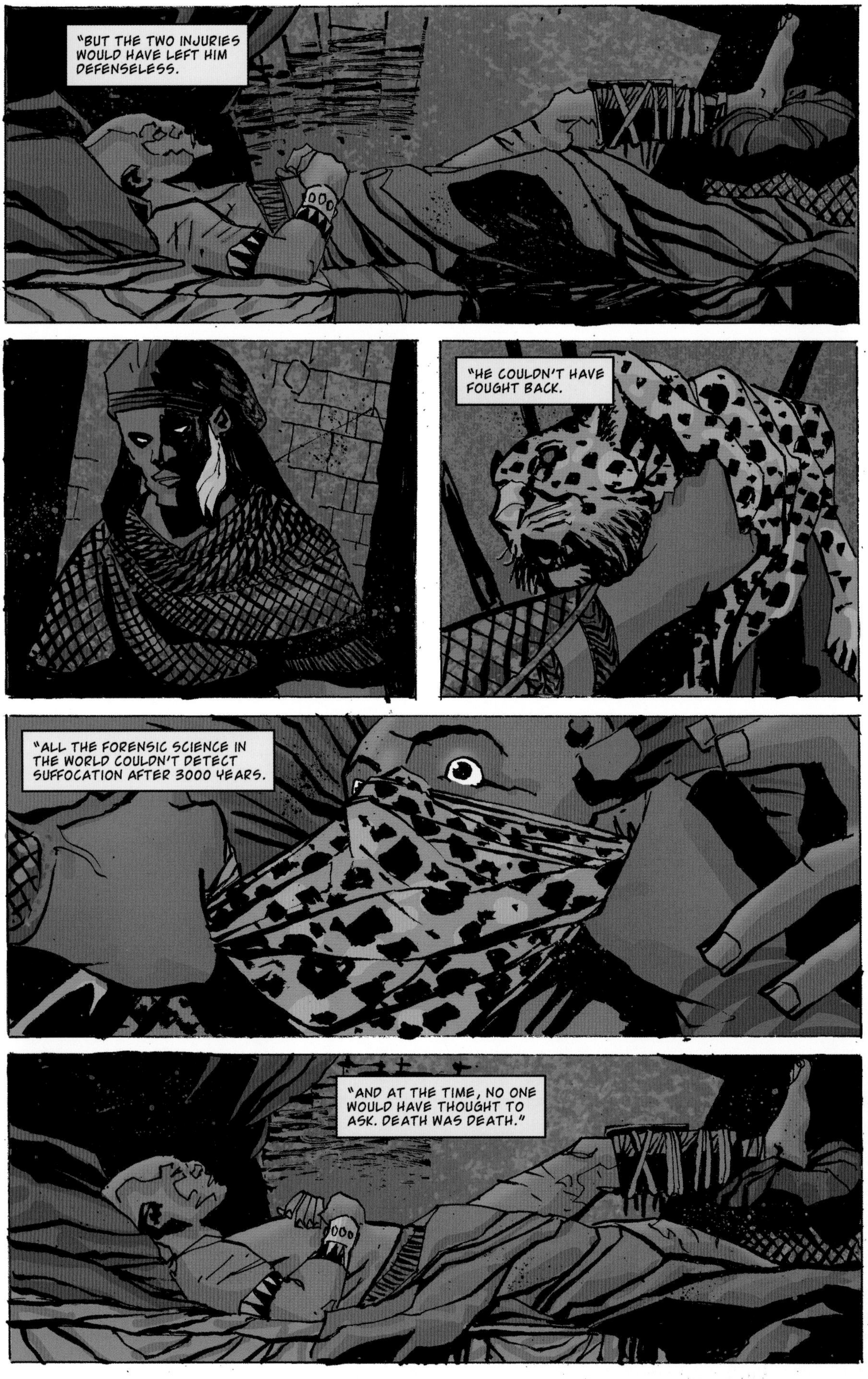
"BUT THE TWO INJURIES WOULD HAVE LEFT HIM DEFENSELESS.
"HE COULDN'T HAVE FOUGHT BACK.
"ALL THE FORENSIC SCIENCE IN THE WORLD COULDN'T DETECT SUFFOCATION AFTER 3000 YEARS.
"AND AT THE TIME, NO ONE WOULD HAVE THOUGHT TO ASK. DEATH WAS DEATH."

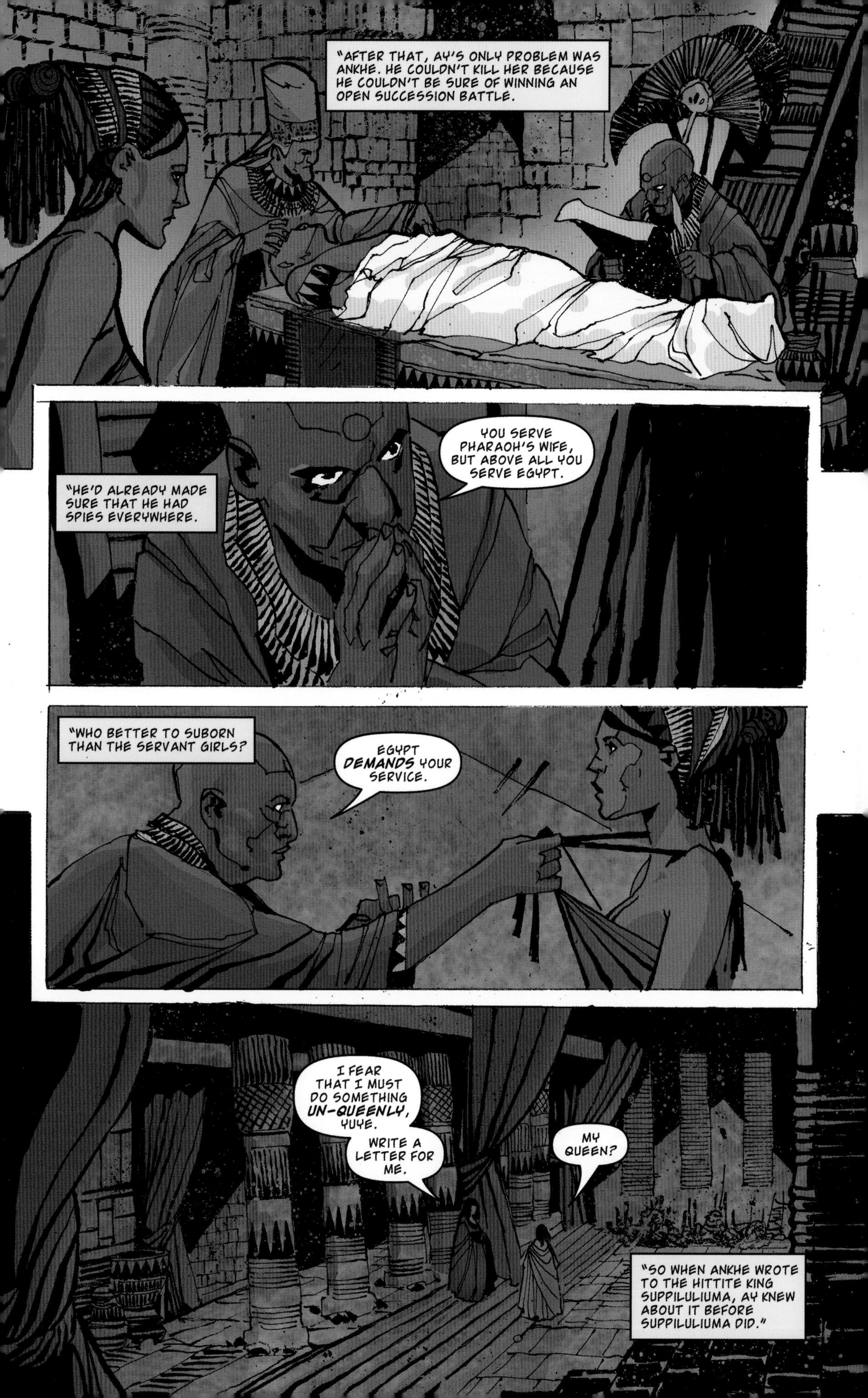
"AFTER THAT, AY'S ONLY PROBLEM WAS ANKHE. HE COULDN'T KILL HER BECAUSE HE COULDN'T BE SURE OF WINNING AN OPEN SUCCESSION BATTLE.
"HE'D ALREADY MADE SURE THAT HE HAD SPIES EVERYWHERE.
YOU SERVE PHARAOH'S WIFE, BUT ABOVE ALL YOU SERVE EGYPT.
"WHO BETTER TO SUBORN THAN THE SERVANT GIRLS?
EGYPT DEMANDS YOUR SERVICE.
I FEAR THAT I MUST DO SOMETHING UN-QUEENLY, YUYE.
WRITE A LETTER FOR ME.
MY QUEEN?
"SO WHEN ANKHE WROTE TO THE HITTITE KING SUPPILULIUMA, AY KNEW ABOUT IT BEFORE SUPPILULIUMA DID."

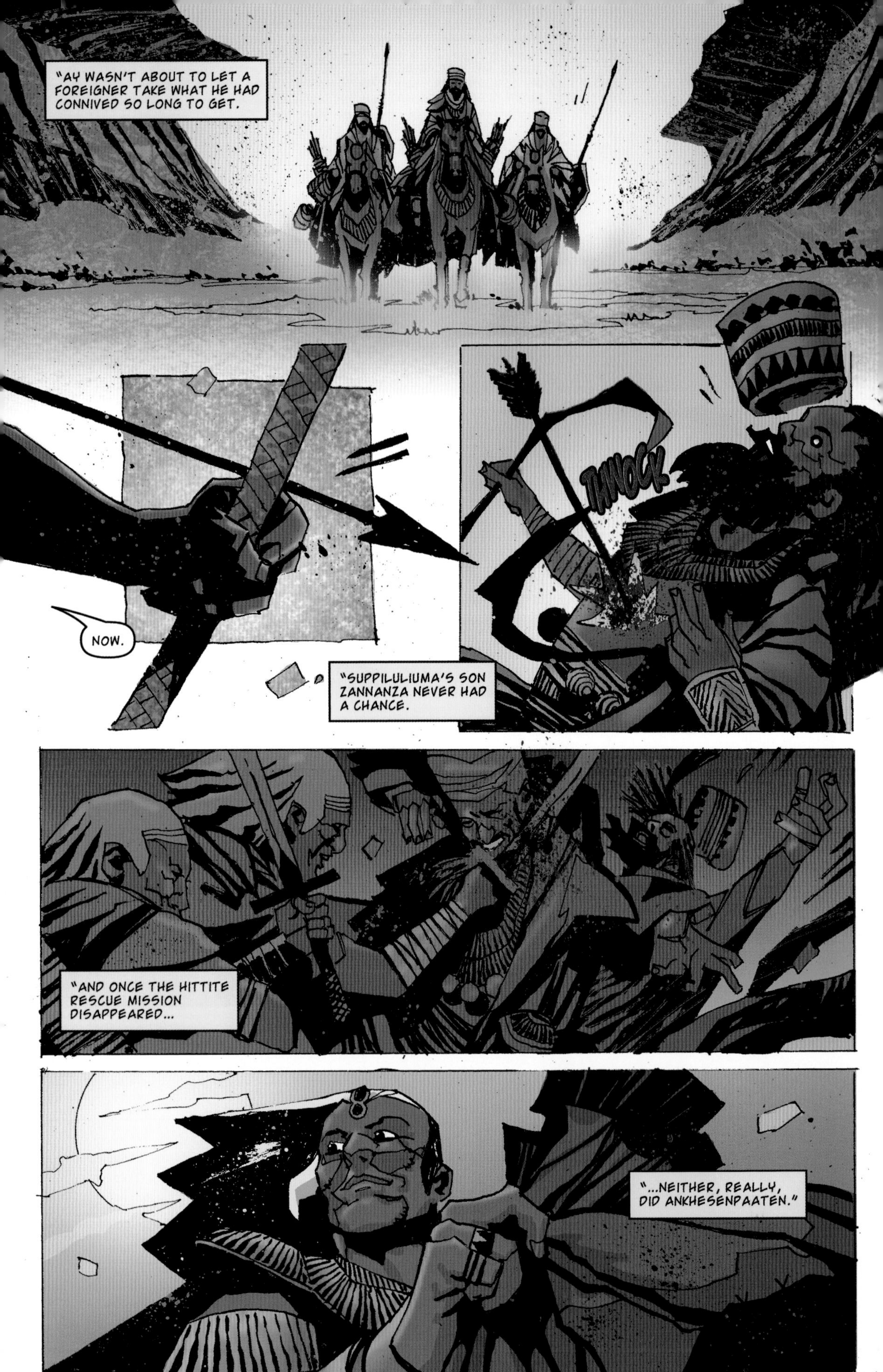
"AY WASN'T ABOUT TO LET A FOREIGNER TAKE WHAT HE HAD CONNIVED SO LONG TO GET.
NOW.
THWOCK
"SUPPILULIUMA'S SON ZANNANZA NEVER HAD A CHANCE.
"AND ONCE THE HITTITE RESCUE MISSION DISAPPEARED...
"...NEITHER, REALLY, DID ANKHESENPAATEN."

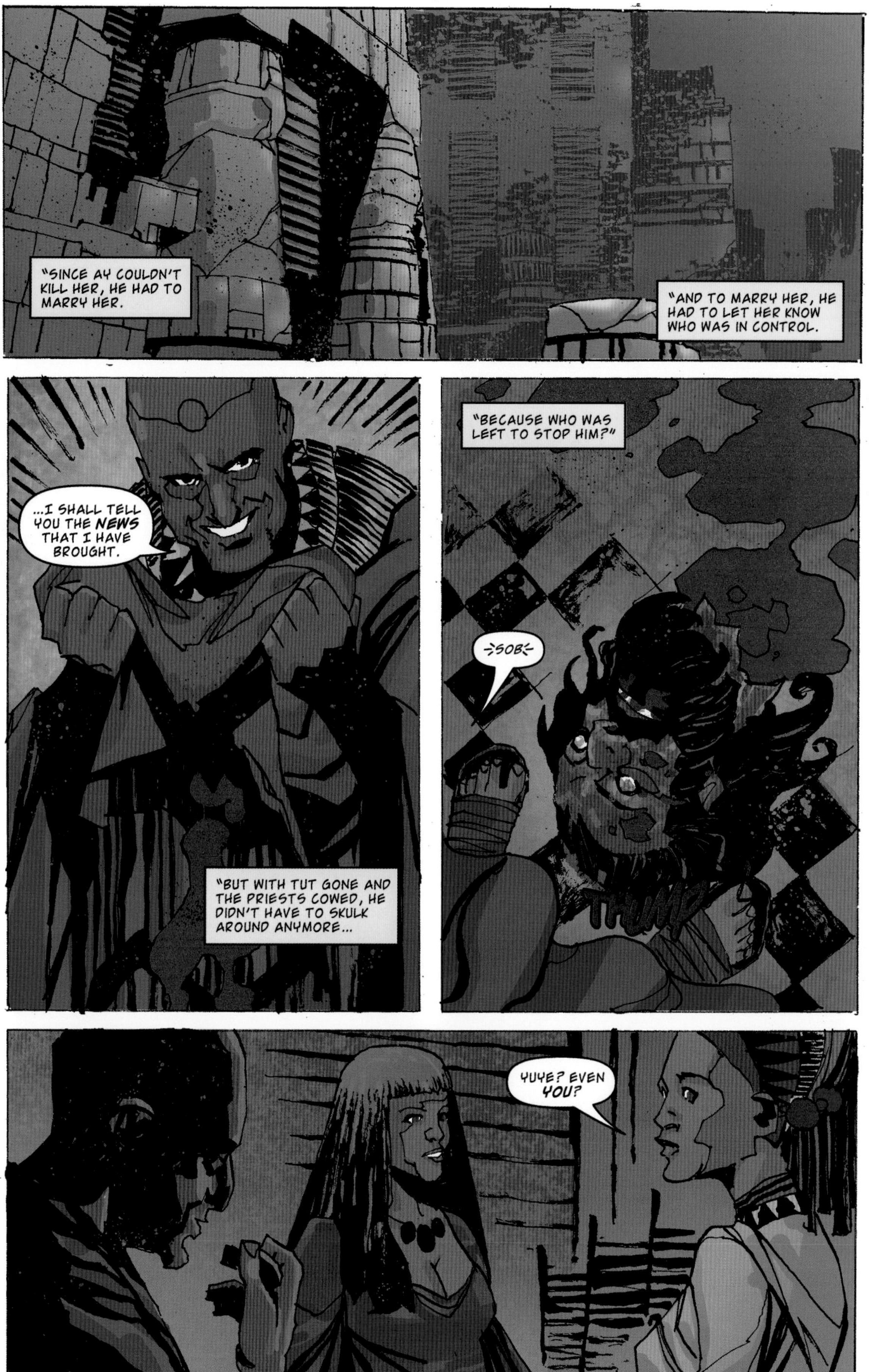
"SINCE AY COULDN'T KILL HER, HE HAD TO MARRY HER.
"AND TO MARRY HER, HE HAD TO LET HER KNOW WHO WAS IN CONTROL.
...I SHALL TELL YOU THE NEWS THAT I HAVE BROUGHT.
"BUT WITH TUT GONE AND THE PRIESTS COWED, HE DIDN'T HAVE TO SKULK AROUND ANYMORE...
"BECAUSE WHO WAS LEFT TO STOP HIM?"
SOB
THUMP
YUYE? EVEN YOU?

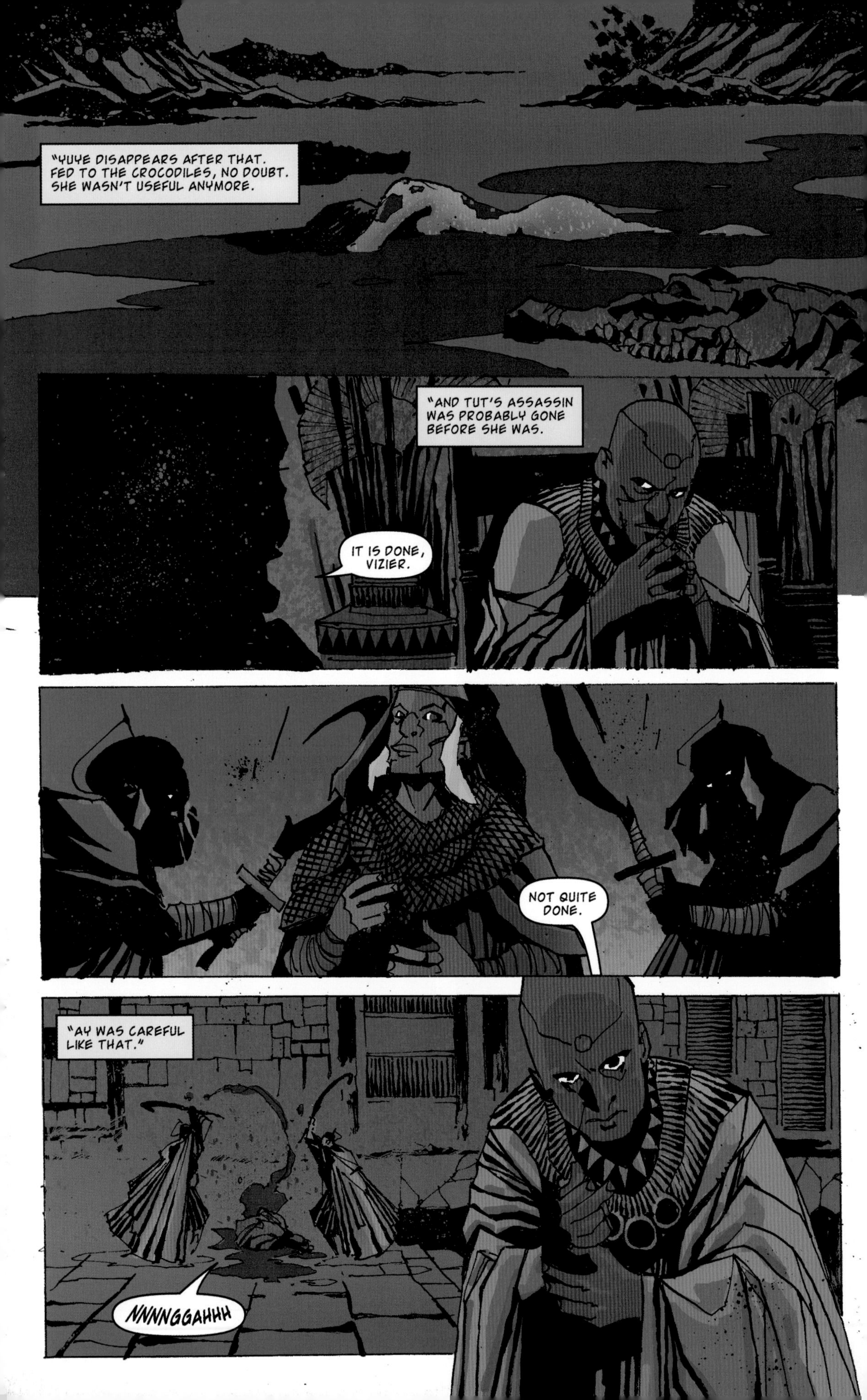
"YUYE DISAPPEARS AFTER THAT. FED TO THE CROCODILES, NO DOUBT. SHE WASN'T USEFUL ANYMORE.
"AND TUT'S ASSASSIN WAS PROBABLY GONE BEFORE SHE WAS.
IT IS DONE, VIZIER.
NOT QUITE DONE.
"AY WAS CAREFUL LIKE THAT."
NNNNGGAHHH

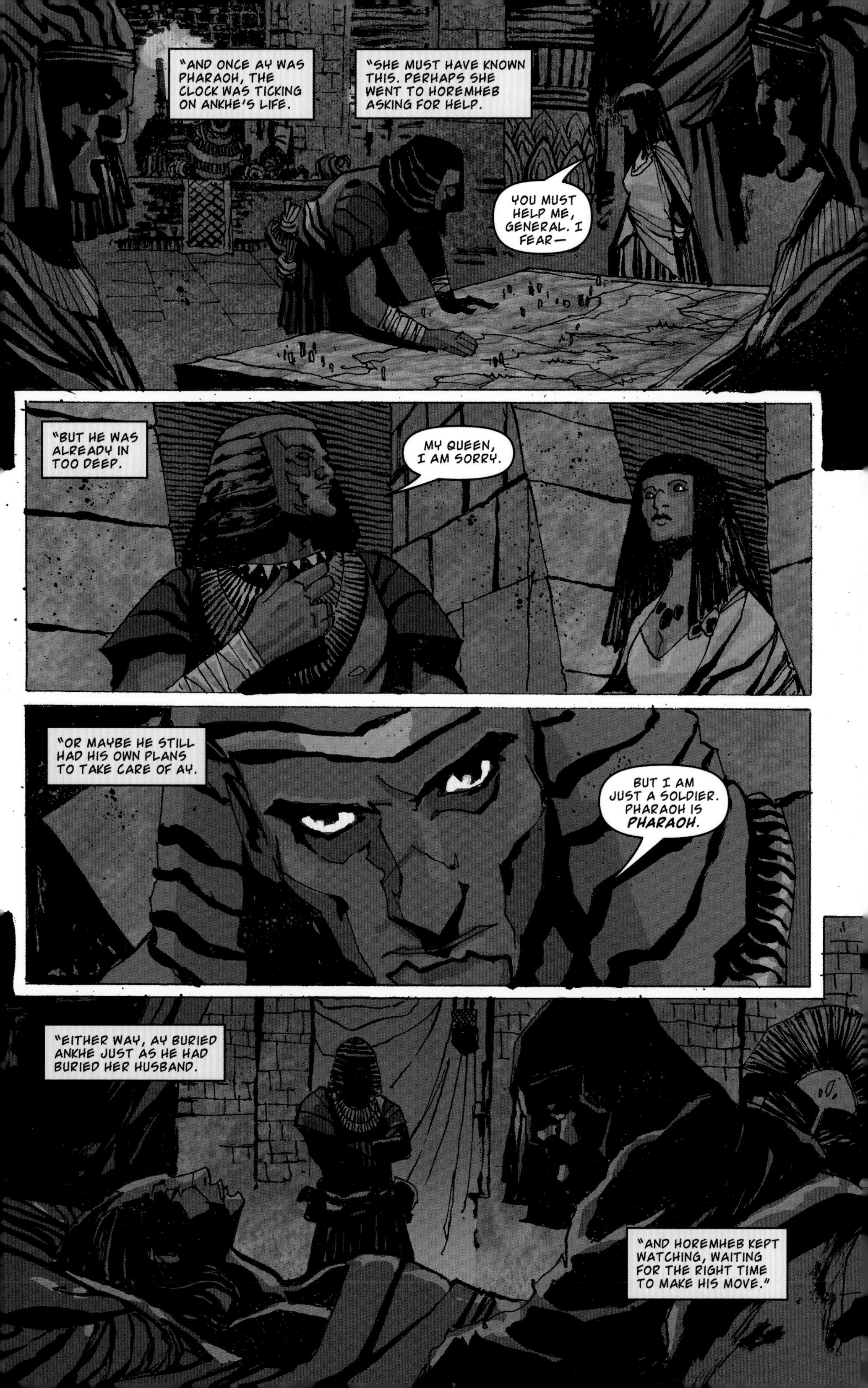
"AND ONCE AY WAS PHARAOH, THE CLOCK WAS TICKING ON ANKHE'S LIFE.
"SHE MUST HAVE KNOWN THIS. PERHAPS SHE WENT TO HOREMHEB ASKING FOR HELP.
YOU MUST HELP ME, GENERAL. I FEAR—
"BUT HE WAS ALREADY IN TOO DEEP.
MY QUEEN, I AM SORRY.
"OR MAYBE HE STILL HAD HIS OWN PLANS TO TAKE CARE OF AY.
BUT I AM JUST A SOLDIER. PHARAOH IS *PHARAOH*.
"EITHER WAY, AY BURIED ANKHE JUST AS HE HAD BURIED HER HUSBAND.
"AND HOREMHEB KEPT WATCHING, WAITING FOR THE RIGHT TIME TO MAKE HIS MOVE."

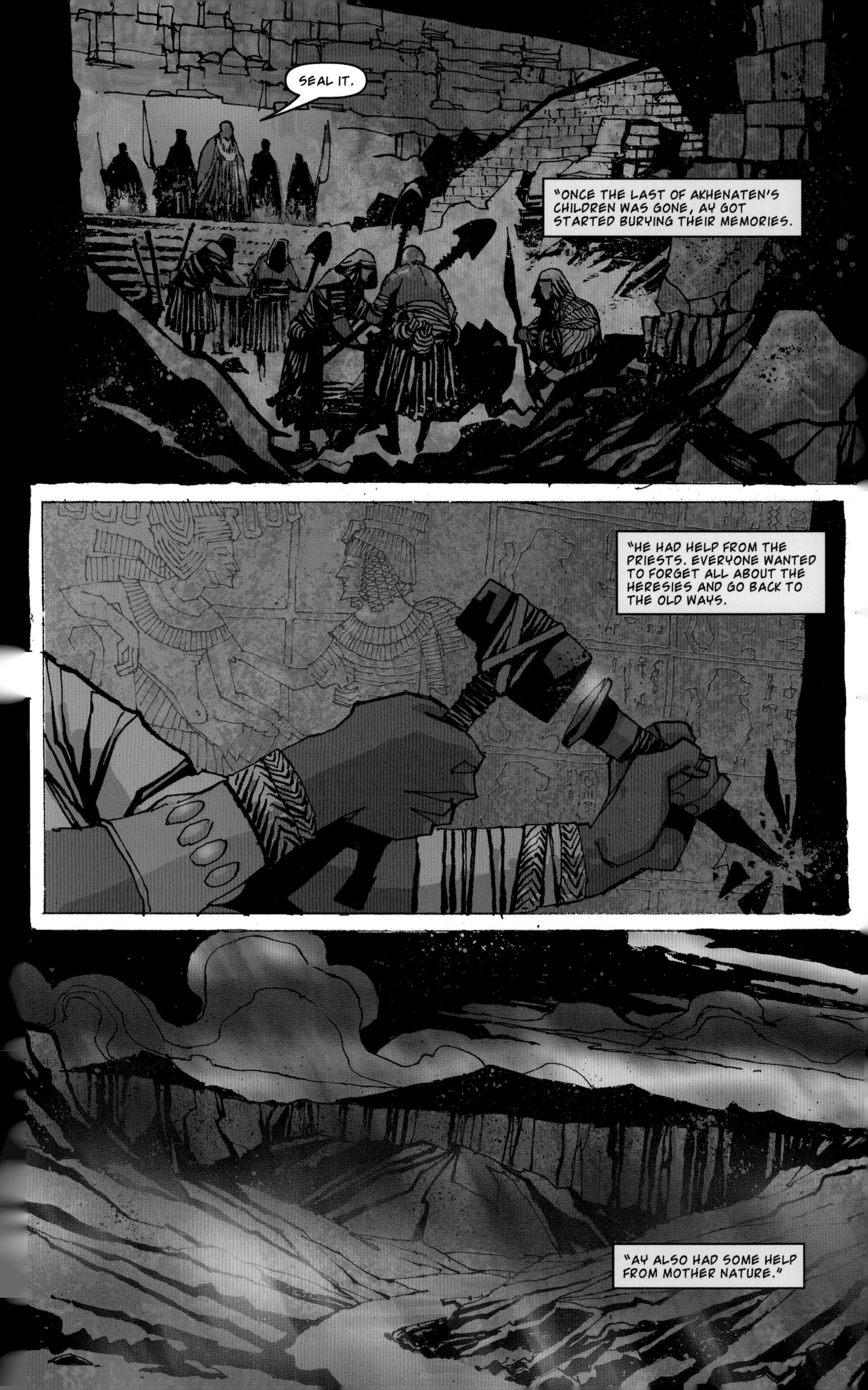
SEAL IT.
"ONCE THE LAST OF AKHENATEN'S CHILDREN WAS GONE, AY GOT STARTED BURYING THEIR MEMORIES.
"HE HAD HELP FROM THE PRIESTS. EVERYONE WANTED TO FORGET ALL ABOUT THE HERESIES AND GO BACK TO THE OLD WAYS.
"AY ALSO HAD SOME HELP FROM MOTHER NATURE."

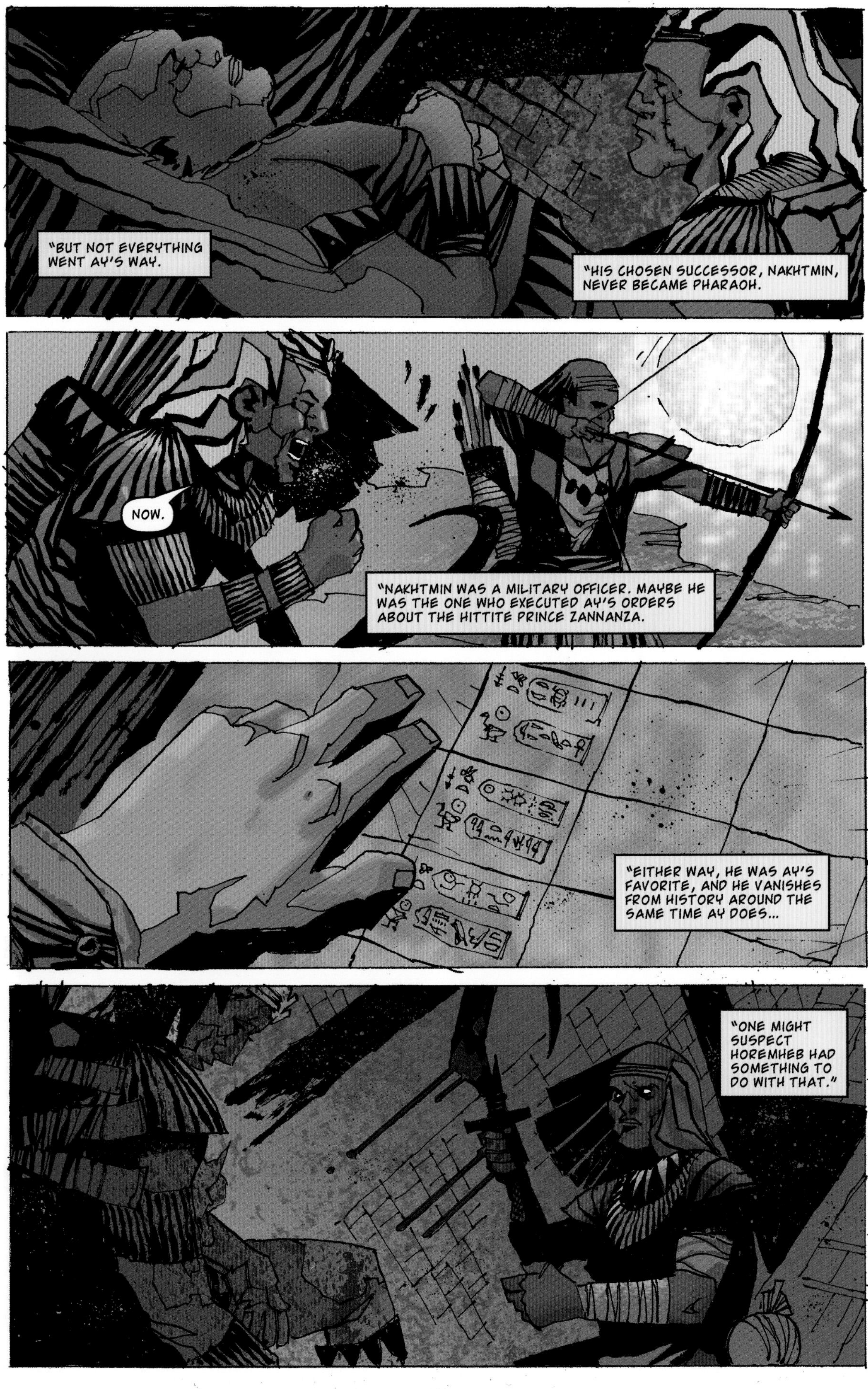
"BUT NOT EVERYTHING WENT AY'S WAY.
"HIS CHOSEN SUCCESSOR, NAKHTMIN, NEVER BECAME PHARAOH.
NOW.
"NAKHTMIN WAS A MILITARY OFFICER. MAYBE HE WAS THE ONE WHO EXECUTED AY'S ORDERS ABOUT THE HITTITE PRINCE ZANNANZA.
"EITHER WAY, HE WAS AY'S FAVORITE, AND HE VANISHES FROM HISTORY AROUND THE SAME TIME AY DOES...
"ONE MIGHT SUSPECT HOREMHEB HAD SOMETHING TO DO WITH THAT."

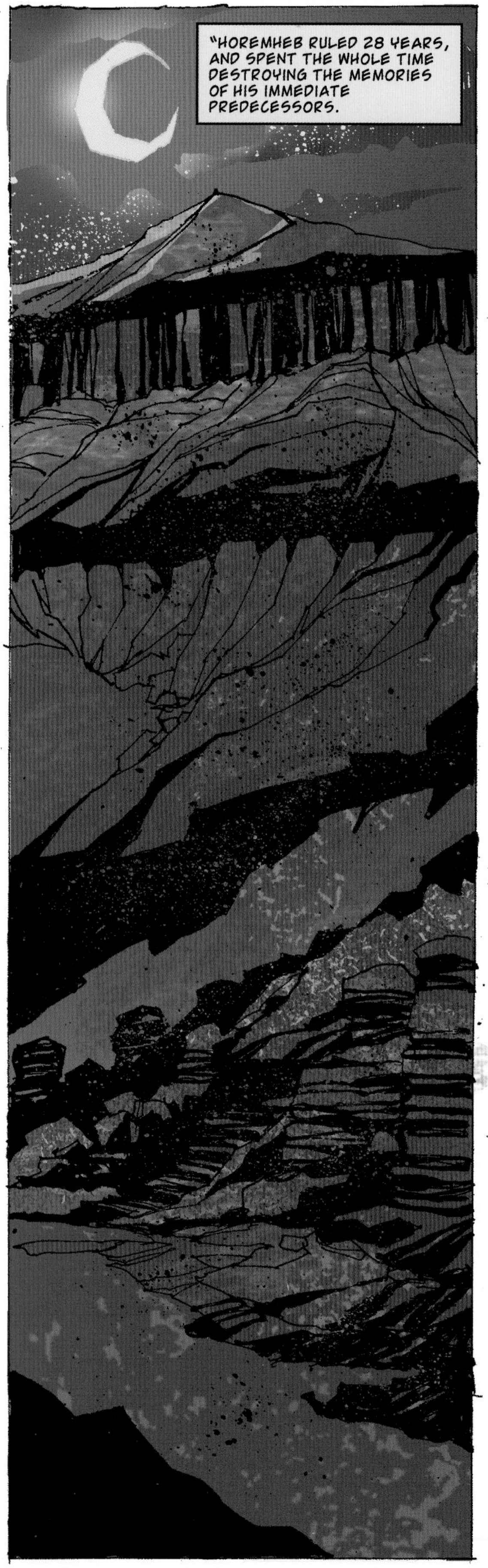
"HOREMHEB RULED 28 YEARS, AND SPENT THE WHOLE TIME DESTROYING THE MEMORIES OF HIS IMMEDIATE PREDECESSORS.

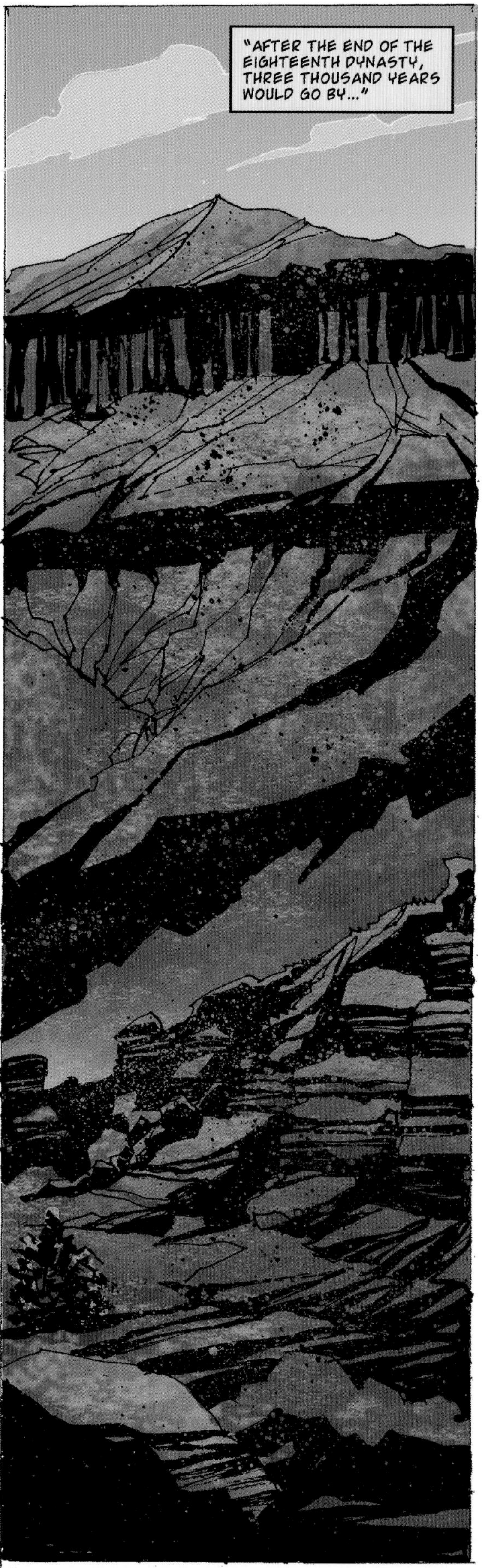
"AFTER THE END OF THE EIGHTEENTH DYNASTY, THREE THOUSAND YEARS WOULD GO BY..."

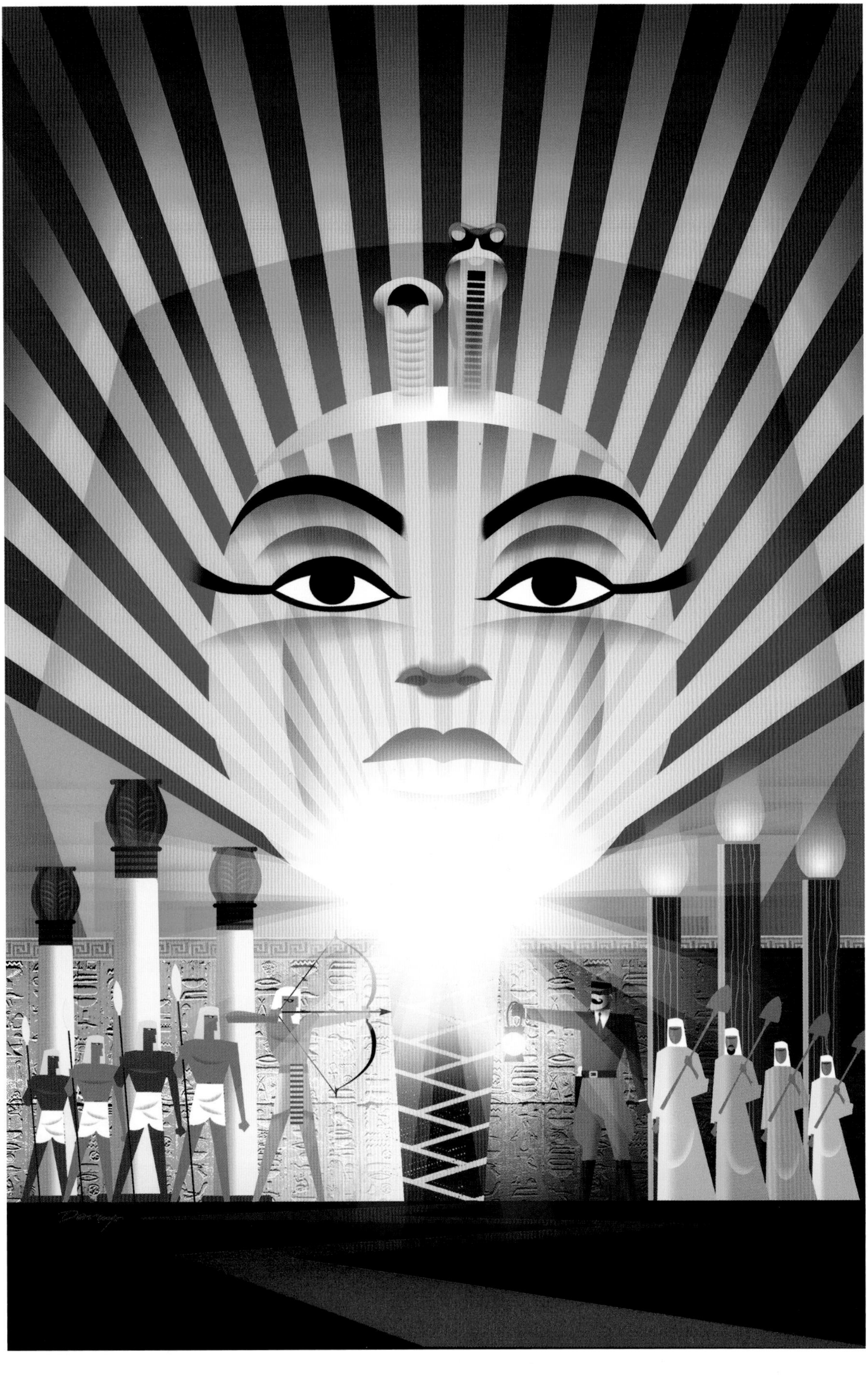

ART BY DARWYN COOKE

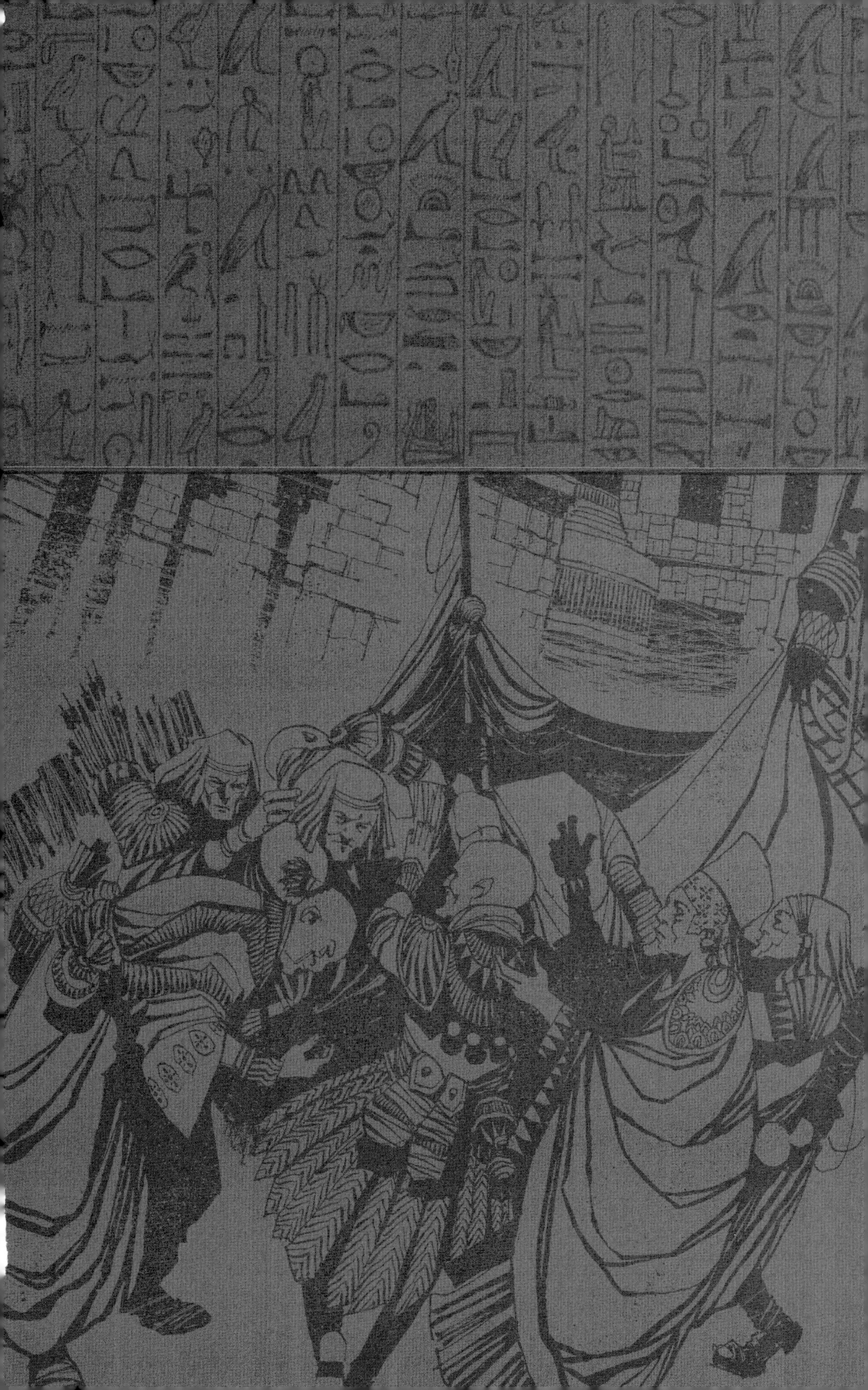

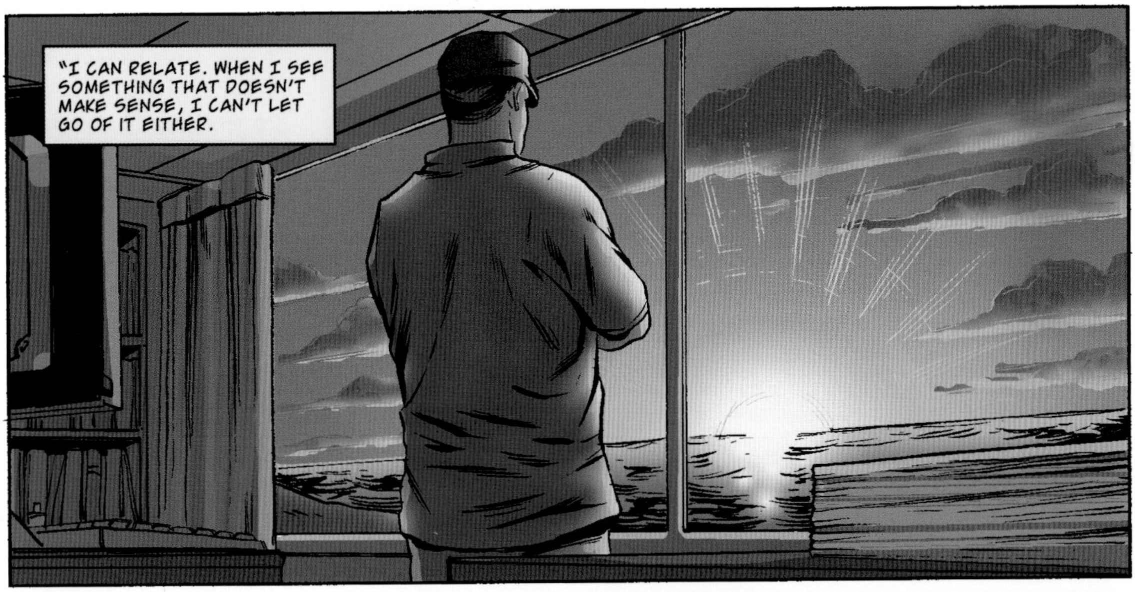
"I CAN RELATE. WHEN I SEE SOMETHING THAT DOESN'T MAKE SENSE, I CAN'T LET GO OF IT EITHER.

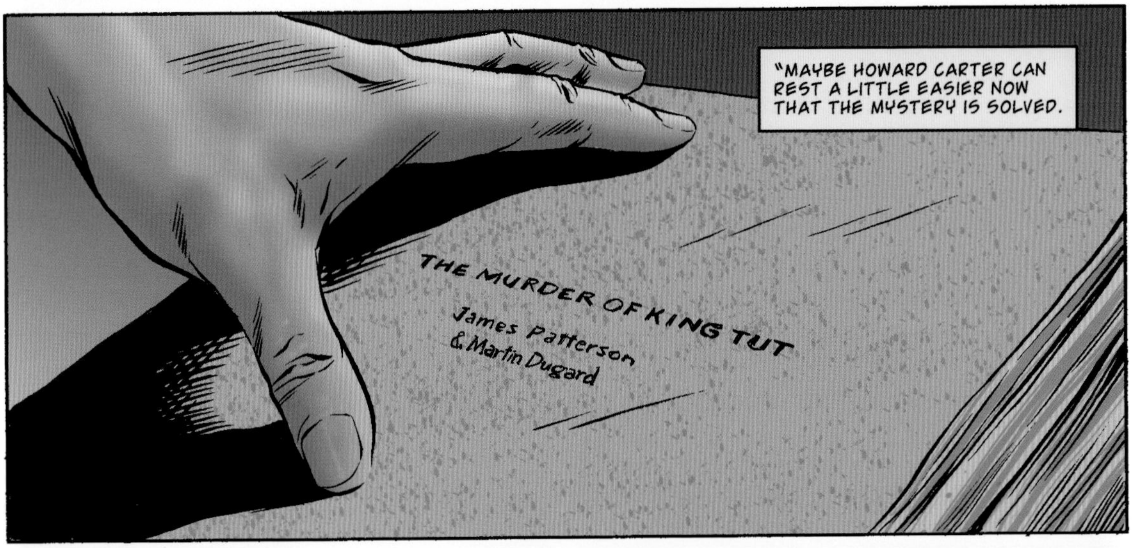
"MAYBE HOWARD CARTER CAN REST A LITTLE EASIER NOW THAT THE MYSTERY IS SOLVED.
THE MURDER OF KING TUT
James Patterson
& Martin Dugard

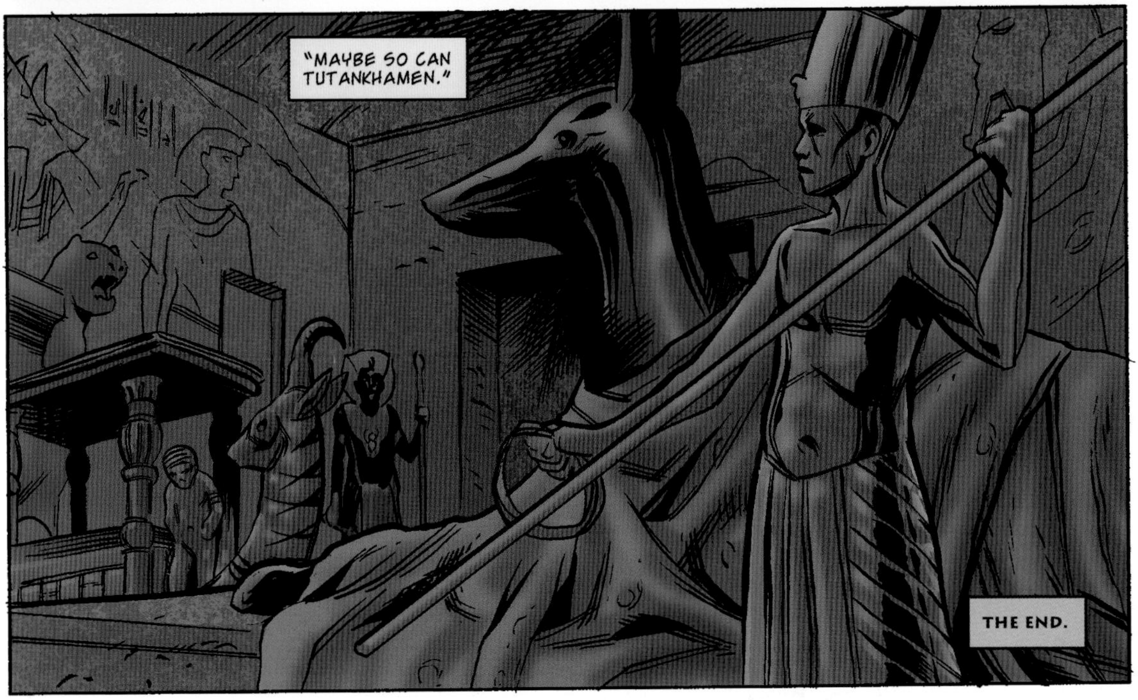
"MAYBE SO CAN TUTANKHAMEN."
THE END.

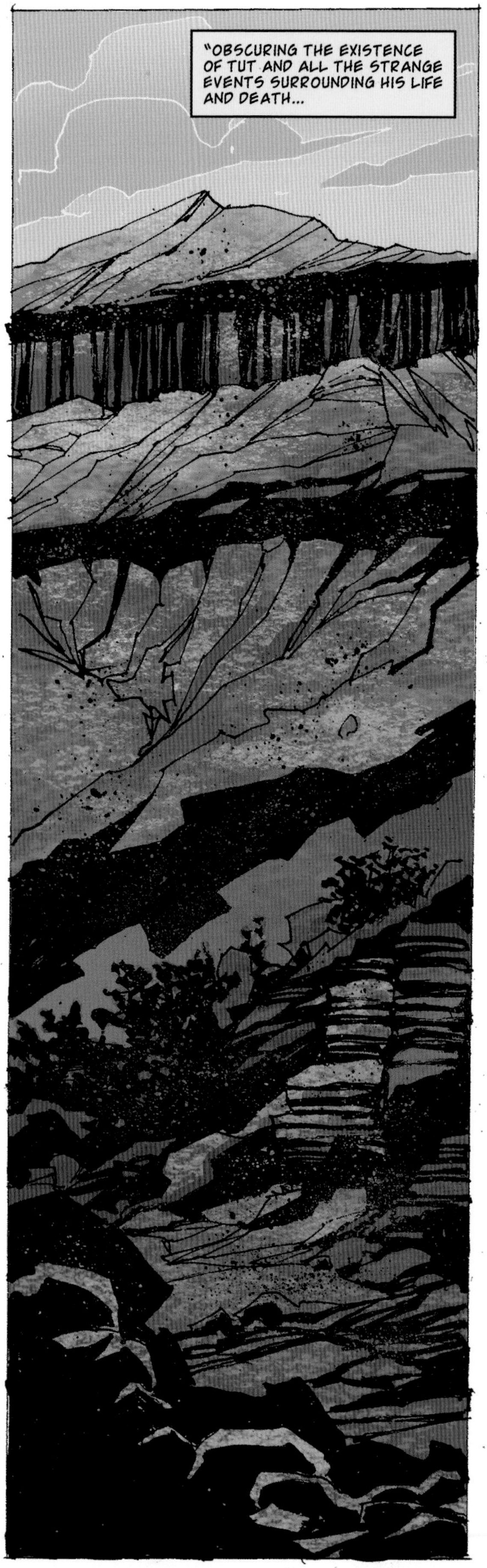
"OBSCURING THE EXISTENCE OF TUT AND ALL THE STRANGE EVENTS SURROUNDING HIS LIFE AND DEATH...

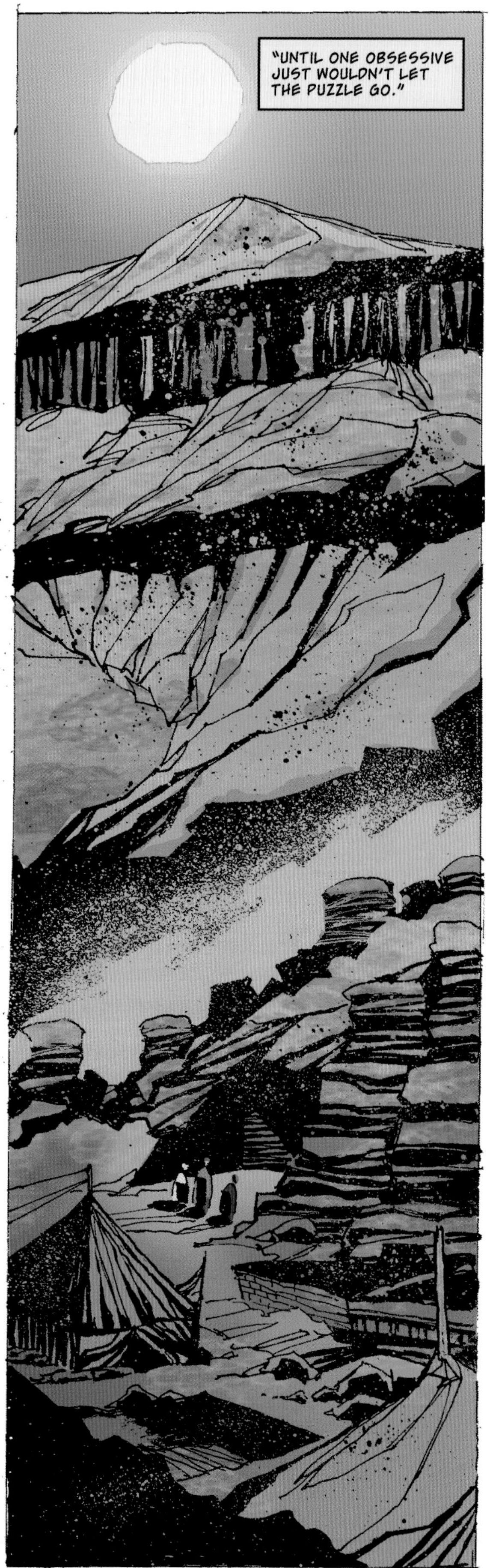
"UNTIL ONE OBSESSIVE JUST WOULDN'T LET THE PUZZLE GO."

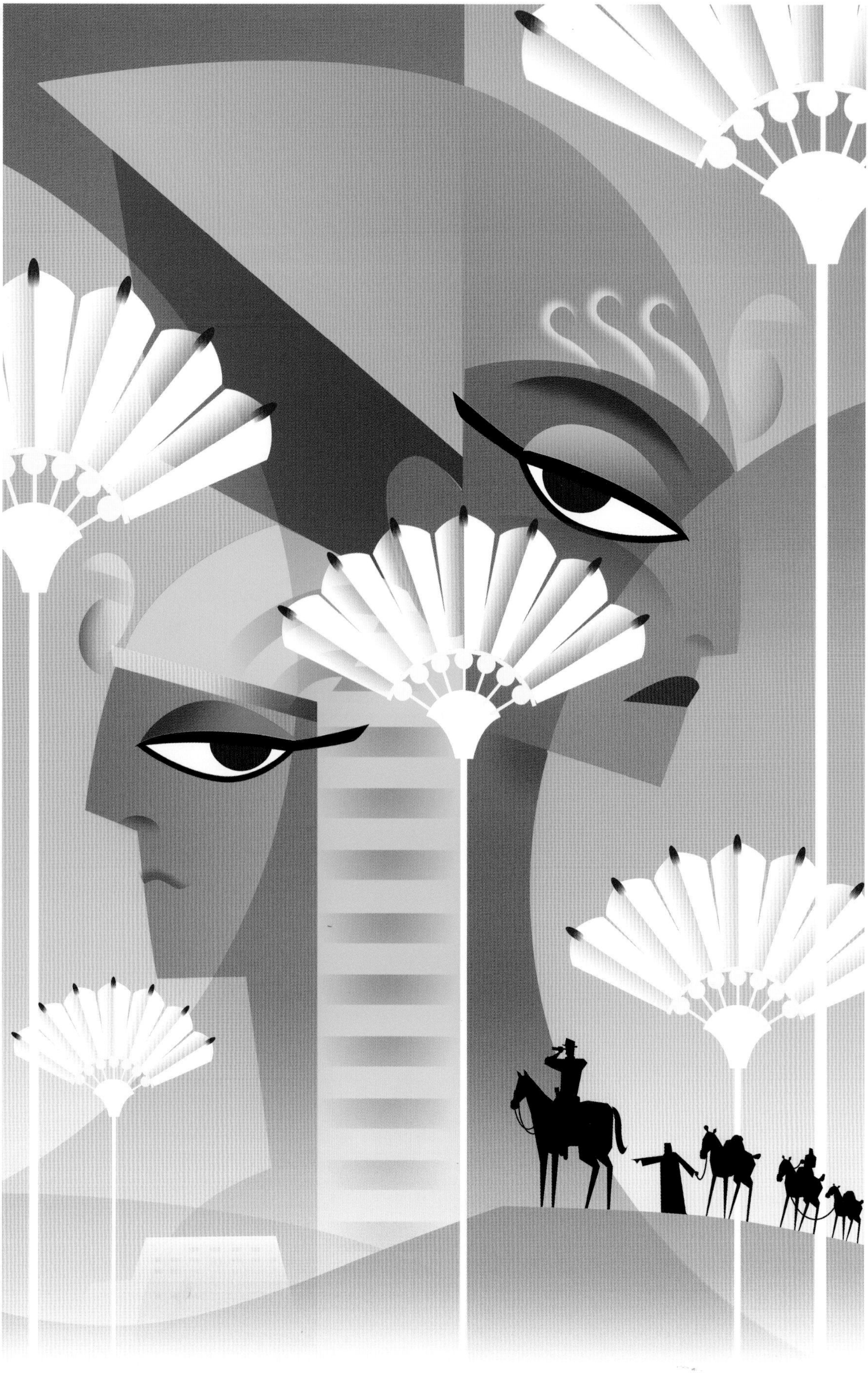

ART BY DARWYN COOKE

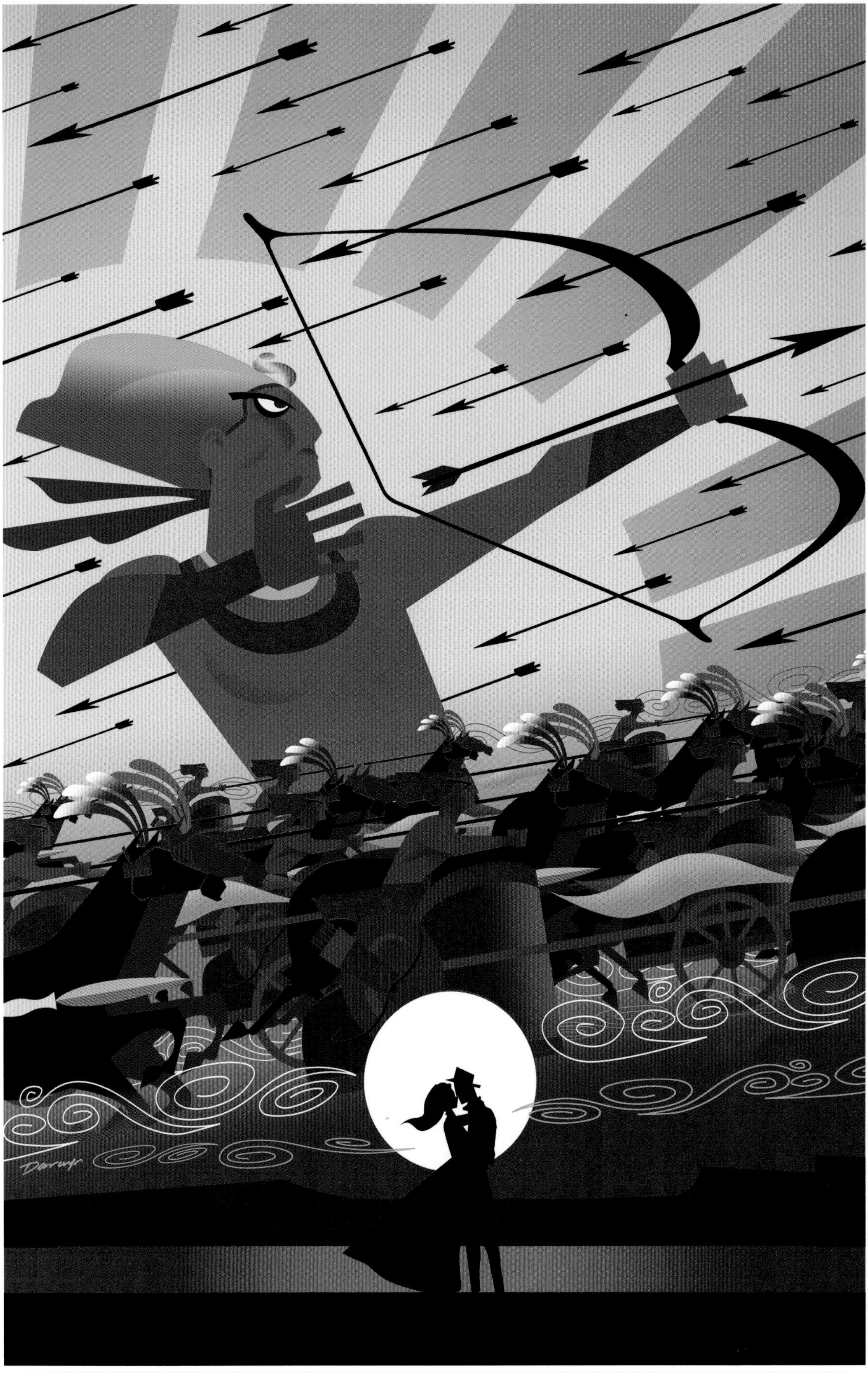
Darwyn

ART BY DARWYN COOKE

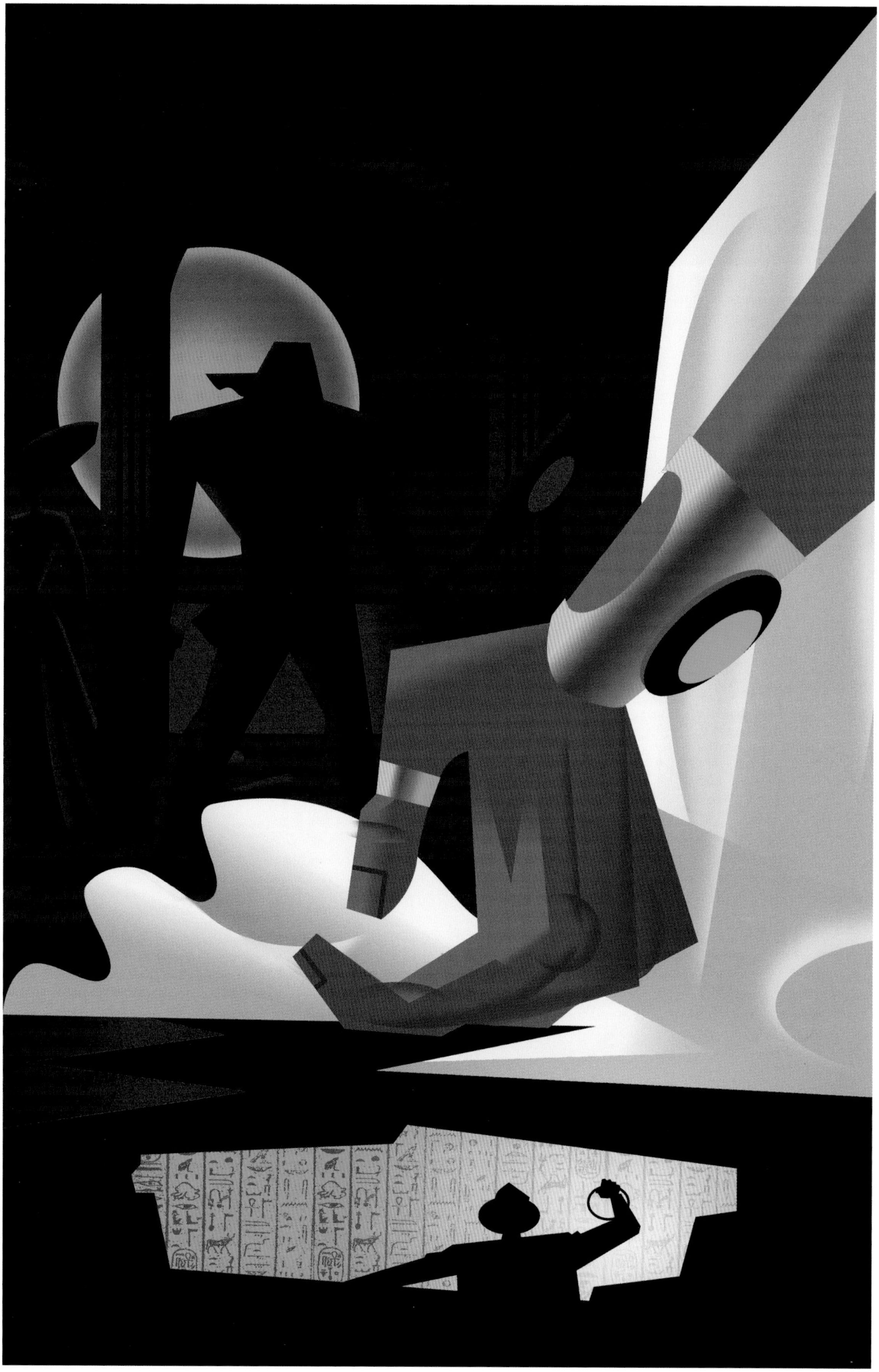

ART BY DARWYN COOKE

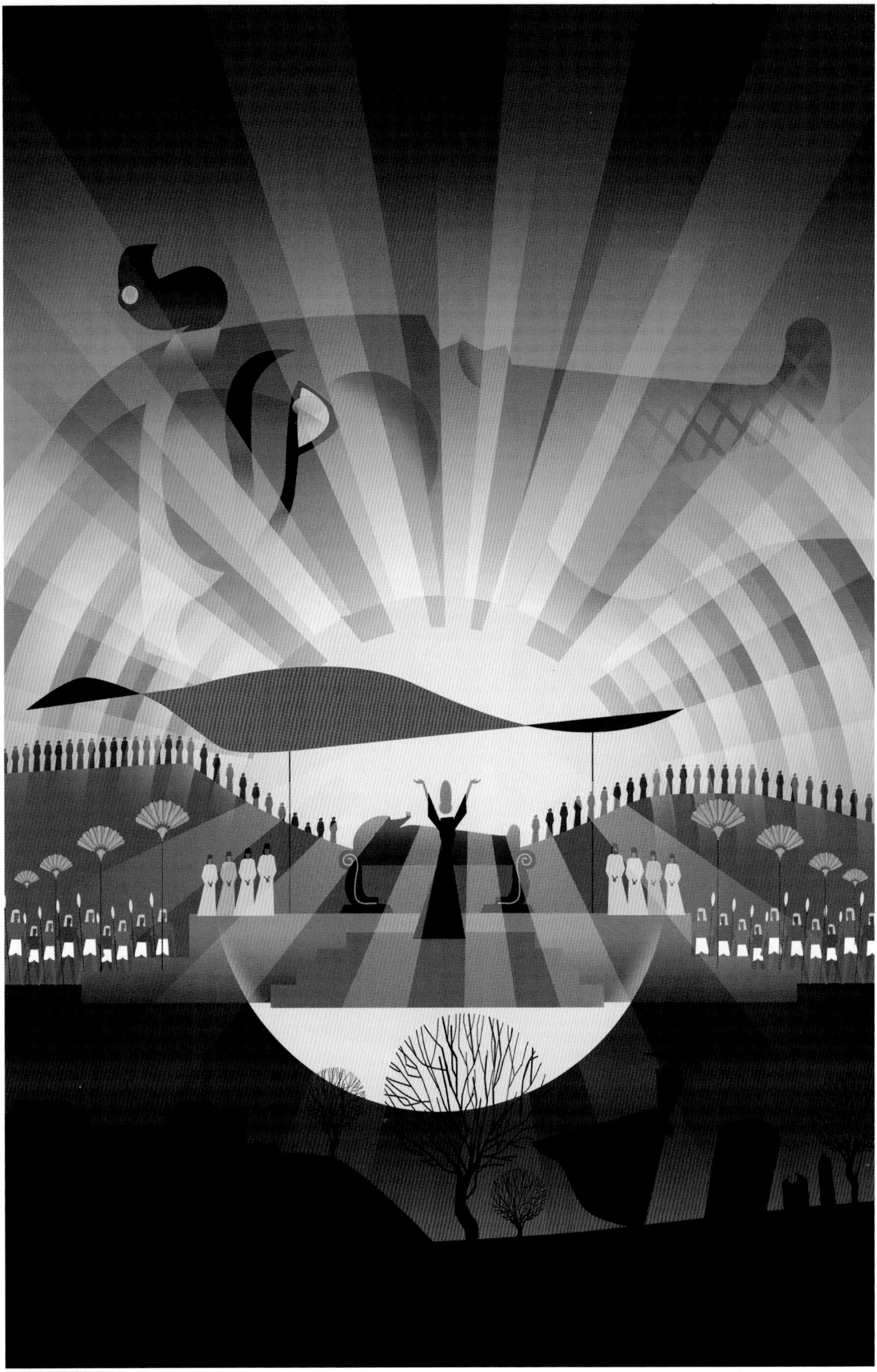

ART BY DARWYN COOKE

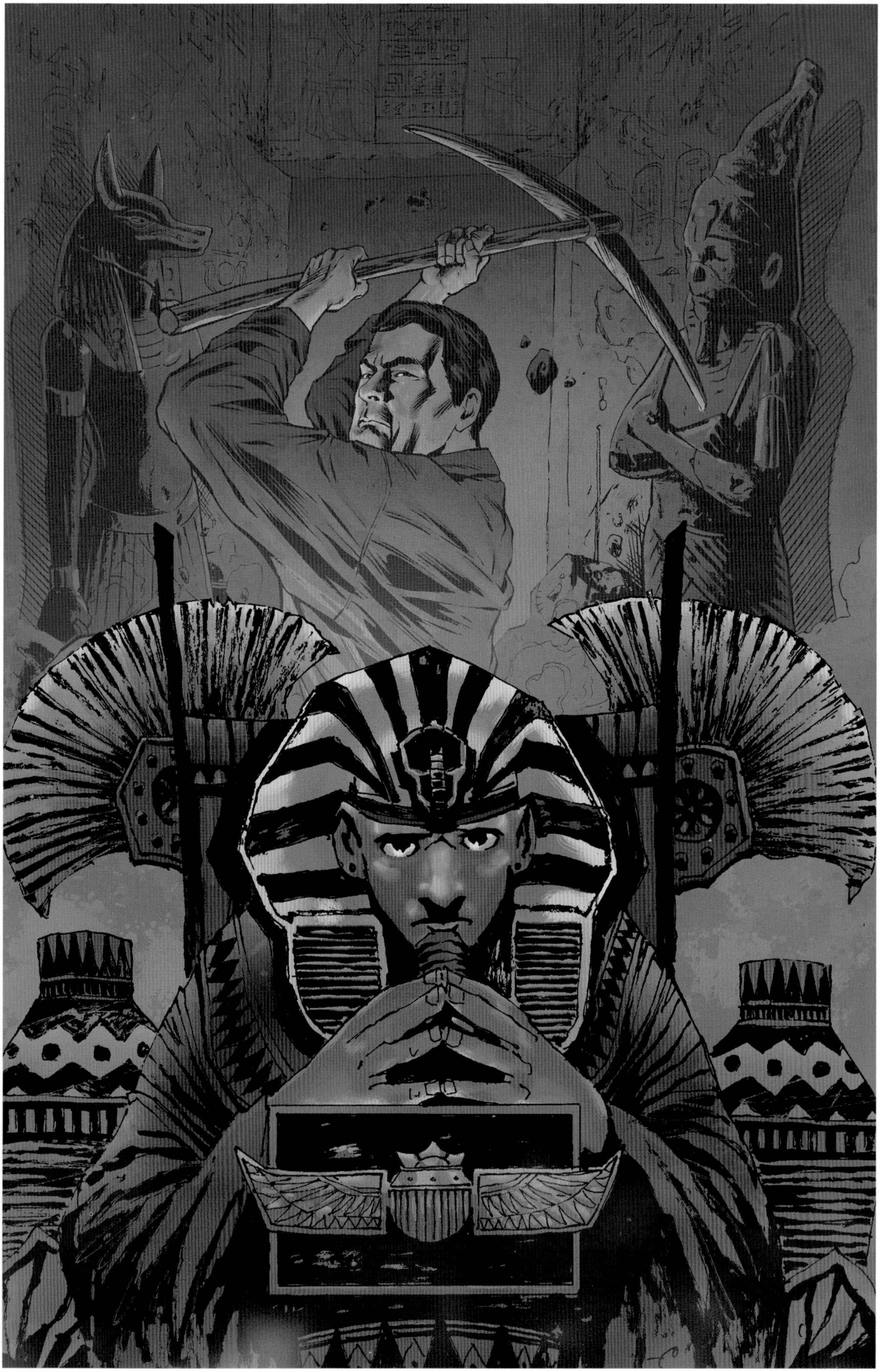

ART BY CHRISTOPHER MITTEN AND RON RANDALL

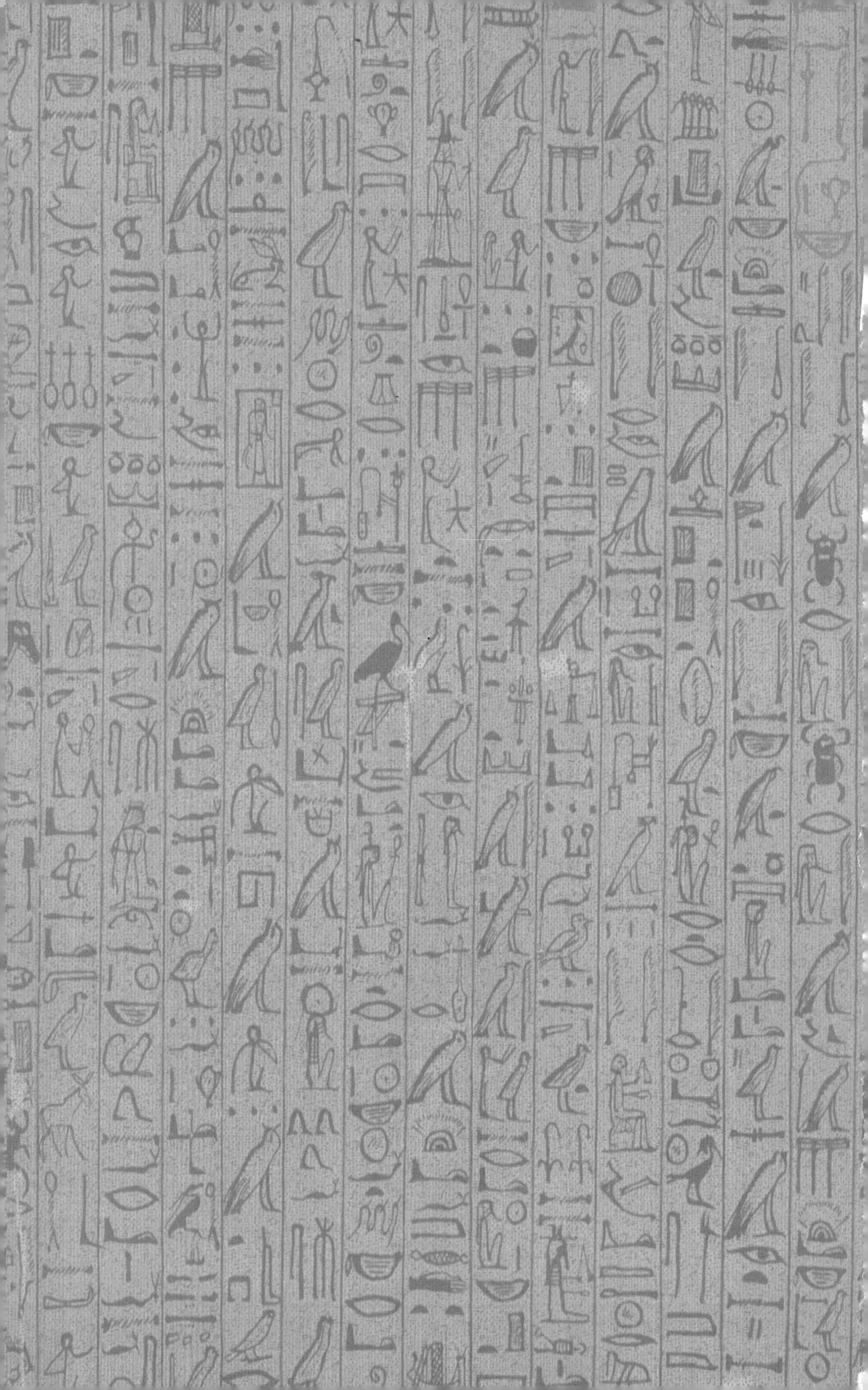